Housing Finance
in Transition Economies

OECD

ORGANISATION FOR ECONOMIC CO-OPERATION AND DEVELOPMENT

ORGANISATION FOR ECONOMIC CO-OPERATION AND DEVELOPMENT

Pursuant to Article 1 of the Convention signed in Paris on 14th December 1960, and which came into force on 30th September 1961, the Organisation for Economic Co-operation and Development (OECD) shall promote policies designed:

- to achieve the highest sustainable economic growth and employment and a rising standard of living in Member countries, while maintaining financial stability, and thus to contribute to the development of the world economy;
- to contribute to sound economic expansion in Member as well as non-member countries in the process of economic development; and
- to contribute to the expansion of world trade on a multilateral, non-discriminatory basis in accordance with international obligations.

The original Member countries of the OECD are Austria, Belgium, Canada, Denmark, France, Germany, Greece, Iceland, Ireland, Italy, Luxembourg, the Netherlands, Norway, Portugal, Spain, Sweden, Switzerland, Turkey, the United Kingdom and the United States. The following countries became Members subsequently through accession at the dates indicated hereafter: Japan (28th April 1964), Finland (28th January 1969), Australia (7th June 1971), New Zealand (29th May 1973), Mexico (18th May 1994), the Czech Republic (21st December 1995), Hungary (7th May 1996), Poland (22nd November 1996), Korea (12th December 1996) and the Slovak Republic (14th December 2000). The Commission of the European Communities takes part in the work of the OECD (Article 13 of the OECD Convention).

FOREWORD

The development of housing finance markets is a dual-dimensional policy issue. On the one hand, a well-developed housing finance system is a quintessential element of the housing policy of a market-based economy. People need reasonable financial arrangements for the construction and acquisition of a dwelling, normally a very costly undertaking relative to an individual's income. Increasing the availability of such financing is an important objective of a housing policy, itself a critical part of a social policy which aims to satisfy the basic needs of the population. On the other hand, the housing finance market represents a significant segment of the financial sector. Not only does it constitute the major part of consumer credit, but it can also initiate the establishment of market based financial instruments, as has been observed in many advanced market economies. An efficient housing finance policy is pivotal for the development of a comprehensive financial system.

The establishment of a well-functioning housing finance system has emerged as an important and urgent policy requirement of transition economies. During the last decade of economic transformation, governments have stepped away from their role under the former economic system as the purveyors of housing for their populations. The privatisation of dwellings has already been carried out in most central and eastern European countries. However, private sector construction and transaction of residences has yet to develop. A situation which can be partly attributed to the lack of effective housing finance mechanisms.

In response to the keen interest among many transition countries and major donors in developing an operational housing finance system in these economies, the OECD held a workshop on the subject in Paris on 19-20 June 2000. It was organised under the framework of its Centre for Co-operation with Non-Members with the co-sponsorship of the Government of Japan. The workshop provided a valuable opportunity for officials and experts to exchange views and experiences on the subject.

This publication consists of a summary of the workshop as well as country reports on eight transition economies -- Czech Republic, Estonia, Hungary, Latvia, Lithuania, Poland, Slovak Republic and Slovenia -- and a few other selected papers submitted to the meeting. All of the papers were updated as of April 2001.

The views expressed in this publication are those of the individual authors and do not necessarily reflect those of the OECD, or the governments of its Members or non-Member economies. Takahiro Yasui, Principal Administrator in the Directorate for Financial, Fiscal and Enterprise Affairs, has edited this volume. This book is published on the responsibility of the Secretary-General of the OECD.

Eric Burgeat
Director
Centre for Co-operation with Non-Members

TABLE OF CONTENTS

SUMMARY OF THE MEETING[*]

Introduction

The establishment of a functioning housing finance system is of major importance for economies in transition. The old housing systems have by now been mostly disposed of: government has ceased being a dominant provider of housing, and land and dwellings have been returned to, or placed in, private hands. However, new systems, which should be based on a market mechanism, have yet to become fully operational. In order for market-based housing transactions to be active, the financial mechanism is a major factor, as homes are usually too expensive for the public to purchase with cash. As housing is a basic need of the public and part of an essential social policy for any government, establishing a well-functioning housing finance system is an important policy issue for transition countries.

Against this backdrop, a Workshop on Housing Finance in Transition Economies was held on 19-20 June 2000 in Paris. It was organised by the Directorate for Financial, Fiscal and Enterprise Affairs (DAFFE) as an outreach activity of the Committee on Financial Markets, under the framework of the Centre for Co-operation with Non-Members (CCNM) Program. The workshop brought together more than 80 officials and experts from 10 non-member transition economies and 15 Member countries as well as the World Bank.

The objective of the workshop was twofold. First, it intended to review the status of housing finance systems in transition countries and to assess the steps needed to develop such systems. Second, the workshop aimed at creating a forum for relevant officials and experts to exchange information and to learn from one another's experiences. The meeting provided an overview of the major issues to be addressed to facilitate the establishment of market-based housing finance systems in transition economies. These include the development of the housing loan business, the necessary institutional arrangements and funding strategies, the practical steps to be taken and the role of government. Eigil Mølgaard, deputy secretary of the Danish Ministry of Economic Affairs, chaired the workshop.

The following is a summary of the presentations and discussions made at the workshop.

Housing finance in transition economies: what is it and what should it be?

Main features of well-functioning housing finance systems

There are a variety of well-functioning housing finance systems in advanced market countries. They constitute an important segment of the financial markets. Housing loans outstanding account for 20%

---

[*]   This summary was prepared by Takahiro Yasui, Principal Administrator, Directorate for Financial, Fiscal and Enterprise Affairs, OECD. He benefited greatly from the comments of Mr Eigil Mølgaard and his colleagues at the OECD on earlier drafts.

to 60% of GDP. Variations in housing finance systems tend to reflect the particular economic and social contexts in which these systems have evolved. In fact, the housing finance systems in advanced market countries have a long history. Several mortgage banks in Europe, such as Germany's Hypothekenbank and the Crédit Foncier de France, were founded in the mid-19th century. Fannie Mae (formerly the Federal National Mortgage Association) of the United States was established in the 1930s. The housing finance systems that have evolved all work well in their own situations, and have been influenced by the economic and social developments peculiar to their respective countries, as well as their particular geographical and demographic characteristics. These systems will continue to evolve as operating environments change, owing to advances in information technology and the globalisation of economic and financial markets.

Some common models can be identified among the various housing finance systems in advanced market countries. One such model is the Southern European model (Spain, Italy and Greece, for example). Housing finance markets in these countries are characterised by very high levels of owner-occupation, low transaction levels, and less favourable terms for mortgage credit.

These markets differ in many respects from those served by the so-called Homeowner model. The latter tend to be characterised by high transaction levels and more favourable credit facilities, supported by highly liberalised financial markets. This type of housing finance system is typically found in the Scandinavian and English-speaking countries, which have owner-occupation ratios of 60% to 70%. The United States has developed the world's largest housing finance market, with very sophisticated financing systems. Historically, the primary (i.e. origination) mortgage market in the United States has been dominated by deposit-taking institutions (thrifts and more recently banks) and mortgage brokers/servicers. After origination, mortgages are either held in portfolio or sold into the secondary market, where they are pooled and repackaged as mortgage-backed securities. Three government-sponsored enterprises (GSEs) -- Freddie Mac, Fannie Mae and Ginnie Mae -- are the primary agents in the secondary market. The first two agencies finance mortgage loans by issuing mortgage-backed securities. Ginnie Mae, part of the US Department of Housing and Urban Development, provides a full faith and credit guarantee on pools of loans guaranteed by the Department of Veterans Affairs or insured by the Federal Housing Administration, but does not itself issue securities. Secondary markets in the United States account for roughly half of outstanding home mortgage credit and in recent years have accounted for some three-fourths of the net increase.

The third model is called the Balanced Tenure model, in which a relatively larger segment of the population tends to live in rental residences and the owner-occupation ratio is as low as 40% to 50%. Housing finance markets in Germany and Austria are examples of this model. In these countries, housing finance systems are rather specialised, highly regulated and integrated, which creates more stable but less active markets than those in countries featuring the Homeowner model.

During the session, several factors were identified as essential for a housing finance system to work effectively. First, the most basic infrastructure is a legal system that supports mortgage transactions. It includes the system for recording titles that not only establish property rights appropriately but ensure the ability to transfer titles at a minimum cost, and also includes efficient foreclosure laws and practices. These are important prerequisites if houses are to act as effective collateral.

The second indispensable factor for any housing finance system is adequate funding. In practice, there are two basic kinds of funding sources: deposits and securities markets. At least one of them needs to be available to channel public savings to housing finance. It was pointed out in this regard that private money had to be used, as a healthy housing finance system could not be maintained with public funds alone.

Third, an appropriate regulatory structure should be in place. Housing finance should be viewed as a means to an end, namely homeownership. Given the importance of housing policy, the government is typically involved in any housing finance system in one way or another. However, housing finance is also part of the overall system of capital allocation. Therefore, regulations concerning housing finance should be designed and implemented in a way that does not distort the efficient allocation of capital in a society. The US experience shows that housing finance can spill over to the whole capital market. Thus, the first asset-backed securities issued in the United States were the mortgage-backed securities developed by GSEs.

The fourth factor needed to ensure that a housing finance mechanism functions properly is macroeconomic stability. A relatively stable macroeconomic environment is especially necessary for housing finance, given its long-term nature.

Current situations and strategies of transition economies

Under the communist regimes of many Central and Eastern European countries, the government was responsible for providing housing for the public. As a result, transition economies tend to have relatively large housing stocks. The number of dwellings per capita is almost comparable to that of advanced market countries. However, the housing markets are not very active, when compared with those in advanced market countries.

There are several factors behind the relative inactivity of the housing markets in transition economies; among them is a very high owner-occupation ratio. In these countries, except for the Czech Republic, Latvia and Poland, owner-occupied housing accounts for more than 90% of the housing stock. This large share is the result of privatisation of real estate in the early 1990s. It should be noted that there are problems with the quality of many existing dwellings. These problems, which were all inherited from the former communist regimes, include inadequate size, poor construction, poor maintenance and insufficient infrastructure. This situation creates significant potential demand for higher-quality housing. However, the supply of such housing is insufficient. As part of the economic transformation, the governments in these countries have largely pulled out of the housing construction business, but private sector activity has not yet expanded sufficiently to compensate. Consequently, the supply of quality housing is constrained and the price is too high for the typical buyer. Moreover, the transition economies have not yet developed effective housing finance mechanisms to help people to acquire such housing.

Under the former system, state-owned banks typically were responsible for extending housing loans with very long maturities and very favourable fixed interest rates, with no required collateral or down payments. This system was obviously not sustainable, especially once the government stopped providing financial support after the economic transformation, and high inflation in the early years of the transformation destroyed it. In lieu of direct support, many governments have made considerable efforts to encourage market transactions by introducing various financing schemes. The development of market-based housing finance systems has become an important policy objective for all transition countries.

The efforts in various transition countries were presented at the meeting. In Poland, the Mortgage Fund was established in the early 1990s as a liquidity facility to finance inflation-proof mortgage loans (mostly dual-indexed mortgages) made by banks on a commercial basis. The Act on Mortgage Bonds and Mortgage Banks adopted in 1997 introduced a German-type mortgage bank system in which specialised mortgage banks may raise funds by issuing mortgage bonds against their mortgage assets. At present, two mortgage banks are in operation; mortgage bonds were first issued in June 2000. In addition, there are two contract savings systems in Poland. One, however, has granted an insignificant amount of loans since it was introduced in 1995. The other was created in 1997 but has not yet begun operation. The Government intends to reorganise and unify both contract savings systems.

In Slovenia, commercial banks are currently the primary suppliers of housing loans to individuals, accounting for almost 60% of the market. However, the loans are largely short-term credits unsecured by mortgage as collateral. Only 16% of these loans are mortgage loans, though the share is increasing yearly. The remaining 40% of housing loans to individuals have come from the state Housing Fund. Established in 1991, the Fund extends credit for purchase or construction of dwellings by individuals and for construction of social rental dwellings by non-profit housing organisations and local communities. The Fund receives a government subsidy, which it uses to provide long-term housing loans on favourable terms. In addition, a contract savings system, the National Scheme of Money Saving for the Purchase of Apartments, was introduced in July 1999. The Scheme is run by selected banks with the support of the government subsidy granted to participating individuals through the Fund.

Thanks to these efforts, market-based housing finance systems have emerged in these countries, though they remain in their infancy. The current volume of housing loans outstanding is nominal -- less than 5% of GDP -- for all transition economies. The low level of transactions reflects the short history of market-based finance and also inactive property markets that can be attributed especially to high prices. However, other obstacles to the development of the housing finance markets have also been identified. First, as many delegates pointed out, residents' income levels are not yet high enough, and only a small portion of the public is deemed financially eligible for loans. Second, relatively high economic uncertainty in transition economies has discouraged both borrowers and lenders from arranging long-term credits. Third, the legal infrastructure for housing finance needs to be improved. Some relatively advanced countries, such as Poland, have set up the necessary legal and institutional infrastructure, but many others have not. Fourth, an underdeveloped financial sector was regarded as an important challenge to the development of housing finance. For example, inefficiency in the banking sector allows a huge gap between deposit and lending rates, effectively deterring households from acquiring housing loans. Finally, problems of mentality were pointed out: many people in transition countries desire exceptionally high-quality housing regardless of its affordability, but also put a high priority on purchasing other durable goods, such as cars.

Development of the mortgage loan business

Practical aspects of mortgage system designing

The mortgage lending business entails certain risks that must be properly managed if the business is to succeed. These risks can be categorised into two types: general macroeconomic and legal/regulatory risks, and operational risks.

As repeatedly pointed out at the meeting, the existence of an adequate legal and regulatory environment that supports a mortgage lending system is essential. There must be laws in place that secure private ownership of land and houses and the ability to use the title to property as security for a mortgage. The legal framework needs to be supported, particularly by the registry system that records the history of title and any liens against a property. Advanced market countries such as Denmark and Sweden have a long history of real estate registration in which every square meter of land has been registered and evaluated for tax purposes. Also important is a foreclosure system that enables a lender to foreclose on a mortgage smoothly if the loan is not repaid.

The establishment of an adequate legal system is obviously a government responsibility. In most transition economies, relevant laws have largely been introduced. However, enforcement is not always effective. Participants reported that in some transition countries the registration of the title to the land book took one year or more. The creation of an appropriate legal environment usually takes time. It was suggested that weak legal enforcement might be supplemented by mortgage insurance, which is often government-supported.

Unstable macroeconomic conditions also create a significant risk beyond the control of the housing loan businesses. Among other factors, a high inflation risk is often regarded as a major obstacle to any long-term financial industry, including housing finance. Alternative mortgage instruments are available to deal with interest-rate fluctuations. For example, Mexico has invented UDI mortgage loans (inflation-indexed loans) and FOVI mortgage loans (dual-indexed mortgage loans linked to both the inflation and minimum-wage rates), influenced by its experience of the Tequila Crisis in 1994. It should be noted that such loans help lenders avoid inflation risk principally by passing the risk on to borrowers; the loans may thus be less attractive to borrowers than standard fixed-rate products. This is probably why adjustable-rate mortgage products are not widely used in advanced market countries, except for the United Kingdom and Ireland. It was suggested that the risk to borrowers might be mitigated through a counter investment fund, though this would increase the financial burden for borrowers to acquire loans. It is also possible that a government could assume the interest rate risk. In Sweden, the Government at one point guaranteed a fixed interest rate of 3.25% for housing loans. However, this measure was abolished due to the heavy budgetary burden and the distorting impact on the financial markets when market rates rose. The direct solution to this problem is the adoption of prudent macroeconomic policies to stabilise macroeconomic fluctuations.

Another macroeconomic or market risk related particularly to mortgage finance is volatility of the property price. Uncertainty related to the future price of land and housing deteriorates their value as collateral for long-term credit. This leads to inefficiency in the mortgage loan market by lowering loan-to-value ratios and possibly necessitating other types of collateral, as is the case in many transition countries. The remedy against this risk is stabilisation of prices, which requires prudent macroeconomic management and the establishment of a deep property market.

Some participants stressed that the availability of appropriate funding for long-term credit is also an important prerequisite for housing finance systems to work. One solution is the creation of mortgage bond markets. A number of transition countries have recently introduced or plan to introduce legislation for mortgage banks and mortgage bonds (see below), similar to that of Germany and other continental European countries.

Effective management of the mortgage loan business

The risks discussed above are beyond the control of individual businesses and thus are left to central governments to handle. There are, however, other risks that housing loan providers have the primary responsibility for managing as part of their normal business operations, although a government can provide some support. These risks include credit risk and operations risk.

The proper management of credit risk is central to the successful provision of housing loans. The logical way to avoid loss via borrower defaults is to avoid taking excessive credit risk, by limiting credit extensions to high-quality borrowers subject to high equity requirements. However, this strategy lowers the overall return on the portfolio and limits its business potential. Thus, it is necessary instead for lenders to adopt a risk management strategy that recognises the need to take some measure of credit risk in order to achieve the desired level of profitability and market potential.

Credit risk management includes three major elements. First is the requirement for a proper assessment of a customer's ability and willingness to pay for the loan for its duration. A lender needs to develop the necessary criteria, taking into account the unique characteristics of the local market. To the extent possible, the assessment should be objective, based on data from reliable and independent sources, and verifiable in some way. Many advanced market countries, such as Canada, have a comprehensive network of credit bureaus that retain electronic data on consumer, retail, finance and other accounts to keep track of missed payments, obviously an important supporting infrastructure for the housing loan business. In contrast, the availability of borrower data remains limited in transition countries. Unreported income, for example, is often too important to ignore, but information is unreliable. Contract savings programs are useful in this regard, as they create a credit record of regular payments.

The second element is equity. A fair equity portion helps to motivate borrowers to continue to pay, and also helps the lender to recover damage in the event of borrower default. However, in transition countries where detailed data are often unavailable, it is not easy to establish an efficient equity requirement (or LTV ratio). The third element in credit risk management is the availability and use of other kinds of collateral when necessary. Mortgage insurance or use of a counter-risk pool of funds, as suggested above, can be beneficial in mitigating credit risk. A public mortgage-loan insurance program established in Canada in the early 1950s has helped one in three Canadians acquire a home. Borrower education is an important guaranty. Maintaining contact with borrowers by providing occasional financial advice not only can help borrowers understand the value of payments but is an effective way to reduce the default risk.

Operations risk also needs to be effectively managed. It occurs at all levels of activity in a mortgage finance operation. If the risk is high because, for example, of operational errors and fraud, the operational cost soars and the business cannot be run at a profit. There are a few important ways to mitigate operations risk. The first is training. A well-trained staff makes fewer errors and can handle higher volumes of transactions. A second step is use of technology, which increases the volume of operations that can be managed with the same staff, reduces errors and fraud and facilitates data collection and analysis. It should be noted, however, that both training and technology are likely to increase short-term costs, though they should be effective, over time, in reducing operations cost.

Simplicity is another useful tool to reduce operations risk. Complex products are more difficult to manage and thus more likely to increase operational cost. Standardisation of documents and operations should lead to lower operational costs, at least in the long term. In addition, qualified external and internal auditors, and the enforcement of quality control by checking loan samples regularly, will help avoid operational problems.

Institutional arrangements and funding strategies

Alternative funding strategies and risks

The development of a well-functioning housing loan business requires the establishment of a system capable of raising financial resources sufficient both in quantity and quality to fund loans. Advanced market countries have developed various instruments to do so. These can be placed into two categories: deposits from the public and products of capital market facilities.

Retail deposits are still the primary financial resources for housing loans, even in advanced markets countries. For example, in EU countries, deposits account for 62% of the funding of mortgage loans.

Deposit financing is even more dominant in transition countries, where the issuance of mortgage bonds began only recently.

A special scheme to mobilise retail deposits for housing loans is the contract savings system. Germany's *Bausparkassen* is a typical example, introduced by many transition countries to develop housing finance. Under this system, a saver enters into a contract with a savings institution to undertake savings up to a specific sum, under a set schedule. Upon the conclusion of the savings period, the saver acquires the right to obtain a loan for a prescribed purpose at a predetermined fixed interest rate. Proponents of contract savings schemes suggest that this system have various advantages. Savers/borrowers can be largely immune to interest-rate fluctuations. The credit records of savers/borrowers can be established by the system itself during the saving period. From a macroeconomic viewpoint, a contract savings system encourages people to undertake long-term savings and to increase the aggregate savings level in a country. The system can be regarded as a transparent basis for subsidies, as the subsidy is directly allocated to individuals for housing. These merits are particularly important for transition economies, which still face macroeconomic uncertainty and difficulty in getting credit records for individuals.

However, others at the meeting noted the disadvantages of contract savings schemes. For example, due to their long-term nature, contract savings schemes may not be flexible enough when faced with a changing economic environment. Moreover, to attract savers, contract savings schemes normally need government support in the form of interest-rate subsidies, which are likely to create substantial budgetary burdens. The schemes may also cause political problems, inasmuch as the required build-up during the initial savings period makes immediate results on housing impossible. While such transition countries as Slovakia and Slovenia are promoting this system to expand housing finance, Poland is moving away from it.

Capital markets are an alternative source of funds for housing loans, and have recently increased in importance in many advanced market countries. There are generally two ways to raise funds from capital markets for mortgage loans: mortgage bonds and mortgage-backed securities. Mortgage bonds issued by mortgage banks have a long history in Europe, dating back more than 100 years. Currently, Germany has the biggest market, amounting to Euro 930 billion. The EU UCITS Directive (Article 22 IV) provides a definition of mortgage bonds. It was argued, however, that the Directive provides only minimum standards: more detailed regulations, such as those on investment, asset and liability valuation, loan-to-value ratio, cover register and trustee, would be needed to protect the reputation of the bonds and develop markets. As a result, actual regulations differ across countries.

Mortgage bonds are gaining attention as an important funding source for mortgage loans, not only in Western Europe but in Central and Eastern European countries. Mortgage bond legislation has been introduced in the Czech and Slovak republics, and in Hungary, Poland and Latvia, and has been drafted in Estonia, Bulgaria and Russia. In the former five countries, issuance of bonds has begun. The outstanding volumes remain trivial, however, with the exception of the Czech Republic, which has carried out 17 issues, amounting to Euro 520 million. It is largely a condition for a bond market that long-term saving be institutionalised by, for example, pension funds and life assurance. This is, however, not the case in most transition economies.

Meeting participants discussed the priority that should be given to mortgage bond legislation as a means of developing housing finance in transition countries. Bond financing has the merit of addressing the maturity mismatch associated with long-term housing loans. And mortgage bonds, it was pointed out, could help connect the expectation of lower inflation with current interest rates when the financial market has an inverted yield curve, as is currently the case in Hungary. Nevertheless, some participants argued that given the relative importance of deposit finance (even in advanced market countries) and the underdeveloped legal infrastructures and capital markets in transition countries, the priority should be the development of housing loan origination's, whatever the means of finance. There was consensus that no single, successful model can fit all transition economies.

In contrast to mortgage bonds, mortgage-backed securities have not been popular among European countries, compared with the United States. Some reasons for this were suggested, including a less favourable weighting in capital requirements, lack of the government-backed agencies found in the United States, lack of standardisation, the existence of competitive on-balance sheet funding instruments, and so on. No issues of mortgage-backed securities have been reported by transition countries.

Institutional arrangements

Various kinds of financial institutions can play a role in the housing finance market. These institutions can be divided largely into specialised and non-specialised institutions. In many countries, one or more financial institutions specialising in housing finance have been established, though their functions vary considerably.

Mortgage banks, such as those developed in Scandinavia, Germany and other continental European countries, are among the most common types of specialised institutions. Though they have historically financed their loans with retail deposits, they are now closely linked with mortgage bond financing. Mortgage banks are often given the exclusive right to issue mortgage bonds, but are subject in turn to tight regulation, especially in terms of their investment. For example, France established legislation in 1999 to introduce a type of mortgage lending institution (*société de crédit foncier*) that is allowed to issue mortgage bonds (*obligations foncières*). In return for the privilege to issue the bonds, these institutions are subject to strict regulation and special insolvency procedures to keep ratings on the bonds high. They are also subject to special supervision by a specific supervisor who is required to report to bondholders for each institution, in addition to the banking supervisory authority (*Commission Bancaire*). As mentioned above, several transition countries have enacted or drafted new legislation to introduce mortgage banks coupled with a mortgage bond system.

Another example of a specialised institution is the *Bausparkassen,* developed especially in Austria and Germany. Bausparkassen specialise in running these countries' contract savings systems. While contract savings can be offered by non-specialised lenders such as commercial banks, Bausparkassen operate the closed scheme in which they provide housing finance with funding obtained from savers under the saving contracts. The closed scheme is considered beneficial in isolating the entire system from interest-rate fluctuations, though it may suffer from liquidity problems in the absence of a steady expansion of the business. In particular, when market interest rates rise, the scheme is likely to face difficulty in securing enough deposits to finance loan demands. Some participants argued that Bausparkassen might not be suitable for transition countries until those countries manage to stabilise their inflation rates. Others pointed out that the system worked adequately in Germany even when the economy was unstable before and after World War II.

While specialised institutions are widespread, non-specialised ones, such as commercial banks, co-operatives, life assurance companies and pension funds, can be important players in the housing loan market. In EU countries, non-specialised institutions account for more than 60% of mortgage markets, while commercial banks hold about 40%. The strengths of non-specialised institutions include flexible risk management using various types of financial products as well as cross-selling. In some European countries, it was reported, mortgage loans are made at a loss, compensated by profits from other activities such as credit-card businesses supported by long-term relationships with the mortgage borrowers.

In transition countries, savings banks, which specialised in individual customer business rather than housing finance, formerly dominated the market. While they remain important in some countries, their business has diminished due to unstable macroeconomic development, large shares of non-performing assets and the abolishment of government support. The establishment of specialised institutions in transition countries is often intended to compensate for the dysfunctioning of non-specialised financial institutions in the housing finance business. Estonia appears to be an exception. There, the major commercial banks have significant foreign capital and thus tend to have sufficient cash available for housing loans. There is no real need for specialised institutions or bond financing.

In addition, it was pointed out that the distinction between specialised and non-specialised institutions has become less important. In some countries, universal banks and specialised institutions such as mortgage banks and Bausparkassen tend to be integrated in groups or conglomerates, so that various financial services can be offered at one window.

Practical steps for establishing housing finance systems

Housing is a basic public need, but it is very expensive. This is a major reason why governments should play a role in the housing and housing finance sectors. Housing costs anywhere from 2.5 to 6 times the average annual income in advanced market countries. It is hardly affordable for lower-income people, often a majority in transition countries.

The high cost of housing is accommodated by savings, subsidies and finance. In transition economies, however, finance is currently scarce, which results in the heavier use of savings and government subsidies than in advanced market countries. To approach the situation of advanced market countries, transition economies will need to increase the use of finance and reduce that of savings and subsidies.

There are two key factors behind the heavy dependence on savings to accommodate housing: an extremely high home-ownership ratio and low energy efficiency. Typically, households in transition economies spend 20% to 30% of their income on energy consumption. This high ratio results partly from relatively high energy prices (many transition countries import energy) and from old-fashioned, low-quality facilities (bad insulation and circulation systems). Under these circumstances, housing subsidies are often used up in paying for utilities. Most residents in transition countries own their residences, thanks to privatisation in the course of economic transformation. However, these residences are in a state of rapid devaluation, because households do not invest in maintenance. Not only is available cash largely directed to energy expenses, but the low marketability of houses does not encourage households to invest in their residences. Therefore, reform is of urgent necessity to increase energy efficiency and to remove obstacles (for example, land-use control) for residences to be placed on the market. The latter is also important for the development of the financial markets, as the owners could issue debt against the marketable assets.

Government subsidies for housing are common even in advanced market countries. They are particularly significant in transition economies, often larger than those for health and education. Clearly, these subsidies need to be reduced. Funds would be better targeted to the limited number of people who really need public assistance, and some transition countries are moving in this direction. Also, subsidies should be structured to complement, not replace, market-based finance systems.

To reduce subsidies, a government needs to develop a functioning housing finance system. Establishing an adequate legal and regulatory environment and achieving macroeconomic stability should be the priorities for policy. Another important government role is to assist in preparing an effective financial mechanism to mobilise capital for mortgages. This can be done by establishing a system to collect domestic savings. For example, in post-World War II Japan, when there was a serious housing shortage and the government budget was limited, the Government Housing Loan Corporation (GHLC) was established. Because the undeveloped private financial sector was unable to provide long-term, low-fixed-rate loans for residential mortgages, the GHLC was designed to raise financial resources from the public in the form of postal savings.

In today's world, however, it may be possible for lenders to tap the bond market, exploiting technology and globalisation. The establishment of the bond market helps transition countries not only to attract global capital to their housing finance markets, but to suppress the high margins that banks are getting in these countries by introducing competition. This would make mortgage finance available to a larger part of the population.

Finally, in designing and implementing government strategies on housing finance in the context of housing policy, co-ordination among relevant authorities is important. In Estonia, a task force was formed to discuss a consistent policy for the development of housing finance; it involves the ministries of Finance, Economic Affairs and Social Affairs, as well as local authorities and practitioners.

Conclusions

The housing finance markets in transition economies are still in their infancy. In order to establish a full-fledged market-based economy, these countries urgently need to develop well-functioning housing finance systems. Many transition countries have made progress toward this end, but none has reached a desired level. They are currently in a position to receive maximum benefit from an exchange of experiences and policy advice from advanced market countries and from other transition countries.

A number of participants expressed their appreciation for this meeting and considered it timely and useful. Many also explicitly urged the OECD to continue this project. These views were confirmed by the evaluation questionnaire, in which participants gave a ranking of 4.4 on a scale of 1 to 5 (with 5 representing "excellent") to the question regarding the usefulness of the workshop. All of them asked the OECD to develop this project further.

HOUSING FINANCE IN TRANSITION ECONOMIES

by
Takahiro Yasui[*]

Introduction

The economic transformation process that began in the early 1990s has completely changed the mechanism for providing housing to the public. The provision of housing used to be a government responsibility, but now it should be left to market mechanisms, possibly with government support. Given the expense of housing, it is important for a functional housing market to have an effective system of long-term finance for housing acquisition. Housing finance is a big market in advanced market countries, though it remains in its infancy in transition economies. In order to promote housing policy within the framework of the economic transition toward a market economy, the Central and Eastern European countries face an urgent need to develop a well-functioning, market-based housing finance mechanism.

This article intends to provide an overview of current housing finance practices in transition economies and to identify the major challenges for its development. Two points should be noted: first, data to analyse and compare the housing finance markets in these countries are of limited availability. Description and analysis may at times need to be deductive. Second, housing finance situations vary significantly among transition economies. This article, however, will attempt to shed light on general trends in transition economies, some of which may not apply to specific countries.

The article consists of five sections. The next section illustrates the current situations of housing finance markets in transition countries. As background, it examines the status quo and potential of housing (property) markets. The third section briefly surveys the housing finance systems developing in these countries; the fourth identifies the major challenges facing these economies in promoting housing finance; and the last section offers conclusions.

Housing finance and housing markets in transition economies

Housing finance markets in transition economies

Housing, though essential as an infrastructure of people's lives, is usually very expensive. It normally costs several times one's annual income, making it impossible for most people to pay cash; generally, financing arrangements are unavoidable. In advanced market countries, the housing loan business is a large industry, although mechanisms and market size vary significantly.[1] Figure 1 shows the amount of residential mortgage loans outstanding relative to gross domestic product (GDP), ranging from approximately 70% for Denmark to 5% for Austria. For the large majority of countries, such loans outstanding exceed 20% of GDP.

---

*   Principal Administrator, Directorate for Financial, Fiscal and Enterprise Affairs, OECD

Figure 1: Size of Housing Finance Market in OECD Countries (Residential Mortgage Loans Outstanding Relative to GDP, 1998)

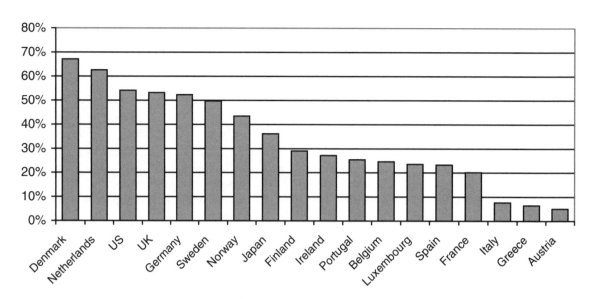

Note: Luxembourg and Portugal are for 1997.   The figure of Austria includes commercial mortgage loans.

Source: European Mortgage Federation - Annual Report 1998, US Federal Reserve Bulletin, Government Housing Loan Corporation of Japan, OECD (GDP figures)

Figure 2: Size of Housing Loan Market in Transition Economies (Housing Loans Outstanding Relative to GDP: 2000)

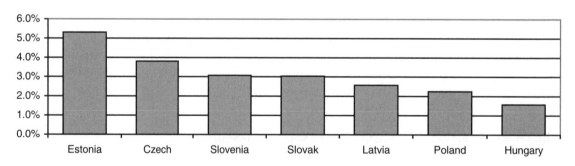

Note: Estonia: Housing loans granted to individuals by credit institutions. Czech: The sum of residential mortgage loans by banks and lending by building societies. Slovenia: Housing loans granted to individuals by credit institutions and the Housing Fund in 1999. Slovakia: The sum of mortgage loans by banks, funds provided by building societies for housing construction, and the loans extended by the State Fund of Housing Development. Latvia, Poland and Hungary: Mortgage loans by banks.

Source: Bank of Estonia, Grabmullerová (2001), Staric (2001), Hlavaèova (2001), Bank of Latvia, Central Statistical Bureau of Latvia, National Bank of Poland, National Bank of Hungary, Szilagyi (2001), EBRD, OECD

In contrast, housing finance markets in transition economies remain in their infancy, as demonstrated in Figure 2 above. The most developed in this respect is Estonia, with a level slightly exceeding 5%. In the other economies, housing loan markets have grown only to 3% of GDP or less. It should be noted that in many of these economies, housing finance markets have grown rapidly in recent years (Figure 3).

Figure 3: Development of Housing Loans in Selected Transition Countries

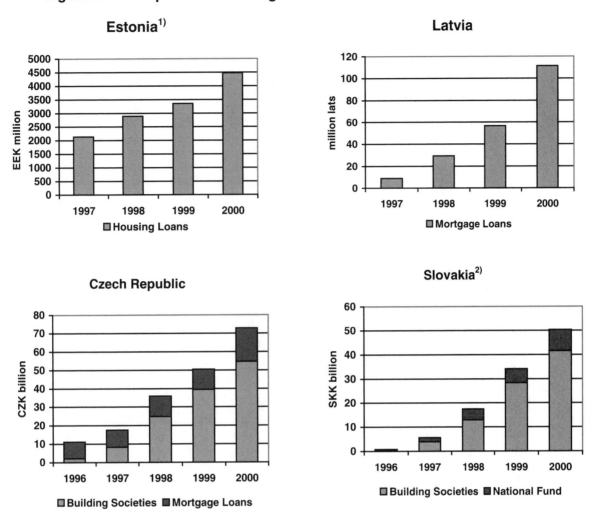

Note: 1) Housing loans granted to individuals. 2) Loans by building societies include those for modernisation of apartments.
Source: Bank of Estonia, Bank of Latvia, Grabmullerová (2001), Staric (2001)

Characteristics of housing markets in transition economies

The current small size of a housing finance market should reflect the fact that the housing (property) market is still rudimentary in transition economies, given the importance of financing for people acquiring expensive residences. This is mainly because of the limited history of such markets. Under the Communist regimes of many transition economies, real estate was in principle owned by the state, and the state had the primary responsibility for providing housing. The state built condominiums in accordance with a particular construction program and let them to the public at very low rents. There was no housing market *per se*, as there were no tradable properties. In some Central and Eastern European countries, some people exceptionally were allowed to own their dwellings, but the owners were generally proscribed from freely moving out and trading their properties with others. A market to exchange properties cannot grow in such circumstances. The housing market therefore effectively emerged from scratch when the economic transformation process began in the early 1990s.

Despite their early similarities, housing markets in the transition economies now vary significantly, reflecting different historical and social backgrounds and economic transformation strategies. The housing markets of these economies do, however, largely share the following features:

- Relatively large housing stocks;

- Significantly high shares of owner-occupied housing;

- Generally poor quality of housing; and

- A low level of housing construction.

Figure 4: Dwellings per 1 000 Inhabitants (1998)

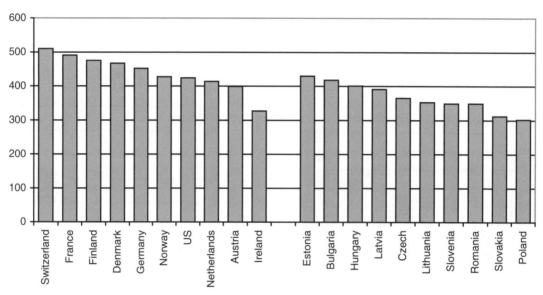

Note: The figures of Ireland and Poland are for 1997.
Source: Annual Bulletin of Housing and Building Statistics for Europe and North America 2000, UN/ECE

First, transition economies have relatively large housing stocks (see Figure 4 for an international comparison). Some transition economies, such as Estonia, have more than 400 dwellings per 1 000 inhabitants, a rate comparable to many EU countries, including Germany. Other transition economies, such as the Slovak Republic and Poland, lag behind but still have more than 300. The relatively large housing stocks in transition economies are essentially the products of former Communist regimes, in which the governments were responsible for building sufficient dwelling space to accommodate the people.

Moreover, in most transition economies, the population has been decreasing in recent years (Figure 5). Without an overall population increase, one can expect no significant new demands for housing in transition economies, unlike the case in many other developing countries. But an examination of demographic structures shows that some countries, such as Romania, have a significant population in the 20-29 age group, which creates housing demands as these young people seek independence from their parents. New demand may also arise from the changing geographical distribution of a population. In many countries, people tend to move to large cities and their surroundings in search of better job opportunities. Nevertheless, one may argue that the transition economies already have sufficient housing levels.

Figure 5: Population Changes in the Last 5 Years (1995-2000)

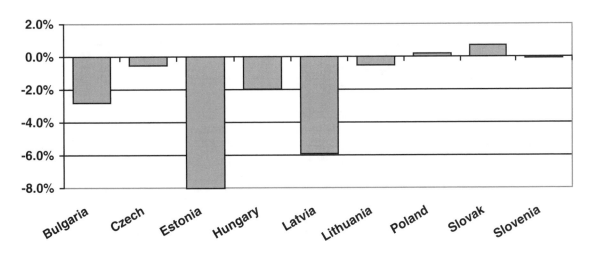

Note: Changes in the population at the beginning of the year, except for Slovakia (mid-year average).
Source: National statistical offices, Country papers

Second, the housing structure in transition economies is remarkable for the significantly high level of owner-occupation. Figure 6 illustrates that the share of owner-occupation housing is exceptionally high in many transition economies, almost 80% in the Slovak Republic and around 90% in Bulgaria, Estonia, Hungary, Romania and Slovenia. This is the obvious result of the privatisation of real estate carried out over the last several years. As part of the economic transformation process, lands and dwellings have been returned to their original owners or sold to the residents at a nominal price. As a result, a large stock of housing has become privately owned and typically owner-occupied, while the amount of public rented housing has decreased dramatically. Some transition economies, such as the Czech Republic, Latvia and Poland, exhibit a moderate share of owner-occupation near 50%; in the Czech and Latvian cases, that probably can be attributed to a pace of housing privatisation that has been slower than in other transition economies. The share of owner-occupation housing is likely to rise as privatisation proceeds. Privatisation has also created structures in which the numbers of commercial rental dwellings are quite limited. Most private rental residences now found in the transition economies resulted from their restitution to the original owners, and rents have been regulated at a notably low level.

It is clear that the high owner-occupation ratio is not the result of free, market-based housing transactions, since the privatisation of real estate only recently set the stage for commercial trading. Therefore, the level would not appear optimal for these economies under an efficient market mechanism. It is likely to decrease over the coming years as housing markets become functional, by degrees that will vary according to the economic and social particularities of the different economies.

Third, while housing stocks in the transition economies are relatively large in quantity, a number of problems have been pointed out regarding their quality. For example, dwellings typically are small in comparison with the advanced market countries (Figure 7). Construction quality is also often described as poor, particularly as regards apartments built in the latter period of Communist control, with poor structural design and budgets applied.

Figure 6: Tenure in Housing[1)]

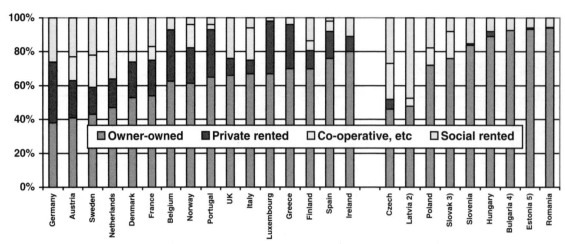

Note: 1) Figures of the EU countries are for 1995 except for Denmark (1997). Those of transition economies are for 1999 except for Bulgaria (1995), Hungary (1997) and Romania (1997). 2) Shares of the aggregate spaces. 3) "Owner-occupied" includes "Private rented". 4) "Owner-occupied" includes "Private rented". "Social rented" includes "Co-operative, etc". 5) "Private rented" includes those resulted from restitution of residences only.
Source: ECODHAS quoted in OECD (1999), national statistics, author's estimates

Figure 7: Average Useful Space per Dwelling (m^2)

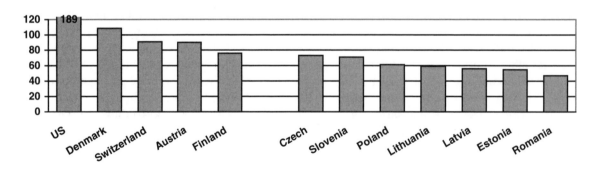

Note: The figures are for 1998, except for US (1997), Switzerland (1990) and Romania (1994). The figures of US and Denmark refer to the living floor space.
Source: UN/ECE Annual Bulletin of Housing and Building Statistics for Europe and North America 2000, National statistics, Budisteanu & Coman (2000)

The quality of existing housing stocks appears, moreover, to be deteriorating because of poor maintenance. In the Communist period, people had little incentive to conduct major renovations for their residences, which were owned not by the inhabitants but by the government. During the economic transformation they have gained ownership of these residences, but have been unable to afford needed renovations.

Housing infrastructure, including sanitation, heating and electricity, is fairly well established. The problem is with efficiency. Equipment and facilities of dwellings are poor and obsolete, impeding efficient use of utilities, especially heat. In addition, circulation systems are old and inefficient, and poorly managed by municipalities. Those factors, coupled with soaring utility prices due to price deregulation, mean that people have to spend a significant portion of their income on utilities. Generally low incomes make it even more difficult for them to invest in their residences. Housing expenses are not very high in transition countries -- they typically account for 15% to 20% of household expenditure -- but the major portion is used for heat and other utilities.

The poor quality of housing is a serious problem for transition economies. For example, the costs of necessary renovation are estimated to amount to USD 2 billion, or 30% of GDP, in Latvia[1,] and to nearly 8% of GDP in Poland[2].

Fourth, turning to the supply side, new construction levels remain low (Figure 8). In the Communist period, the government played a major role in housing construction. Either the central government or municipalities built flats for public rent or had state-owned enterprises and co-operatives build apartments with considerable subsidies. After the economic transformation, the government largely ended such a role and new construction decreased significantly. Housing construction now is predominantly done by the private sector, although a large portion is carried out by individuals in an unorganised way. Some private developers are active in housing construction, but most focus on luxury dwellings intended for the limited numbers of rich people and foreigners. Table 1 shows the trend in the size of new dwellings, indicating that the quality of new housing has been quickly approaching the level of advanced market countries, at least in terms of size. Naturally, these new residences are very expensive, beyond the means of ordinary citizens.

Figure 8: Number of Dwellings Completed per 1,000 Inhabitants (1998)

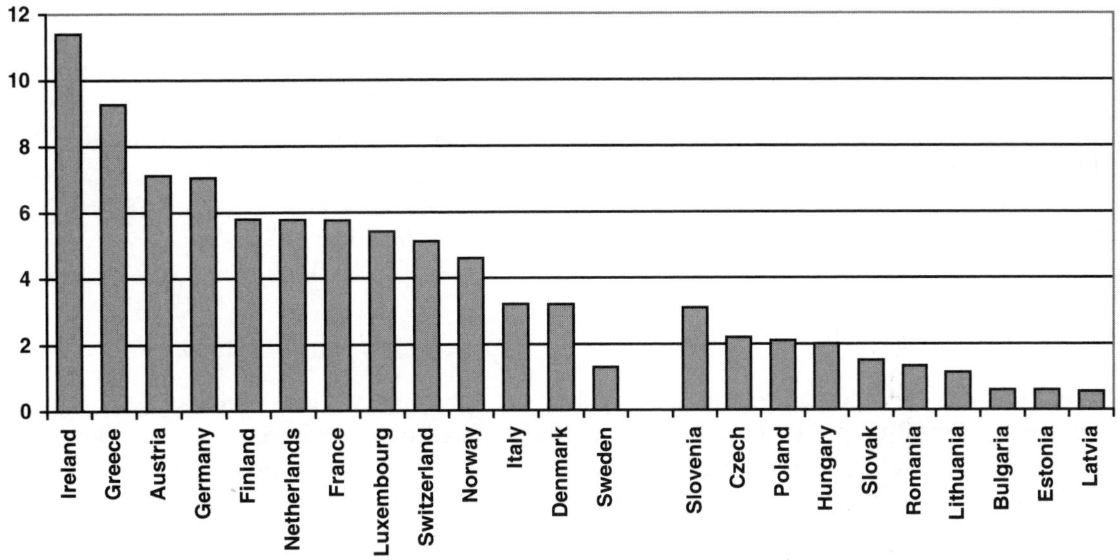

Note: The figures of Germany, Luxembourg, Italy and Slovenia are for 1997.
Source: Annual Bulletin of Housing and Building Statistics for Europe and North America 2000, UN/ECE

Table 1: Average Useful Space per Dwellings Completed
(m^2)

	1990	1995	1997	1998
Bulgaria	71.7	86.1	86.8	85.2
Czech Republic	82.5	93.7	103.0	104.3
Estonia	61.6	91.3	121.2	112.6
Hungary	89.9	99.2	95.4	96.9
Latvia	60.6	123.1	153.9	166.3
Lithuania	64.0	101.0	109.2	119.9
Poland	77.2	89.6	93.3	93.4
Romania	64.5	72.9	82.9	88.1
Slovak Republic		111.2	105.5	121.3
Slovenia	92.9	105.4	105.4	

Source: UN/ECE Annual Bulletin of Housing and Building Statistics for Europe and North America 2000

To date, private sector construction has not developed sufficiently to compensate for the decline in the public sector, resulting in a low level of new construction. Figure 9 illustrates the developments in new housing construction through the 1990s in selected transition economies. In all countries except Slovenia, public-sector housing construction diminished sharply. Private-sector construction has also decreased because of the lack of public support and underdeveloped commercial-base construction.

In summary, the housing markets in transition economies are characterised by relatively large housing stocks typically dominated by owner-occupied housing. Together with decreasing populations, this may suggest that there are no pressing demands in the housing markets and eventually little need for a housing finance mechanism. However, upon closer examination, current housing stocks are poor in quality, and potential demand for better-quality residences is significant. To increase supply, construction of new housing and renovation of current residences need to be promoted, and to facilitate transactions, an effective housing finance mechanism should be established.

Government housing policy

Housing policy is an important part of social policy for any country. Governments pay considerable attention and normally spend significantly from their budgets to secure and improve housing for people. This is true even in advanced market countries. Under the former Communist regime, the state had a direct role in constructing and providing housing. Since the economic transformation began, the governments of transition economies have been stepping away from direct intervention. They are now trying to formulate policies better suited to a market-based economy, essentially similar to the policies of advanced market countries.

Figure 9: New Housing Construction

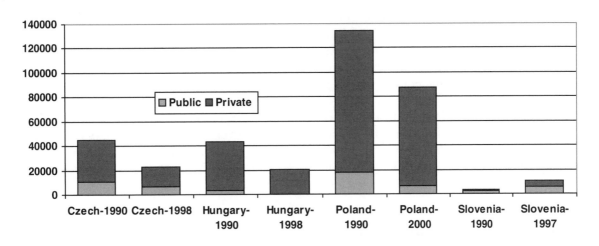

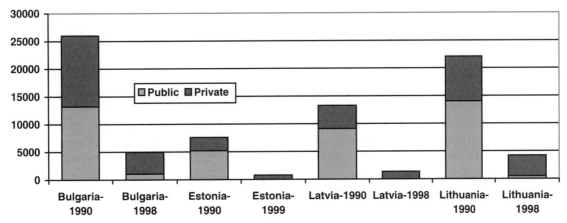

Source: Annual Bulletin of Housing and Building Statistics for Europe and North America 2000, UN/ECE, national statistics

Nevertheless, current strategies in housing policy differ considerably among transition economies, varying according to their geographical, historical, social and economic particularities. As a detailed analysis of housing policies in these economies is beyond the scope of this article, only a few general observations will be made here.

First, to compensate for the decrease in the public supply of new housing, government housing policy emphasises the promotion of new private-sector housing construction. Various public incentives have been prepared to that end, including subsidies and preferential tax treatments related to housing construction. In addition, countries such as the Czech Republic have begun to pay more attention to the better use of current housing stock, creating support measures for maintenance and improvements of existing dwellings.[3]

Second, governments try to centre their direct responsibility on targeted groups, such as low-income and young families, in accordance with overall social policy. State support measures focus increasingly on these socially disadvantaged citizens. In this context, countries such as Poland emphasise construction of social rental housing.[4]

Third, governments are making considerable efforts to establish market-based housing finance systems to promote the acquisition of housing by households through market transactions. For the government to withdraw from its traditional responsibility of providing housing, it is indispensable to develop a market in which people can trade dwellings. In addition to promoting supply by stimulating construction, effective demand has to be created, and that requires reasonably available financial arrangements. The lack of a well-functioning housing finance system, while not unique, is a major reason for the current illiquid housing market in transition economies.

An important objective of the establishment of a market-based housing finance system is to alleviate the fiscal burden of the state in pursuing housing policy. However, significant budgetary amounts have been allocated to support the operation of the systems (see below). In this respect, the strategy aims generally to promote the provision of housing on a commercial basis, coupled with focused fiscal support to address the needs of households less able to afford adequate housing.

Housing finance systems in transition economies[5]

While no housing market developed under the former Communist regime, a certain housing finance scheme existed in many transition economies. While real estate was in principle owned by the state, some people were allowed, in effect, to purchase residences from the state, though they could not trade the properties. A certain financial arrangement was available for such housing purchases, typically a long-term, low-interest, fixed-rate loan from the Savings Bank. In essence, such loans were provided automatically, with no credit assessment being performed. Such a system obviously cannot be sustained in a liberalised market economy. It continued to operate in countries such as Poland and Bulgaria in the initial stages of economic transformation, but largely fell into ruin, however, when governments became unable to support it with the considerable subsidies needed to compensate for low-interest-rate loans in a highly inflationary economic period, early in the transformation process. To develop the housing finance market, new housing finance systems, functional and sustainable under a market mechanism, needed to be established.

Efforts have been made to set up various financial mechanisms, and housing finance markets have emerged in many transition economies. However, the current picture of these markets varies remarkably among the economies, depending on the strategies each country has pursued in the reform process. Generally, the major providers of housing finance in these economies are (i) commercial banks, (ii) mortgage banks issuing mortgage bonds, (iii) contractual savings schemes, and/or (iv) public funds.

Commercial banks

As a credit institution for households and corporations, commercial banks are the natural provider of housing finance in a market economy. They have the largest share in the mortgage loan market of the EU region. Commercial/universal banks are providing housing loans in transition economies as well, though the business remains at a rudimentary stage. The loan products are still very expensive:

- They are mostly short-term products with a maturity of less than 10 years or even 5 years, though longer-term loans are starting to be provided in a few economies.

- The loan-to-value ratio for mortgage loans is typically much lower than the standard of advanced market countries.

- They require high interest rates, both in nominal and real terms. In some economies, housing loans are provided mainly with a floating interest rate, such as dual-indexed mortgage products in Poland, which effectively pass the interest rate risk on to borrowers.

- Moreover, residential mortgage loans are often denominated in foreign currencies, such as US dollars or Euro, so that customers bear the currency risk.

These products hold little attraction to homebuyers, and as a result, housing loans remain a minor component of bank assets. Some transition economies, however, have witnessed rapid growth in mortgage loan business in recent years, reflecting macroeconomic stabilisation (Figure 10).

Figure 10: Share of Housing Loans in Bank Assets (2000)

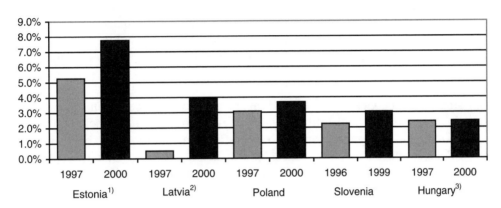

Note: 1) Housing loans granted to individuals. 2) Mortgage loans granted by credit institutions. 3) Mortgage loans. Source: Bank of Estonia, Bank of Latvia, National Bank of Poland, Zawislak (2001), Staric (2001), Szilagyi (2001)

To mitigate the expense of mortgage loans and promote housing finance, some governments have provided fiscal support for these loans in the form of interest-rate subsidy and/or preferential tax treatment. In Lithuania, a few selected commercial banks (including the former state-owned Savings Bank) can offer mortgage credit for the purchase or construction of dwellings with a fixed 5% interest rate; the difference with the market financing rate is covered by a public fund. This scheme resembles the above-mentioned financing mechanism applied in the Communist period, which has been abolished in many other transition economies. In contrast, the Czech and Slovak Republics have a subsidy to cover a prescribed level of interest payments (equivalent to interest rates of 4% of mortgage loans for new housing construction and 6% for purchase).

Another way to improve people's access to housing credit is a guarantee mechanism on housing loans. Such a guarantee could be provided on a commercial basis, but countries such as Canada have developed a public guarantee system to promote housing/mortgage finance in the economy. Among transition economies, Estonia, Lithuania and the Slovak Republic are developing a loan guarantee or insurance scheme backed by the government. Lithuania established the Housing Loan Insurance Company in 1999 to provide insurance on loans for house purchase, construction or renovation. The Slovak Republic adopted in 1999 a state guarantee program on bank loans for housing construction, particularly for rental apartments for lower-income residents. And in 2000 the Estonian Housing Foundation, in co-operation with three commercial banks, launched a mortgage guarantee project primarily targeting young families.

Notably, mortgage credit is not always dominant in housing loans in transition economies. While all housing credits in Bulgaria reportedly are secured by mortgage, the share of mortgage credit in housing loans to individuals accounts for as little as 16% in Slovenia, though that ratio has been increasing rapidly. The low use of mortgage in housing finance can be attributed largely to the still incomplete enforcement of mortgage, in particular foreclosure, procedure. It has been noted that even when lenders use a mortgage as collateral, they do not put much value on it, eventually allowing a low loan-to-value ratio and/or requiring other collateral such as a third-party guaranty.

Mortgage banks and mortgage bonds

Mortgage banks are the banks that specialise in mortgage credit. In advanced market countries, mortgage banks traditionally rely on deposits from the public to finance their loan extensions, as commercial banks do. In Western European countries, however, mortgage banks have also raised funds by issuing mortgage bonds, taking advantage of the high credit ratings backed by high-quality assets and stringent regulation. A typical example is the German mortgage banks issuing mortgage bonds (*Pfandbriefe*). Supported by financial innovation and deregulation, financing by mortgage bonds has expanded significantly in recent years, though their issuance appears to have declined lately in some countries.

Taking inspiration from the German system, Hungary and Poland recently introduced legislation on mortgage bonds and mortgage banks. In Hungary, a few mortgage banks, including the state-owned Bank for Land Credit and Mortgage Loans, have been founded, and mortgage bonds have been issued since 1998. In Poland, under the Act on Mortgage Bonds and Mortgage Banks adopted in 1997, two mortgage banks have come into operation, and a few others have applied for licenses. Two mortgage bond issues have been made to date.

The framework of mortgage banking financed by mortgage bonds has been introduced in some other transition economies, including Latvia, the Czech and Slovak Republics and, more recently, Bulgaria. However, the structure adopted by these economies differs from the German model in that the establishment of a separate institution is not required for conducting mortgage banking and issuing mortgage bonds. Commercial banks can obtain a mortgage banking license and issue mortgage bonds so long as mortgage banking operations and assets are segregated internally in accordance with the legislation. This suggests that the new legislation effectively provide universal banks with an alternative tool to raise funds, though they are earmarked for mortgage credit. Most licensed mortgage banks in these countries are in fact universal banks, while only a few, including the state-owned Mortgage and Land Bank of Latvia, specialise in mortgage, and other real-estate-related, lending. The issuance of mortgage bonds has just started. In Latvia, the Mortgage and Land Bank has made three bond issues to raise USD 5 million.

The use of mortgage bonds in financing mortgage loans has two merits. One is that bond issues normally can raise longer-term funds than the collection of deposits, which are generally short-term in transition economies. This should help alleviate the duration mismatch between the assets and liabilities of the intermediary institutions, improving their risk management. The other merit is the possibility of attracting more funds from foreign investors, benefiting from the increasingly globalise financial markets. It should also be pointed out, however, that mortgage bond financing requires strong legal settings and a broad investor base, both of which pose a significant challenge to transition economies. For them, a well-functioning judiciary that can effectively enforce both the mortgage bond legislation recently introduced and foreclosure procedure is of urgent necessity. In advanced market countries, insurance companies and pension funds are the major investors for mortgage bonds, as they need long-term assets. While one may expect foreign investors to play a role in the market, domestic investors have to be developed to permit sustainable growth of mortgage bond financing.

Another form of securitising mortgage assets is the issuance of mortgage-backed securities. This is very popular in the United States, and has been used increasingly in the EU countries in recent years. In transition economies, however, no such issues have been reported.

Contractual savings schemes

The scheme of contractual savings for housing is fairly popular among transition economies. Such a scheme currently operates in the Czech and Slovak Republics, Hungary, Latvia, Poland and Slovenia. The basic function of the scheme is common: the scheme operator obtains deposits from applicants, usually at a below-market interest rate, and extends housing credits to them at favourable terms once accepted deposits have accumulated to a certain level. However, the schemes in these countries vary. For example, the systems adopted in the Czech and Slovak republics and Hungary are modelled after German or Austrian *Bausparkassen*, which requires the establishment of separate, specialised institutions to manage the scheme. In contrast, the systems in Poland and Slovenia are administered principally through existing commercial banks.

The contractual savings scheme is now the dominant provider of housing finance in the Czech and Slovak Republics, which introduced the system in the early 1990s. The Hungarian and Slovenian schemes, which began respectively in 1997 and 1999, have also been attracting savers quickly, though it is too early to evaluate their performance (lending has not started yet due to the required minimum period of saving). Poland has established two types of contractual savings schemes. One is *kasa mieszkaniowa,* adopted by the law of 1995, and the other is *kasa oszczednosciowo-budowlana,* stipulated in the law of 1997. The former began operating in 1996, though its volume remains modest, while the latter, which is modelled after *Bausparkassen*, has yet to begin operations.

The success of contract savings for housing in these transition economies can be attributed largely to state-provided incentives. In the Czech and Slovak Republics as well as Hungary and Slovenia, savers can benefit from a state subsidy that provides premiums on their savings, making the system highly attractive to them. This, however, creates a considerable fiscal burden for the state. In the Czech and Slovak republics, the subsidy to the contractual savings scheme has occupied the dominant portion of the housing budget. For this reason, the Polish government has frozen operations of the *Bausparkassen* system enacted in 1997.

It should be noted that even in Germany, which has the most developed contractual savings scheme, it constitutes only a part of the finance arrangement for homebuyers. Typically, a loan from the scheme is used for a downpayment in the overall financial package for housing purchase, and the much larger amount is often financed by mortgage loans from commercial and/or mortgage banks. The dominance of contractual savings schemes in the housing finance of some transition economies may end once mortgage loan markets develop on a larger scale.

Public funds

In some transition economies, the state has been providing housing loans directly by establishing a public fund to promote housing construction and purchase. Typical of such funds are the Housing Fund of Slovenia, which was established in 1991, and the State Fund of Housing Development of the Slovak Republic, set up in 1996. The Slovenian fund aims to extend loans at favourable terms for housing purchase and construction by individuals and for the construction of social-rented housing by local communities or non-profit organisations. It also pays subsidies to savers in the contractual savings scheme. The Slovak fund is designed to accommodate finance principally for apartment construction. It used to provide both loans and grants, but stopped giving the latter in 2000 to reduce the budgetary burden. Supported by allocations from the state budget, these funds have played significant roles in the housing markets of the respective economies. The Slovenian fund accounts for 40% of total housing loans to individuals in the country. The Slovak fund contributed 36% of funding for housing construction in 1992-1999.

Many other transition economies have public funds to promote housing finance, though their purposes and functions vary. For example:

- The Estonian Housing Foundation, originally established by government decree of 1994, has been providing favourable loans to narrowly defined recipient groups, including young families and flat-owners associations and co-operatives, and the owners and tenants of dwellings restituted in the privatisation process.

- Poland established the Mortgage Fund in 1992 in co-operation with the World Bank and USAID; its primary function is to provide liquidity for banks to originate dual-indexed mortgage loans. The Notional Housing Fund was created in 1995 to grant very concessional mortgage credit to housing co-operatives and non-profit associations for construction of social rental housing.

- The Lithuanian General Support Fund for Housing Construction and Acquisition, founded in 1992, provides deeply subsidised mortgage loans for construction or purchase of dwellings through banks, as described above.

The popularity of the new public funds to promote housing policy among transition economies may owe partly to the windfall revenues that the states have gained from housing privatisation in the economic transformation process. Many of these funds were established with the capital raised through privatisation, though they often require further financing by the state budget thereafter.

In addition to loan collection and the contribution from the state budget, the Housing Fund of Slovenia has been issuing bonds to become more self-financed.

Others

In advanced market countries, insurance companies and pension funds often play a role in the housing/mortgage finance market, not only as an important holder of mortgage bonds and mortgage-backed securities but as a direct provider of housing loans. In some transition economies, insurance companies also engage in the housing (mortgage) loan business, though the volume remains marginal.

Challenges for development of housing finance markets

Even in countries that have functioning housing finance systems, their business remains rudimentary, largely because of their short history. In fact, as discussed above, some countries have seen rapid growth in the housing finance market. For the robust development of housing finance markets in transition economies, however, various challenges need to be addressed. Four of these are identified below.

Low financial affordability

The first challenge is households' low ability to afford housing. In general, income levels remain considerably lower than in advanced market countries. In all transition economies except Slovenia, GDP per capita remains near USD 5 000 or less, not even one-fourth the average of the OECD countries (Figure 11). Saving ratios are low as well. Consequently, only a small portion of the population (10% to 20% in Estonia and Latvia) is considered financially eligible for loans.

In addition, as mentioned, a large portion of newly constructed residences are deluxe, intended for foreigners or the richest locals. These residences are very expensive by local standards, and unaffordable for ordinary people.

People in transition economies also tend to put more importance on acquiring other durables, typically automobiles, than new housing. This is likely the case because new residences are too expensive for them seriously to consider buying, and as a result of privatisation most of them have their own dwellings, even if of less than satisfactory quality.

Figure 11: GDP per Capita (1999: USD)

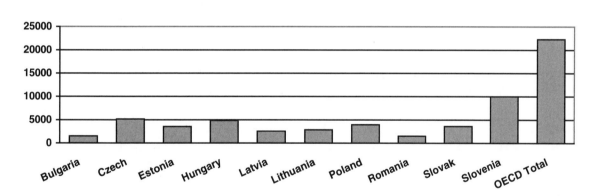

Source: EBRD Transition Report 2000, OECD in Figures 2000

Economic uncertainty

Second, economic uncertainty is an important obstacle for households in applying for and obtaining housing loans. Economic shocks following the economic transformation and the recent financial crises have made it exceptionally difficult for households to feel comfortable about the medium- or long-term future. As a result, both households and lending institutions tend to refrain from long-term housing loans. Table 2 shows how real GDP growth has evolved in the transition economies since 1989. Many countries experienced a difficult period after the economic transformation began. The situation has improved in recent years, however, except in those economies most affected by the financial turmoil that began in 1997. Continuing economic growth should not only increase people's ability to afford housing, but strengthen their confidence in the economy and, more importantly, their job security, thereby improving attitudes toward long-term housing loans.

Table 2: Real GDP Growth
(%)

	1989	1990	1991	1992	1993	1994	1995	1996	1997	1998	1999e	2000p
Bulgaria	0.5	-9.1	-11.7	-7.3	-1.5	1.8	2.1	-10.9	-6.9	3.5	2.4	4.0
Czech	1.4	-1.2	-11.6	-0.5	0.1	2.2	5.9	4.8	-1.0	-2.2	-0.2	2.0
Estonia	8.1	-6.5	-13.6	-14.2	-9.0	-2.0	4.3	3.9	10.6	4.7	-1.1	5.0
Hungary	0.7	-3.5	-11.9	-3.1	-0.6	2.9	1.5	1.3	4.6	4.9	4.5	6.0
Latvia	6.8	2.9	-10.4	-34.9	-14.9	0.6	-0.8	3.3	8.6	3.9	0.1	4.5
Lithuania	1.5	-5.0	-5.7	-21.3	-16.2	-9.8	3.3	4.7	7.3	5.1	-4.2	2.2
Poland	0.2	-11.6	-7.0	2.6	3.8	5.2	7.0	6.1	6.9	4.8	4.1	5.0
Romania	-5.8	-5.6	-12.9	-8.8	1.5	3.9	7.1	3.9	-6.1	-5.4	-3.2	1.5
Slovak	1.4	-2.5	-14.6	-6.5	-3.7	4.9	6.7	6.2	6.2	4.1	1.9	2.0
Slovenia	-1.8	-4.7	-8.9	-5.5	2.8	5.3	4.1	3.5	4.6	3.8	4.9	5.1

Note: 1999 estimate, 2000 projection
Source: EBRD Transition Report 2000

Table 3: Inflation (Change in Annual Average Retail/Consumer Price Level)
(%)

	1989	1990	1991	1992	1993	1994	1995	1996	1997	1998	1999e	2000p
Bulgaria	6.4	26.3	33.4	82.0	73.0	96.3	62.0	123	1082	22.2	0.7	7.0
Czech	1.4	2.7	52.0	11.1	20.8	10.0	9.1	8.8	8.5	10.7	2.1	3.9
Estonia	6.1	23.1	211	1076	89.8	47.7	29.0	23.1	11.2	8.2	3.3	3.8
Hungary	17.0	28.9	35.0	23.0	22.5	18.8	28.2	23.6	18.3	14.3	10.1	9.5
Latvia	4.7	10.5	172	951	109	35.9	25.0	17.6	8.4	4.7	2.4	2.9
Lithuania	2.1	8.4	225	1021	410	72.1	39.6	24.6	8.9	5.1	0.8	1.0
Poland	251	586	70.3	43.0	35.3	32.2	27.8	19.9	14.9	11.8	7.3	9.9
Romania	1.1	5.1	170	210	256	137	32.3	38.8	154	59.1	45.8	45.0
Slovak	2.3	10.8	61.2	10.0	23.2	13.4	9.9	5.8	6.1	6.7	10.6	11.9
Slovenia	1306	550	118	207	32.9	21.0	13.5	9.9	8.4	8.0	6.1	8.6

Note: 1999 estimate, 2000 projection
Source: EBRD Transition Report 2000

Another critical macroeconomic factor is inflation. In a highly inflationary environment, any financial system becomes dysfunctional. This is particularly true for long-term financial mechanisms, such as housing finance. It was the severe inflation early in the economic transformation process, and not the process itself, that ruined housing finance systems left over from the former Communist regimes in some transition economies. On the other hand, low inflation should help in reducing the interest rates of loans, effectively giving people greater access to long-term housing loans. The recent robust developments in the housing finance markets of Western European countries are attributed at least partly to the lowered inflation of the last several years. Table 3 exhibits inflation rates since 1989, indicating that after the early shocks in the transition process, most Central European countries have been fairly successful in stabilising the inflation rate to single-digit levels. Lower inflation should favourably affect the development of housing finance markets in these economies, and in fact housing credits have rapidly expanded in some of them in recent years, as described above.

Underdeveloped financial sector

The third challenge relates to the financial sector as a whole. The housing finance market is a part of the financial sector and so is inevitably affected if the overall financial sector is not well developed and efficient. Residential mortgage lending by commercial banks provides an example. When commercial banks are not run efficiently in a competitive environment, the spread between the interest rates of loans and deposits is wide, discouraging the development of mortgage loans, as currently is the case of transition economies.

Yet if the financial sector is not developed enough to attract sufficient funds, the financial needs for housing acquisitions cannot be met. The generally undeveloped capital market poses a significant challenge, for example, to the financing of mortgage loans by the issuance of mortgage bonds.

Moreover, housing loan origination requires various administrative techniques, such as risk assessment, collateral arrangements, contract documentation, loan services and risk management, which are common to other financial businesses. The level of such techniques hardly improves without an efficient financial sector.

Figure 12: The Size of Credit by Banks to Private Sector relative to GDP (1999)

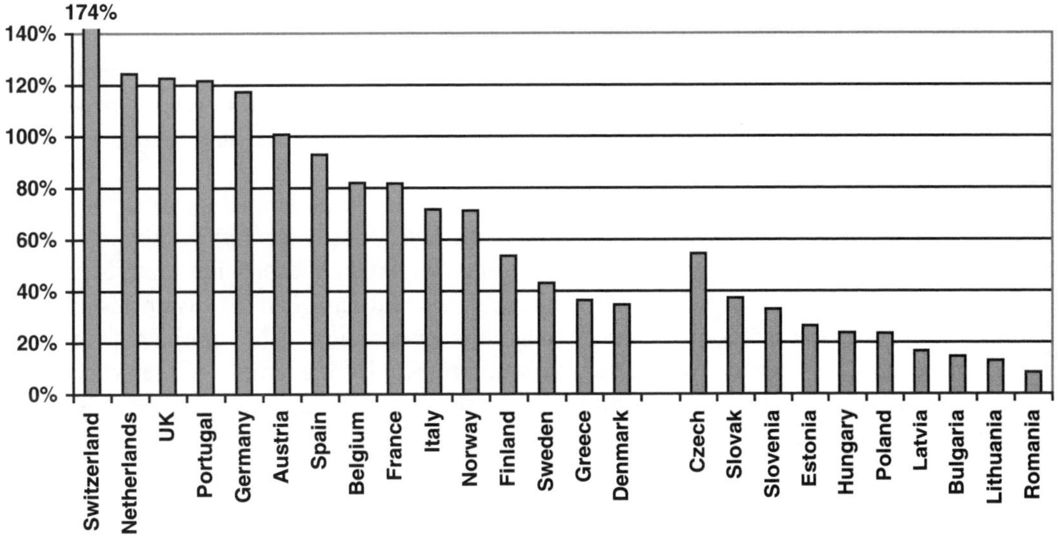

Note:
The figures of Slovenia and Hungary are for 1998.
Source: IMF International Financial Statistics

The financial sector in transition economies has not developed sufficiently. Figure 12 provides an international comparison of the size of credit by financial institutions directed to private sector, and clearly indicates that the credit market has yet to develop in most transition economies. For the sound development of housing finance, the establishment of an efficient financial sector -- perhaps through further privatisation and increased competition, as well as improved regulation -- is an indispensable step. Figure 13 illustrates that the spreads between lending and deposit rates are still very wide in transition economies. The efficiency of the financial sector can therefore be improved significantly.

Figure 13: Interest Rate Spread (Lending Rate-Deposit Rate, 1999)

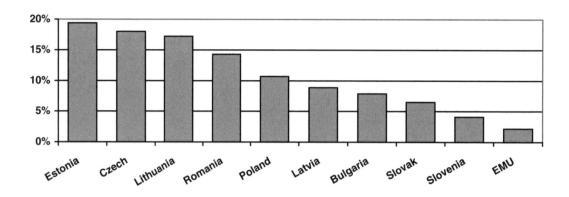

Note: The interest rate charged by banks on loans to prime customers minus the interest rate paid by commercial or similar banks for demand, time, or savings deposits.
Source: World Bank World Development Indicators

Ineffective legal infrastructure

Lastly, it is often noted that legal infrastructure in transition economies remains weak, hindering the development of housing finance. For housing finance, as well as other financial arrangements to some extent, to function appropriately, solid legal systems are needed. A set of legal systems necessary for housing finance can be divided into two groups: basic civil law systems and regulatory systems specific to housing finance.

The first group relates mainly to property and contractual rights. Most essentially, property rights on real estate have to be established, so that people can trade properties and provide them as collateral. This right was dogmatically denied under Communist regimes, but has been legally (re)established in the economic transformation process in all transition economies. The problems arise with enforcement. Property rights on real estate cannot be well protected, for example, if the property is not properly registered. In many transition economies the registry lacks full and accurate records, as many were lost or grew outdated during the Communist period. Even now, new registration reportedly can take more than a year to appear on the book.

Contractual rights have to be established with credit and collateral laws. An important aspect of collateral law concerns the quality of the pledge securing the loan -- the mortgage -- which needs to be established in law, as it is the ultimate security for mortgage lending. Again, many transition economies have introduced reasonable legislation in this respect, but enforcement remains weak. Foreclosure is cumbersome and time-consuming, if possible at all. The judiciary is inefficient and inexperienced in commercial cases. The improvement of law enforcement mechanisms is imperative, though this may take time.

The second type of legal infrastructure for housing finance is the adequate regulatory framework for mortgage loan business. This covers a range of aspects. There must be proper consumer protection rules to protect client borrowers from fraudulent or abusive conduct by the loan originators. Financial soundness of mortgage lenders should be regulated and supervised, especially when they finance the lending by raising funds from the public in the form of deposits or securities. Such regulation and supervision could be the same system as applies to all deposit-taking institutions, but some economies have established a specific scheme for specialised housing finance institutions, such as the contract savings organisations. Moreover, the particular legal framework is normally introduced for mortgage-related securities to ensure their marketability with standardisation and high credibility backed by stringent regulation. Some transition economies, such as Bulgaria, have introduced special regulation on mortgage bonds. In spite of the recent efforts to improve the regulatory settings for housing finance in many transition economies, they have not yet established public confidence in the system.

Conclusions

In the economic transition process, the establishment of a well-functioning housing finance system is an important component in transforming the system of government-provided housing under the former Communist regime to one based on market mechanisms. Although there is potentially a strong need for new, better-quality housing in the transition economies, the housing market remains shallow, not only because of a low level of new construction but also the underdevelopment of housing finance mechanisms.

Efforts have been made to introduce various housing finance systems, and housing finance markets are emerging in most transition economies. However, current market structures differ remarkably across the countries. Commercial and mortgage banks are the driving force of housing finance in Bulgaria, Hungary and Poland as well as the Baltic countries, while the contractual savings scheme plays a significant role in the Czech and Slovak republics. In Slovenia, the government-established Housing Fund is the most important promoter of housing finance. Regardless of structural differences, however, housing finance remains at a rudimentary stage in all transition economies. Emerging-market transactions are supported heavily by government subsidies, and those on a commercial basis remain marginal.

Various challenges are identified for the development of housing finance markets. These include the low loan eligibility of the large portion of the households, the still unstabilised macroeconomic situation, inefficiency in the overall financial markets, and weak legal infrastructure for mortgage credit. None of these has an instant solution. Rather, they require well-intended and continued efforts for improvement within an overall framework of economic transformation strategy. There are encouraging movements. Most notably, the macroeconomy has grown more stable and essential legal frameworks have been introduced, creating the current expansion of the housing finance markets. Further efforts, especially in developing an efficient financial market and improving law enforcement practices, are needed to establish a well-functioning housing

NOTES

1.   See Stephens (2001) for various models of housing finance in EU countries.

1.   Vecvagare (2001)

2.   Zawislak (2001)

3.   See Grabmullerová (2001)

4.   See Zawislak (2001)

5.   This section is benefited from the country reports submitted to the workshop on housing finance in transition economies held in Paris in June 2000, most of which have been revised and included in this publication.

HOUSING FINANCE IN THE CZECH REPUBLIC

by
Daniela Grabmullerová[*]

Macroeconomic characteristics

From the end of World War II until 1989, housing policy was implemented in the environment of a centrally governed state. Its primary role was the construction of new dwellings, with the Government as the investor. The approach was aimed at construction of government-sponsored dwellings and support for co-operatives. Although the Government focused on constructing multiple-story buildings in localities selected by the central authorities, there was some support for individual construction of family homes. The Government's paternalistic approach deformed public perceptions of housing because it failed to motivate people to secure their own accommodations. Despite the wide-ranging activities of the state -- the number of apartments constructed was large, reaching 100 000 apartments annually in the 1970s – substantial problems plagued the housing sector, and public dissatisfaction rose with the quality of housing services (persistent shortage of apartments, low quality, etc.). The former administrative rationing system proved economically nonviable. Whereas at the beginning of the 1950s the Czech Republic was a European leader in the number of apartments per 1 000 citizens, by the early 1990s the country found itself at the bottom of the list.

Since 1990, however, the economy has undergone a transformation. Fundamental changes aimed at eliminating the housing administrative rationing system and creating a market-oriented structure took place, notably from 1991 to 1993. However, this period, as well as the following few years, was marked by a "neo-liberal approach" and a generally narrow perception of the housing sector. Consequently, while elements of the housing administrative rationing system were eliminated, this was not followed in timely fashion by the creation of support measures to ensure accessibility to housing for all layers of society.

The first step -- besides restitutions -- was the transfer of state-owned housing stock to the municipalities. Municipalities received loss-making housing units that were often in a state of utter disrepair. Yet, the municipalities were not provided with adequate conditions for administration, maintenance or repair of these structures. As a result, municipal authorities tried to privatise these newly acquired dwellings. Privatisation took place chiefly on the basis of municipal decrees that allowed the sale of entire buildings to legal entities, most often co-operatives, formed by tenants. Privatisation trends were further emphasised by the Apartment Ownership Act, which allowed the ownership titles to apartments to be transferred to individuals. This measure, lacking a systemic character, failed to define the manner of administration and maintenance of privatised housing. In addition, the Government underestimated the purchasing power of tenants. Combined with a pragmatic stance of municipalities, this law has caused numerous problems, above all the fact that new owners lack funds to maintain privatised dwellings, which could lead to a worsening of the existing problem of neglect.

---

[*]   Director, Housing Policy Department, Ministry for Regional Development, Czech Republic.

Privatisation of apartments has also had a negative effect on co-operative housing, understood at the beginning of the 1990s as a remnant of the former regime. Measures adopted by the Government focused on liquidating co-operatives rather than on eliminating deformations caused by the Communist administration. This course of action was based on the Apartment Ownership Act. Fortunately, the planned liquidation of co-operatives was never fully carried through.

Table 1: Macroeconomic Developments

	1994	1995	1996	1997	1998	1999	2000
Population (thousands)	10 336	10 331	10 315	10 304	10 295	10 280	10 270
GDP current price (billion CZK)	1 182.8	1 381.1	1 572.3	1 668.8	1 798.3	1 833.0	1 910.6
GDP per capita (USD)	3 975	5 034	5 610	5 146	5 400	5 200	4 820
GDP per capita in purchasing power standard (USD)	11 300	12 400	13 000	13 100	12 900	13 000	13 873
Gross saving ratio (% of GDP)	27.8	29.9	28.1	26.3	27.3	26.6	25.7
Gross fixed capital formation (% of GDP)	29.0	34.2	38.2	34.2	30.4	28.2	30.4
CZK/USD (annual average)	28.786	26.545	27.138	31.711	32.274	34.600	38.590
Inflation (annual)	10.0	9.1	8.8	8.5	10.7	2.1	3.9
Unemployment (year-end, %)		2.9	3.5	5.2	7.5	9.4	8.8
Wage (monthly average)	6 894	8 172	9 676	10 691	11 693	12 658	13 491

General description of the current housing situation

Following restitutions and privatisation, the housing structure in the Czech Republic is consistent with the housing situation in other European countries. Although the quality of housing is lower, it roughly corresponds to the economic power of the Czech Republic. Neglected maintenance of dwellings caused by prolonged under-capitalisation has caused considerable problems.

Measures accepted thus far are not sufficiently interrelated and focused, and thus are not fully effective. In addition, their effectiveness is limited by the overall economic and social situation in the country, which in many respects is still in transformation. As a result, the system does not function in a manner comparable with advanced countries.

The housing market is structurally and territorially differentiated. The housing situation is quite diverse in different parts of the country, with substantial disparities between regions and municipalities. Most measures adopted in the past had an across-the-board character.

The housing situation is affected by many external factors. The most pressing problem is the territorial distribution of enterprises and the situation on the labour market -- these aspects cause local discrepancies between the availability of housing and employment opportunities. Demand in large cities with sufficient numbers of jobs is considerably higher than supply, causing shortage of housing and related problems. Conversely, regions with high unemployment have vacant dwellings for which there is no demand. Discrepancies between employment opportunities and available housing are further deepened by poor transport infrastructure, especially in rural areas.

Situation in individual housing sectors

The *co-operative sector* consists mostly of co-operatives. They own approximately 19% of all housing stock and their importance is considerable. The situation is more or less satisfactory from the users' viewpoint, although the consequences of injudicious legislative decisions made in the early 1990s are becoming evident. Unfinished privatisation poses some problems, and housing construction is stagnating as a result of inadequate government support.

The *private rental sector* is relatively small, amounting to approximately 6% of all housing stock. There are significant problems due to lack of maintenance of buildings, rent control regulations that cover most apartments, and poor relations between tenants and property owners.

The *municipal rental sector* amounts to approximately 24% of all housing stock. It faces problems similar to the private rental sector;. However, new units are being constructed thanks to government subsidies. The function of municipal housing is not clearly defined as a result of different stands of individual municipalities and continuing liberation of rent control.

The *owner-occupied sector* consists chiefly of family homes. The sector is being expanded with privately owned apartments as a result of both privatisation and new construction.

Housing sector overview

Condition of the housing stock, housing construction

Size of housing stock

According to the 1991 public census, the housing stock in the Czech Republic comprises 4 077 193 dwellings, of which 371 512 units, or 9.1%, are permanently vacant. The greatest number of vacant dwellings is family homes used as weekend cottages (without certification). These rural dwellings are usable for permanent living purposes only to a limited extent due to their location in areas with low employment opportunities. The greatest proportion of temporarily vacant private residences is units not used as a result of unresolved privatisation claims.

Table 2: Number of permanently used dwellings

1991 (public census)	3 705 681 dwellings (90.9% of the housing stock)
1999 (selective research)	3 731 165 dwellings

According to the 1991 public census, the Czech Republic had 360 permanently occupied dwellings per 1 000 inhabitants. A selective statistical survey conducted by the Czech Statistical Office in the first quarter of 1999 found that there were 365 such dwellings per 1 000 inhabitants.

Considering that at the time of the 1991 census approximately 400 000 families did not have their own dwellings and lived in common households with other families (two-thirds of these were cases of unwanted cohabitation) and that housing construction remains relatively low, it can be assumed that the number of households without their own dwelling has increased.

Quality of the housing stock

51% of the housing stock consists of apartments in multiple-story buildings. Approximately 1.2 million apartments are located in prefabricated panel buildings. The size of apartments is especially unsatisfactory, particularly compared to international standards. Moreover, a large portion of the housing stock is technically obsolete as a result of neglected maintenance. Particularly alarming is the condition of panel buildings. Sanitation and heating standards in the housing stock are, however, considered acceptable.

The poor functioning of the housing market is exacerbated by difficulties pertaining to commuting possibilities (worsening transportation services and increasing fuel costs) and the low supply of accessible housing in localities with relatively numerous employment opportunities. In addition, the average age of dwellings is relatively high: family homes, 60.3 years, apartment buildings, 36.2 years.[1]

Table 3: Existing Structure of the Housing Stock - Basic Forms of Housing (1999)

	Rental sector[1)	Co-operative sector[2)	Private sector	Other
Number of dwellings	1 219 000	704 000	1 722 000	87 000
Share	33%	19%	46%	2%

Note: 1) Municipal, state-owned, and private rental housing, and housing owned by legal entities created for the purpose of privatisation of apartment buildings. 2) Construction and civic co-operatives.
Source: Study of the structure of the housing fund (1998), Czech Statistical Office.

After 1989, gradual changes in the structure of housing took place:

–   The private rental sector, created chiefly as a result of restitutions, currently amounts to about 6%, or 215 000 dwellings (most of them apartments with regulated rent).

–   In 1991 state-owned apartments were transferred to municipalities. This action created the municipal rental-housing sector, currently comprising 24% of the total housing stock, or 880 000 units (this sector is gradually declining, as municipalities are privatising some buildings, most often selling them to existing tenants).

–   Ownership of dwellings in co-operative buildings is gradually being transferred to co-operative members; these units amount to 19% of the housing stock, or 704 000 units.

–   Privately owned apartments in apartment buildings (including transferred co-operative units) amount to approximately 6% of the housing stock, or 230 000 units. Privately owned family homes amount to about 40% of the housing fund, or 1 490 000 units.

As regards the rental and privately owned sectors, the structure of the housing stock corresponds roughly to the housing structure in European Union countries.

New housing construction

New housing construction slowed down substantially after 1990, and the decline lasted until about 1993. Since 1994, construction starts have gradually increased, leading to an increased number of completed dwellings as shown in Figure 1. Despite positive developments of the last several years, the Czech Republic is lagging behind the European Union average.[2]

Figure 1: New Housing Construction (number of dwellings)

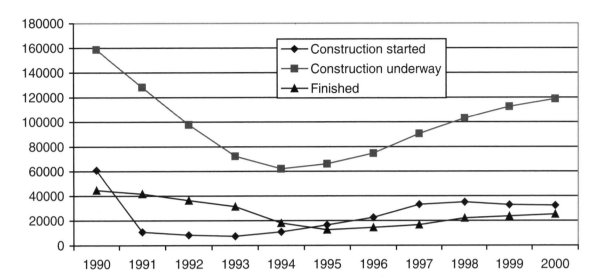

Total housing costs, affordability for households

On average, total housing costs in all types of housing amount to CZK 2 990 per month. Housing expenditures amount to 18.9% of average net household income. Due to rapidly increasing rent levels and different structures of housing expenses, total accommodation costs are higher in rental units, amounting to 19.4% of the average household income.

Housing costs differ significantly depending on housing type (privately owned, co-operative, rental), size and category of dwellings, size of the municipality, and the technology used for heating, hot-water production and cooking.

The affordability of individual types of housing differs substantially. As for acquisition, the affordability of new privately owned dwellings is low. Acquisition costs grew substantially in 1990-99, a fact caused by price liberalisation, relatively high demand for good-quality housing, and a sharp increase in land prices, especially in the mid-1990s.

The affordability of privately owned dwellings has increased as a result of lower interest rates on mortgage loans, which in 1999 ranged from 8% to 11%, depending on the financial institution. If the state interest rate subsidy (4%) is used, it means that a CZK 750 000 loan repayable in 20 years involves monthly instalments of CZK 4 545 and CZK 5 815 respectively. These amounts correspond roughly to 200% to 300% of the regulated rent for a 60-square-meter apartment in Prague.

Support measures for housing

Support for mortgage loans

Mortgage loans are long-term loans secured with real estate and used especially for purchases of dwellings by individuals. Such loans have been available in the Czech Republic since 1995, when the applicable legislation took effect.

Government support for mortgage loans has several forms of differing focus. Mortgage-certificate interest revenues were exempted from income-tax payment in order to strengthen the accumulation of funds in mortgage banks. Two other approaches -- subsidising interest on mortgage loans and subtracting instalments from the income base for the calculation of personal income tax -- are intended to make mortgage loans more accessible for households.

The most important measure is subsidy of a part of interest on mortgage loans. This measure, available only for new-dwelling purchases, aims to encourage housing construction. Based on the latest legislation, the interest rate ranges from 0% to 4%, depending on current developments.

Although support instruments exist, mortgage loans are not widely used. The main reason is the low level of income of most households. Few households are able to obtain and then repay a mortgage loan sufficiently large to allow the purchase of a new dwelling. Subsidised mortgages are available only for newly constructed dwellings; older apartments and family homes, however, are currently sold for lower prices.

Support for construction of municipal rental apartments and technical infrastructure

Investment subsidies for construction of rental apartments and the related infrastructure are granted on the basis of programs announced yearly. This non-returnable subsidy amounts to a maximum of CZK 320 000 per unit and a maximum of CZK 80 000 per unit for related infrastructure. The subsidy purposely covers only a part of the costs of construction and needs to be combined with municipal or private funds.

Substantial funds have been allocated to this program since its beginning in 1995, a fact reflected in the extent of new housing construction. Nonetheless, the program alone is unable to encourage sufficient construction of rental apartments. Experience has shown that municipalities seek additional resources to finance construction of new dwellings. The planned form of housing organisations will rectify and legally define multiple-source financing on a non-profit basis. Thus, housing non-profit organisations will gradually take over the investor role of municipalities.

Support for construction of rented housing with community care services

Investment subsidies for construction of nursing homes have been granted since 1991. The maximum subsidy is CZK 750 000 per unit, and the grants are intended for persons with reduced self-sufficiency, such as disabled and retired individuals. Nursing homes include so-called protected housing. Municipal rental apartments are available for virtually all groups with specific housing needs.

Construction savings plans – building societies

Construction savings plans provide a system for financing of housing based on clearly defined savings and loan stages. These construction savings plans offer access to low-interest loans linked with low-interest savings plans. Available in the Czech Republic since 1993, construction savings plans are used to finance varied housing needs, from acquisition of a dwelling to purchase of furnishings.

The main form of government subsidy is a non-returnable contribution of 25% of the annually saved amount (maximum CZK 4 500 per person); the objective is to encourage households to save money and thereby accumulate the funds necessary to provide low-interest loans. Support also comes through the exemption from income tax of interest on construction savings deposits, and the possibility of deducting repaid interest on loans from the income tax base.

Thanks mainly to the government subsidy, construction savings plans are used to the maximum possible extent, especially in the savings stage. Almost 40% of already granted loans have been used to purchase a dwelling, often as part of privatisation projects. However, only one-fifth of loans have been used to acquire new dwellings. This shows that the funds that can be accumulated through construction savings plans are insufficient, given the cost of new construction.

Interest-free government loans for municipalities

The government loan (interest-free and repayable within 10 years) is intended for municipalities and, through them, for private property owners (loans with maximum 7% interest totalling at least 20% of the allocated subsidy) for repair and maintenance of neglected housing. Such government support was designed to initiate the creation of municipal funds (a condition for obtaining the subsidy) for the modernisation of the housing stock. Thus, loans are turning to low-interest credits granted by the State Housing Development Fund.

Subsidies for repair of the housing stock

These subsidies are intended for all owners of buildings constructed with the prefabricated panel technology, namely municipalities, housing co-operatives, private owners and legal entities in which the government does not own a stake. Not exceeding 50% of budget costs, the subsidy is intended for repair of very serious defects and emergencies.

Other instruments

Besides the important instruments mentioned above, numerous other measures aim to provide support for the housing sector. Direct subsidies include payment of bank losses for persons repaying subsidised loans (1% and 2.7%) granted in the past for co-operative and private construction and subsidies for heating insulation. Fiscal measures include a deduction of paid interests from the income tax base, exemption from property tax for 15 years from certification of a new dwelling, and accelerated depreciation (30 years) aimed at creation of funds for the repair of apartment buildings (various tax relieves are listed in Annex). Besides these forms of support, the state pays substantial sums in aid to areas affected by floods. A range of housing allowances should also be mentioned as a part of government support.

Mortgage loans

Universal Czech banks can obtain licenses for mortgage banking activity so long as they keep separate legal and accounting records on the activity. The "mortgages" that provide the collateral for the mortgage bonds are not physically segregated from other assets of the bank, but they are legally segregated in case of default or bankruptcy, so that they serve exclusively as first-rank collateral for the bonds.

The Czech banks do have to pay a small price for taking this approach. They are required to conform their mortgages to a norm of mortgage banking, having fixed-rate loans (for one or five years), in contrast to the flexibility of US, UK and French banks, which offer both variable- and fixed-rate loans. To the extent that they are funding the loans out of short-term deposits, this has introduced an element of interest-rate risk that would not be required otherwise.[3] On the other hand, the Czech mortgage banking law is not as restrictive as the German one, in that it permits the loan-to-value ratio to be as high as 70 percent.

Nine mortgage banking licenses have been issued so far. As noted, all but one of these licenses have been given to universal banks, not specialised mortgage banks, and the one specialised bank has found it uneconomical to operate in that fashion. One of them is focused exclusively on making loans on commercial real estate and another is oriented toward commercial loans, loans for rental residential developments, and loans for high-cost houses.

Currently, the standard design for mortgages is a 20-year term, with a rate fixed for one or five years and prepayment subject to high, but negotiable, fees. It is advantageous for most households to take the full 20-year term and it appears that most do. The advantage is particularly great if the borrower qualifies for the 4-percentage-point subsidy from the Government, since this is payable out to 20 years. Even if the borrower is not eligible, the interest on the loan is currently tax-deductible, which reduces the effective real rate of interest to about zero percent, at least for high-income borrowers.

Table 4: Development of Mortgage Loans

	1996	1997	1998	1999	2000
New mortgage loans (billion CZK)	6 188	4 092	4 988	6 414	10 228
New mortgage loans (% of GDP)	0.58	0.55	0.6	0.59	0.95
of which: for individuals	5 676	3 407	4 594	6 103	9 820
for corporations	512	685	394	311	448
New mortgage loans with State subsidy (number of flats)	126	2 031	2 761	3 053	4 765
New mortgage loans with State subsidy (billion CZK)	127	1 557	2 336	3 403	5 601
of which: for individuals	114	1 294	1 689	2 443	2 995
for corporations	0	22	43	11	0
for co-operatives and municipalities	0	0	0	0	144
Mortgage loans total (billion CZK)	9 088	9 247	10 987	10 922	18 180
Mortgage bond issuing (billion CZK)	1.8	1.1	2.2	11.9	5.35
Mortgage bond outstanding (billion CZK)	1.8	2.9	5.1	17.0	22.35

As of June 2000, these loans are being offered at rates of about 9 percent for the first five years. One variant of this design is an option of a one-year adjustable rate mortgage, convertible to a five-year rate at time of renewal.

Underwriting on these loans is based on calculations designed to ensure that remaining discretionary income exceeds 1.6 times the minimum living income for that family size. The net effect, apparently, is for a payment-to-net income ratio of about 30%-35%. In making these calculations, the 4-percent subsidy is deducted from the rate (if applicable) and a share of the tax savings due from deducting the interest paid is removed from the net mortgage payment.

Notably, mortgage banking regulations allow loans with loan-to-value ratios of up to 70% to be used as collateral for mortgage bonds. Loans for up to another 20% of the appraised value can be obtained at a higher, floating rate.

Table 5: Average Terms of Mortgage Loans

	1996	1997	1998	1999	2000
Basic interest rate (A)	N/A	12.31	13.58	10.28	8.79
State subsidy (B)	4.0	4.0	4.0	4.0	4.0
Result interest rate (A-B)	N/A	8.31	9.58	6.28	4.79
Average period (months)	182	184	185	186	181

Mortgage subsidy

After adopting the necessary legislative conditions in October 1995, the Government approved the terms of the state financial support for mortgage loans in order to stimulate new housing construction. The purpose of this program is to increase the availability of long-term loans from commercial banks to private builders of family homes and apartment buildings. The support is provided in the form of interest rate subsidy of four percentage points on mortgage loans. Mortgage loans are granted for a maximum of 70% of the value of the property to be built. Builders who lack initial capital can obtain the necessary funds from swing loans or loans granted under the Construction Savings Plan.

The financial aid can be used for construction of apartment buildings or family houses, purchase of land for housing construction, purchase of a new apartment or a house (within one year of certification), and for repayment of a loan received after 1 January 1995. A Government decree specifies that borrowers are entitled to receive government financial aid until full repayment of mortgages, providing that the repayment period should not exceed 20 years. This measure applies to mortgages (or parts thereof) which do not exceed:

– CZK 2 million (house with two apartments).

– CZK 1.5 million (single-family house).

– CZK 12,000 per square meter of an apartment, but no more than CZK 800 000 per unit in an apartment building.

Housing finance systems: building societies

The Building Society system was introduced in the Czech Republic in 1993. The amount of yearly premium is 25% of savings, up to CZK 4 500. Annual optimal savings is CZK 18 000, or twice the average monthly wage in 1993 (but 150% in 1998). Minimum saving period is five years to get housing contractual loan (usually at 6%) if 50% of the contracted sum is saved. Saving for five years is required to cash the premium, but not required to use for housing. Loans are provided only for housing purposes; to be demonstrated by invoices (initial provisions allowed for loan for non-housing purposes).

In addition, the interest and premium on savings are exempt from taxation. Premiums are paid into the account within one or two months after the end of the "contract year" (the 12-month cycle since start of the account). The interest paid on loans made for new construction is not tax-deductible (in contrast to interest on such loans by mortgage banks). Accounts can be tied to issuance of a market-rate housing loan immediately (by the parent commercial bank), repayable by a bridge loan from the Building Society after 2 years. The parameters of the state premium are embedded in law, and Parliament must act to reduce or increase it.

Figure 2: Development of Contract Savings

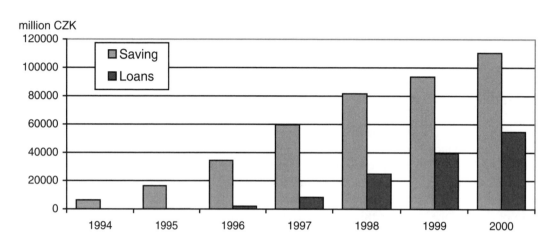

The Building Society system has grown quickly in the Czech Republic. Four institutions were able to begin operations in the first year, and two more in 1994. The first, the Czecho-Moravian Building Society, has remained in the lead since then. All six institutions have strong minority participation by German or Austrian *Bausparkassen*, with majority ownership resting with a Czech universal bank.

Basic objectives of the new housing policy

All the proposed measures are based on the fundamental objective of creating a situation in which every household will be able to find accommodation that is adequate in size, quality and price. Attaining this goal will require an increase in the volume of funds allocated to housing, namely funds for maintenance of existing dwellings and construction of new units. Another requirement is to develop adequate economic, legal and other instruments, strengthening the role of the state such that public funds are used as productively and economically as possible. At the same time, market principles need to be developed to weaken lingering paternalism and to emphasise individuals' responsibility for their housing situations. Multiple-source financing will have to be used to reach these objectives (combinations of private and public funds, public-private partnerships, incorporation of employers' support). The Government role is to stimulate the flow of private investment, not to replace private initiatives. In this regard, public funds will be used to supplement creation of the State Housing Development Fund, an important non-budget source for the financing of housing development.

Housing policy aims to increase availability and affordability of housing

The overall availability of housing depends on the interaction between available and suitably located housing and the needs for accommodations. It is affected by the scope of housing construction, the use and maintenance of existing dwellings, and demographic developments. The Housing Policy Concept emphasises the preparation of land for housing construction, support for suitable technologies that reduce new-construction costs, and use of existing structures, including non-residential premises, for additions, modifications and conversions to residential purposes. For optimal use of existing housing, people must be sufficiently mobile. Currently, areas offering employment often do not coincide with the location of available housing. In this regard, it will be important to improve the transportation infrastructure, particularly those services that allow daily commuting to large cities.

Affordability of housing, based on price and the proportion of household financial resources, must be increased, as it is one of the greatest obstacles to satisfying the needs of people in most income brackets. Subject to economic growth, the situation can be improved by ensuring the development of rental housing on a non-profit basis, revising the system of social housing allowances, reworking the approach to home ownership accommodation, and some other measures.

Expansion of housing policy priorities

The above facts and analysis show a need to expand the priorities of housing policy. Government housing policy has focused mainly on support for new construction and increasing the number of new dwellings. Past measures have yielded some improvement since the first half of the 1990s; more than 22 000 new apartments were completed in 1998, and the number of new dwellings is continuing to grow. Yet, it is apparent that further intensification of new housing construction cannot be secured solely through another massive increase of subsidies; instead, external restricting factors and deformations must be eliminated.

Besides continuing support for new construction, the Government proposes to pay closer attention to maintenance and optimal use of existing dwellings, including the elimination of obstacles that prevent this objective. The result is expected to be a substantially more effective use of existing capacities, an increase in the number of available dwellings, improvement of quality, and increased investor interest in the housing sector.

New objectives of housing policy

Moving beyond the transformational framework of the past, the new objectives focus on specific issues of the housing policy to deal with specific problems. The first one is support for acquisition of new and older dwellings. This measure is based on the assumption that older dwellings will more easily satisfy accommodation needs because they are always less expensive than newly constructed units. Hence, the Government is proposing to adopt support measures (notably providing loans under special terms) to reduce the predominant orientation of households on new construction and facilitate purchases of older dwellings.

The second focus is placed on stronger support for selected groups of the disadvantaged. The situation in the housing sector and the existence of support instruments make it possible to focus housing policy on groups of people disadvantaged by low income, poor health, age, origin, etc. The adoption of adequate measures, such as low-interest loans or subsidies, will help groups such as the young, handicapped or the homeless to obtain suitable housing.

Decentralisation of housing policy

Effective housing policy can be executed only if the roles of Government authorities are adequately divided. Especially important is the vertical distribution of powers between central, intermediary (regional) and local authorities; long-term studies of housing patterns have shown that accommodation problems need to be dealt with at the lowest levels possible to satisfy the different and complex needs of people. The main near-term goal will be fundamentally to reinforce the role of municipalities in housing matters.

In addition to the irreplaceable function of municipal housing policies, especially in the executive stage, a rapid analysis will be needed of the distribution of powers by the forthcoming regions in the housing sector.

New instruments of housing policy now under preparation

The Act on Public Beneficial Housing Co-operatives provides support in the forms of low-interest mortgage credit for new co-operative housing construction; and direct non-returnable subsidy for new co-operative housing construction.

New measures aimed at easing acquisition of first housing by young people include mortgage credit with interest subsidy for the purchase of an older dwelling; and low-interest credit up to CZK 200 000 for acquisition of a co-operative or owner-occupied dwelling.

So-called supported housing is granted for people disadvantaged in the sphere of housing – seniors, physically and mentally disabled people, people living in poor social conditions, and so on. This measure takes the form of a direct non-returnable subsidy to municipalities for new rental housing construction.

NOTES

1.   Estimated by the Ministry for Regional Development

2.   International comparisons are somewhat misleading because statistical methodologies differ. In many EU countries, unlike in the Czech Republic, the size of the housing stock includes modernised dwellings or recreational units (including seaside cottages and mountain resorts), thereby increasing the volume of housing construction.

3.   It is not clear how important this issue is. Banks do offer a one-year fixed rate loan that could easily be funded out of shorter-term deposits, but it appears that it is not popular.

Annex: Tax Relief for Housing

Aim of measure	Support for greater use of mortgage loans	Promotion of mortgage loans and loans under the Construction Savings Program	Creation of financial resources for repair of privately owned buildings	Support for new housing construction
Form of support	Income tax exemption on yield from mortgage bonds	Paid interest may be deducted from income tax base	Property tax exemption up to 2007	Property tax exemption which applies to new privately owned apartment buildings for 15 years from building certification
Applies to	All holders of mortgage bonds	Borrowers	Buildings returned under the restitution program	New apartment buildings
Applicants	Mortgage bonds holders	Borrowers	Property owners	Building or apartment owners
Terms	Specified in Act	Specified in Act	Specified in Act	Specified in Act
Where to apply	On tax return form		On tax return form	On tax return form
Note			The tax exemption applies even if property has been transferred to a related person	

Aim of measure	Creation of financial resources for repair of apartment buildings	Replacement of heating system	Creation of financial resources for repair of houses owned by low income or disabled people	Creation of financial resources for repair of houses owned by low income or disabled people
Form of support	Tax exemption which applies to income from apartments (garages) in buildings owned by co-operatives	Five year property tax exemption for buildings with a new heating system (not using solid fuel) or thermal insulation	Property tax exemption	Property tax exemption
Applies to	Houses owned by the Builders' Co-operative, the People's Co-operative, and corporations founded by apartment owners	Buildings with new heating system or thermal insulation; the five year tax exemption period starts in the year following building certification	Houses or dwellings owned by low income and handicapped persons	Houses or dwellings owned by low income and handicapped persons
Applicants	Property owners	Property owners	Property owners	Property owners
Terms	Specified in Act	Specified in Act	Specified in Act	Specified in Act
Where to apply		On tax return form	On tax return form	On tax return form
Note			The tax exemption applies to the proportion of the property which is used as the applicant's permanent residence	The tax exemption applies to the proportion of the property which is used as the applicant's permanent residence

Annex: Tax Relief for Housing *(cont.)*

Aim of measure	Creation of financial resources for repair of privately owned apartment buildings built before 1948	Creation of financial resources for repair of apartment buildings	Creation of financial resources for repair of privately owned buildings
Form of support	Property tax exemption up to 2007 for restituted buildings built before 1948	Accelerated depreciation, up to 2 1/4% annually, of the acquisition cost of property	Property tax exemption up to 2002
Applies to	Privately owned apartment buildings in which more than 50% of apartments are rented	All buildings	Privatised apartment buildings
Applicants	Property owners	Property owners	Property owners
Terms	Specified in Act	Specified in Act	Specified in Act
Where to apply	On tax return form		On tax return form
Note	The tax exemption applies even if the property has been transferred to a related person		The tax exemption applies even if the property has been transferred to a related person

THE HOUSING SECTOR IN ESTONIA

by
Igor Jakobson[*]

Macroeconomic developments

Estonia is a small country with the population of 1.44 million. Like the other Baltic countries, the Estonian economy suffered from sharp contraction after the independence in 1990. In the first few years, real gross domestic product (GDP) fell, and inflation hiked, reaching 1 078% in 1992. The economy started to stabilise in 1995 when real GDP growth turned to be positive. In 1997, the economy showed rapid expansion over 10%, suggesting that it was overheating. The asset prices soared and the trade deficit widened. The economic boom ended shortly, however, resulting that real GDP growth slowed to 4.0% in 1998 and -1.1% in 1999. The Russian financial crisis in 1998 also had a negative impact on the Estonian economy despite the fact that Russia had become far less important as a trading partner. The economy showed recovery in 2000, led largely by increased industrial production and export to Scandinavian and other EU countries.

Table 1: Macroeconomic Indicators

	1991	1992	1993	1994	1995	1996	1997	1998	1999	2000
Real GDP growth (%)	-10.0	-14.1	-8.5	-1.8	4.3	4.0	11.4	4.0	-1.1	
GDP at current prices (billion USD)			1.6	2.3	3.6	4.4	4.7	5.2	5.1	
Gross industrial output (% change over previous year)	-7.2	-35.6	-18.7	-3.0	1.9	3.4	15.2	2.3	-1.7	9.1
Exports (billion USD)		0.4	0.8	1.3	1.8	2.1	2.9	2.7	2.4	3.3
Imports (billion USD)		0.4	0.9	1.7	2.5	3.2	4.4	3.9	3.4	4.3
Consumer price index (%)	202	1 078.2	89.6	47.9	28.9	23.1	11.1	8.2	3.3	4.0
GDP per capita (USD)			1 076	1 522	2 392	2 967	3 178	3 586	3 553	
Gross saving ratio (% of GDP)				19	24	26	33	29	28	
Gross fixed capital formation (% of GDP)			24	27	26	27	28	30	23	
Exchange rate (kroon per USD, end of period)		12.9	13.9	12.4	11.5	12.4	14.3	14.1	14.7	17.0
Population (thousands)				1 499	1 484	1 469	1 458	1 450	1 443	1 439
Employment (% change over previous period)	-2.3	-5.2	-7.5	-2.2	-5.3	-1.6	-0.5	-1.3	-3.5	-1.3
Unemployment (%)	1.8	4.5	7.8	8.9	9.7	10.0	9.7	9.9	12.3	14.3
Wage (monthly average USD)			80	134	207	248	257	293	302	

Source: The Estonian Statistical Office

---

* Chairman of the Board, Estonian Housing Foundation

Table 2: Main Trading Partners, 1999 (% of total)

	Exports to	Imports from
Finland	22	37
Sweden	21	10
Russian Federation	5	8
Germany	8	10
Latvia	8	4

Source: The Estonian Statistical Office

Housing sector overview

According to the Estonian Statistical Office (ESO), as of 1 January 2000, Estonian housing stock included about 623 100 housing units -- apartments and privately owned single-family homes (residences) -- with total floor space of about 33.56 million square meters. Of these, about 37 400 housing units were in public ownership and the remaining 585 700 in private ownership. Today there are about 432.0 dwelling units per 1 000 residents.

Table 3: Housing Stock

(Beginning of year)	1995	1996	1997	1998	1999	2000
Total housing stock						
Number of dwellings (1000)	618.3	620.2	622.1	623.1	623.0	623.1
Dwellings per 1000 inhabitants	412.4	417.9	423.4	427.4	430.0	432.0
Average usable floor space per dwelling (m^2)	53.5	53.6	53.5	53.6	53.7	53.8
Public housing stock						
Number of dwellings (1000)	347.9	240.0	118.4	63.7	44.0	37.4
Average usable floor space per dwelling (m^2)	48.1	46.8	44.4	44.6	41.9	39.2
Privately owned housing stock						
Number of dwellings (1000)	270.4	380.2	503.7	559.4	579.0	585.7
Average usable floor space per dwelling (m^2)	60.3	57.9	55.7	54.7	54.7	54.8
Average floor space per inhabitant (m^2)	22.1	22.4	22.6	22.9	23.1	23.3

Source: The Estonian Statistical Office

Table 4: Total Floor Space and Living Space of Dwellings

(1 January 2000)

Type of ownership	Number of dwellings (1000)	Floor space (1000m²)	Of which living floor space (1000 m²)	Number of permanent inhabitants (1000)	Average floor space per inhabitant (m²)
Public housing stock	37	1 465	1 040	87	229
State	5	214	150	11	26.9
Local government	32	1 251	890	76	22.3
Private housing stock*	586	32 095	21 824	1 363	23.3
TOTAL	623	33 560	22 864	1 439	23.3

Source: The Estonian Statistical Office (* Data on private housing stock are estimated.)

Housing stock can be classified into three basic groups:

- – Apartment houses with 5-16 stories; average age 10-35 years   35%

- – Apartment houses with 1- 4 stories; average age more than 30 years   30%

- – Small residences (single-family homes); average age over 50 years   35%

Although the average age of small residences is quite high (over 50 years), this type of housing has become prevalent in the 1990s when developing new units. Only 300 private homes were built in 1991; this number increased to a yearly average of 500 from 1992 to 1996, and by 1997 the number had increased to 739, but by 1999 the number commissioned had dropped to 384 units. Unfortunately, housing stock of this type represents only about 0.5% of national housing stock.[1]

The infrastructure and communications supplies for housing stock do not meet contemporary standards. The major installations of buildings developed in the period after World War II and prior to 1975-80, are in rather poor repair and require substantial replacements. A rapid trend toward adopting electricity-based heating and hot-water systems, and the increased use of household appliances, will necessitate substantial rebuilding of electrical installations.

Engineering surveys have found that the technical condition of brick-and-mortar multi-flat blocks is much more complicated than that of large-panel concrete apartment houses. Construction defects specific to brick-and-mortar apartment houses are hard to diagnose, and in general are difficult and costly to eliminate.

In 1997, work began to investigate the technical condition of small residences. The stock of small residences is rather old; half of these single-family homes and up to two-thirds of wooden residences predate 1940. Most of this stock, both the older residences and the newer ones built in the 1950s and 1960s, was built by its owners.

National housing stock offers low variety for consumers, resulting in limited choices -- about 75% of living space is located in large apartment houses. Apartments, thus, are the primary type of housing in Estonia. The share of households living in private single-family homes (detached houses) and in houses with few apartments is relatively small when compared to the numbers in other European countries. The average number of rooms per resident (an indicator of privacy) is estimated to be about one, considerably below that in most countries in Western or Northern Europe. Cramped living quarters become less adequate as the size of a household increases. Thus, 72% of four-person families live in units with fewer than four rooms. Families with small children face the greatest space shortage.[2]

The majority of housing units, irrespective of ownership, are in poor repair, especially as to thermal insulation. Some buildings present increased hazards to their occupants due to the considerable decay of structures and technical services. With limited opportunities for households to receive loans in the current market situation, most occupants are unable to fund the renovations needed to maintain the housing stock and to ensure decent housing quality.

Public housing stock

As of 1 January 2000, the public housing stock of Estonia accounted for six percent of total stock. Of a total 37 000 units, 5 000 were state-owned and 32 000 were owned by local authorities. 29% of this stock is in Tallinn, 44 % in other cities and 27% on the territories of rural municipalities.

Table 5: Share of Dwellings by Type of Ownership
(%)

Type of ownership	1995	1996	1997	1998	1999	2000
Public housing stock	**51**	**34**	**16**	**9**	**7**	**6**
State	8	5	2	2	1	0,8
Local government	43	29	14	7	6	5,2
Private housing stock*	**49**	**66**	**84**	**91**	**93**	**94**

Source: The Estonian Statistical Office (*Data about private dwelling stock are estimated.)

The largest share of dwelling units (44%) are tiny one-room apartments with kitchen; 36 % are small two-room apartments with kitchen; and only 20% of these dwellings are three-room or bigger apartments with kitchen. 56% of these dwellings were completed from 1961 to 1990. A total of 860 dwelling units, with total floor space of 45 000 square meters, accommodate more than one household per unit, the so-called communal flats.

There are 2 016 vacant dwellings, having total floor space of 81 100 square meters; 18% are in Tallinn, 25% in other cities, and 57% in rural regions. In 1999, 388 dwellings were declared unsuitable for habitation and 129 dwellings were refurbished for non-residential use.

In 1999 the average monthly rent of publicly owned dwellings was 3.96 kroon per square meter; average rent was 4.60 kroon in units with modern facilities. These levels had increased by three percent from the previous year. Average monthly maintenance charges and repair costs were 5.22 kroon per square meter. These charges and costs had increased by four percent from 1998.

Private housing stock

As of 1 January 2000, the number of dwellings in private ownership was 585 700, of which 23% were dwellings with flat-owners associations and housing co-operative associations. The other housing units were run entirely by private individuals.

There were a total of 134 700 flats run by different associations, of which 79% were run by flat-owners associations and 21% by housing co-operative associations. Of flats run by flat-owners associations, 83% were in Tallinn. Thirty-six per cent of flats run by housing co-operative associations were in Harju County – the administrative unit for Tallinn and its environs – of which 20% is located in Tallinn. In addition, 19% of these flats were in Tartu County, and 13% in Ida-Viru County.

The number of different flat-ownership-based associations had grown by 20% from 1 January 1999, with the largest increase (56%) in Ida-Viru County. Growth had more than quadrupled since 1 January 1995.

53% of flat-owners associations were in five-story buildings, and 29% in blocks of flats with nine stories or more. 66% of housing co-operative associations were in residential buildings of one to four stories.

The majority of the flats (75%) had two to three rooms with kitchen, and 89% were completed from 1961 to 1990.

Management and maintenance charges and repair costs

In 1999, the average monthly management charges for flats in blocks run by associations was 4.47 kroon per square meter; it was 5.23 kroon in those run by co-operative associations and 4.26 kroon in those involving flat-owners associations.

The average monthly maintenance charges and repair costs of flats were 4.84 kroon per square meter; charges were 6.16 kroon with co-operative associations and 4.46 kroon with flat-owners associations. Maintenance charges and repair costs of flats run by associations have grown by 21% since 1998.

Ownership relations in housing

The current state of Estonian housing is affected heavily by the problematic consequences of Soviet-era housing policy and management. Government directives then required construction costs to be reduced annually by five to seven percent. Maintenance costs were to be increased as a result, but in fact no additional funds were allocated to run the stock. Market relations have since expanded to housing, but there is a huge gap between the needs for capital and the possibilities for covering these needs. The results of ownership reforms have merely extended this unbalanced situation.

Housing privatisation has led to a situation where the majority of apartment owners are unable to invest sufficiently to carry out first-priority works in their housing units to assure that technical quality be maintained.

The ownership reforms have resulted in a situation where the sitting tenants in restituted houses and the owners of these houses lack the opportunities to implement individual housing strategies. This is a problem for the 22 500 families living in 5 226 houses restituted to the previous owners. About 2 000 restituted houses are in Tallinn.[3]

With the existing owner population, and the creation of so-called compulsory tenants, demand for rental apartments has increased considerably. This imbalance has left municipalities with little flexibility and few options in attempting to assure housing for all households, beginning with the most needy. This is true primarily in the bigger cities.

The mixed social composition of residents in multi-apartment houses, whether panel-built or brick-and-mortar, has made it difficult to manage and maintain these properties, as solvent and insolvent owners occupy flats in the same block. This also creates problems in establishing and managing flat-owners associations. As of January 2000, according to the Register of Companies, 4 201 associations had been established in the blocks, but residents had shown very little interest in establishing flat-owners associations (this varies considerably by region).

The main reasons for low success are the following:

- Subjects obliged to privatise are not interested in creating flat-owners associations.
- Registration of flat-owners associations is legally complicated and cannot be carried out in local county-centres.
- Apartment owners lack motivation to create associations.

Moreover, flat-owners associations have offered few examples of managing housing more successfully than the preceding property-management companies, keeping in mind the opportunity to ensure residents an opportunity to pay relatively lower maintenance fees. The majority of blocks of flats are maintained based on contracts signed directly by flat owners and property-management companies. The services provided by these companies cost more but tend to be more reliable and professional. In the future, owners will make their choices based on the price-to-quality ratio for the service provided.

In the case of blocks, one has to consider that realistically, associations will not be founded in all of them. The procedure for registering flat ownership as immovable has been established legally; the procedure must be initiated by the subject obliged to privatise the property. Yet legally the management of a block of flats is unresolved when no association is created there. According to the Ministry of Justice, only 69,954 apartment properties (12%) had been registered as of 1 January 2000.

The main problem for owners of detached houses, as well as for owners of summer cottages under renovation or soon to be, relates to the lifetime of their property. Depreciation levels of technical infrastructure are high, and many properties completely lack utilities. The average age of detached houses is more than 50 years, and that figure is rising, as detached housing built recently represents a dramatically small proportion of total housing stock.

To extend the structural life expectancy of existing detached houses and to ensure residents' safety, considerable renovation work is required. Detached houses hold 11.4 million square meters of housing, up to 35% of Estonia's housing stock. Newer and better houses from the 1960s and 1970s with insufficient thermal insulation comprise about 7.2 million square meters, and older ones with very poor thermal insulation comprise 4.2 million square meters.

Privatisation of housing stock management companies, which have been municipally owned, should be carried out in stages and linked to the pace of registering flat-ownership in multi-flat blocks to flat-owners associations or to any alternative form. To protect residents, whether renters or owners, from any monopoly in the housing-services market, larger municipalities should not force all housing-management companies into private ownership. The local authority can thereby reserve the ability to influence the housing market until it (presumably) normalises and normal competition arises among private-sector companies. Local authorities should, in any case, retain regular inspection and supervision over housing management services.

To develop normal competition it is important that in parallel to improving the professional competence of housing managers -- at least during the first years -- state funding should be allocated to support any training schemes provided for housing owners and managers. "Third sector" organisations -- universities, and training and consultancy companies -- should initiate these training schemes and guarantee their continuity. This plan should assure flat-owners that management of housing blocks would be conducted only according to reliable and sound strategies. When funding is required for large-scale reconstruction work pursuant to these strategies, favourable funding schemes for loans should be applied.

The majority of companies providing housing services are in monopoly situations, and price-calculations, under the Competition Act and the Energy Act, should be clearly interpreted for consumers. Consumer-protection organisations and their representatives should continuously monitor any changes in prices and rates by these monopoly companies; and tenant representatives should participate in the work of the boards of these companies.

Housing market

The number of dwellings changing owners has increased yearly. The year 1997, when commercial banks fixed a relatively low interest rate on housing loans, proved especially successful. More than half of dwellings were purchased or sold using loans. A decline in the real estate market in 1998 was caused by commercial banks imposing restrictions on loan conditions, coupled with a rapid increase in the interest rate on housing loans.[4]

The Property Law -- adopted by the Riigikogu, or Parliament, on 9 June 1993 -- is the main Estonian legislative act regulating the creation of security interest in residential (real) property. This Act, which took effect on 1 December 1993, is based on the general principles of German civil law (the German Bürgerliches Gesetzbuch, or BGB).

Under current regulations, privately owned residential property such as detached houses and flats are treated either as movable or immovable property. The legal status of such property -- including the rules establishing security interest for such property -- is determined by the registration of the land under this property, whether a house or an apartment, in the Registry of Real Property. Detached houses and apartments located on land listed in the Registry are considered as real or immovable property; all other houses and apartments are treated as movable property.

The Estonian Statistical Office distinguishes four types of property transactions: sales of immovable property (real property transactions); building title agreements (long-term land lease); residential space (separate-dwelling houses and flats); and non-residential space.

The first two categories are legal transactions with real property and are registered in the Title Book, whereas the latter two are legal transactions with movable property and thus are not registered in the Title Book. The huge increase of real property transactions is due mainly to the land reform -- in 1998 the number of real properties increased by 103%, according to the Estonian Land Board.

Therefore, the scheme used by the Statistical Office to record transactions based on legal definitions is not quite adequate in assessing housing-market activities, as only a portion of dwelling units (mainly detached houses) are sold as real property. According to national statistics, the number of transactions with residential space in 1998 decreased by 15% from 1997, while single-family houses decreased at a higher rate (28%) than apartments (11%).

From spring 1998 to spring 1999, sale-prices for residential spaces declined up to 20%, depending on location and quality, although some market segments witnessed a slight increase. The largest reduction in prices took place in the second half of 1998, when the economic situation and more conservative credit terms considerably reduced housing demand. By spring 2001 price levels were near what they were in 1997.

The price-scale has become wider and prices less transparent. Compared to the years of rapid market growth, buyers are paying more attention to cost-saving measures. When buying, households are more often prepared to have only a superstructure, and new owners are ready to do finishing work. Smaller and less luxurious spaces are often preferred; brokers are also used less, to save on transaction fees.

In large-scale housing estates, the supply of flats for sale is slightly higher than the demand, so prices have dropped, particularly for flats of poor quality and in poor locations. But prices for larger flats -- especially for four-room ones -- have dropped as well. In central Tallinn, expensive and exclusive flats are in oversupply, particularly on the rental market. Foreigners purchase most of the expensive new apartments. Demand and prices have not dropped solely for flats in attractive locations, but elsewhere there is a considerable oversupply.

The number of transactions involving single-family houses has decreased relatively more than that for the flats. Prices for larger detached houses built in the 1970s and 1980s have also dropped slightly, but the supply of smaller and cheaper houses built in the 1950s and 1960s is limited, so prices have not changed considerably.

Table 6: Average price level of dwellings (February 2001):

Prices of Apartments (kroon/m^2)

	4 rooms and kitchen	3 rooms and kitchen	2 rooms and kitchen	1 room and kitchen
Tallinn, existing	3 800-10 200	3 900-10 200	4 000-10 300	4 000-10 200
Tallinn, new	13 000	13 200	13 400	13 500
Tartu, existing	2 400	2 500	2 800	3 200
Pärnu, existing	2 800	3 000	3 100	3 300

Prices of Single Family Houses (kroon/m^2)

	New	Renovation needed
Tallinn	8 000-13 000	7 000-15 000
Tartu	3 000-8 000	2 500-4 000
Pärnu	5 000-12 000	3 300-6 300

New housing construction

In 1993-94, the share of housing expenditure increased in relation to GDP and also in relation to private consumption expenditure. Since 1995 the share of this expenditure has remained almost level. In 1997, it was 13.7% of GDP, and 23.4% of private consumption expenditure.

Table 7: Housing Investment

Year	Housing investment		New (commissioned) residential buildings	
	% of housing expenditure in GDP	% of residential construction to national construction turnover	Number of units (flats, detached houses)	Average size of new housing units (sq. m)
1992			3 405	70.3
1993	8.4	14.5	2 431	74.3
1994	12.0	10.0	1 953	81.5
1995	13.7	8.8	1 149	91.3
1996	13.8	7.2	935	110.7
1997	13.7	9.0	1 003	121.2
1998		9.3	882	112.6
1999		9.4	785	110.9

Source: The Estonian Statistical Office

The sale of new dwelling units involves difficulties. For new flats and single-family houses supply considerably exceeds demand, as in recent years several single-family housing projects have been launched and new multi-flat houses have been completed. The increase in supply was especially notable in 1998, when demand had already decreased. In 1999, the volume of new construction decreased due to considerable oversupply.

Table 8: New Housing Construction

Year	Total floor space of the housing stock (1 000 m^2)	Total floor space of new housing units (1 000 m^2)	% of total housing stock
1992		239.5	
1993	32 217	180.5	0.56
1994	32 423	159.2	0.49
1995	33 063	104.9	0.32
1996	33 250	103.5	0.31
1997	33 308	121.6	0.37
1998	33 435	99.3	0.30
1999	33 500	87.1	0.26
2000	33 560		

Source: The Estonian Statistical Office

During the period of market growth, along with some excellent examples of housing development, several average and poor projects were initiated, which are not attractive in the current market situation. Demand has declined considerably and potential buyers have better choices. As an alternative, any buyer may prefer a single site to develop a unique single-family housing project. Therefore, there are really no ready-built detached houses on the market, but sites to be developed once a contract is signed.

Table 9 indicates the major sources used when financing new housing construction. Public-based (local authority) funding has been reduced to zero, and the major share is for private individuals. Funding from other sources is mainly for multi-flat housing construction by developers. Both of these groups represent home ownership and involvement of households with housing loans. It is important to note that the numbers above indicate new housing units commissioned or completed, but there are also renovation and reconstruction projects on existing residential buildings.

Table 9: Financing of Dwelling Completions

Year	Total Number of completions	By local authorities	By private individuals	Other sources
1994	1 953	26	507	1 420
1995	1 149	58	472	619
1996	935	30	500	405
1997	1 003	1	739	263
1998	882	-	525	357
1999	785	-	571	214

Source: The Estonian Statistical Office

In 2001 no great increase in demand is likely, although loan terms have become more favourable. The chief reason is the slightly unstable economic situation, coupled with labour-market difficulties and the slight decline in per capita income.

The first cycle has been completed on the housing market, and the majority of people who wanted and could sell or buy residential space have now done so. In the long term there will never be as rapid an increase in housing demand as we saw in 1995-96, when the number of transactions with residential space grew by 1.6 times and the value of transactions rose 2.4 times.

In the short term, prices of new family houses and apartments will remain stable for good projects, or decline for less attractive housing projects.

On average, households' spending for housing constituted 13% to 16% of their outlays in 1994 and 19% in 1998-99. Housing costs have risen faster than the overall cost of living, with heating accounting for over half of these expenses. Over the past four years, the costs of management, maintenance, repair and heating have risen about 2 times, at about the same rate as the consumer price index; but electricity has gone up about 3.5 times, and water and sewage costs by 11.5 times.[5]

About 15% to 20% of residents are assessed as financially eligible to obtain loans, but this differs considerably by region. This effectively means families belonging to the upper two income deciles, which have average disposable income of, respectively, 3 049 and 5 591 kroon per household member. Presumably, only these household segments are able to bear the full economic responsibility for their homes, being able to make the necessary investments for improving the condition of their homes.

Table 10: Disposable Income per Income Decile

Income-deciles	I	II	III	IV	V	VI	VII	VIII	IX	X
Disposable income per a household-member (kroon)	454	939	1 145	1 281	1 434	1 660	1 950	2 381	3 049	5 591
Proportion of transfers in all the total income (%)	59	43	45	52	40	29	20	18	11	5

Source: Monthly of ESO, No. 7, 1998

Figure 1: Survival Subsidy

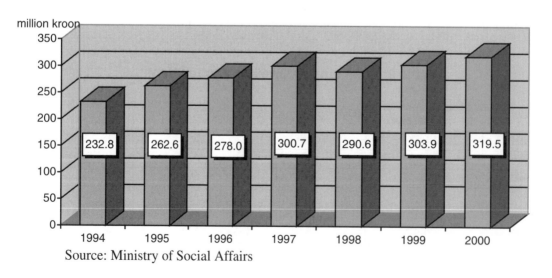

Source: Ministry of Social Affairs

60

The so-called survival subsidy is an allowance provided for households facing difficulty in covering housing-related expenditures. To assign the subsidy, household incomes and expenditures are compared. Social Security Offices provide these subsidies directly, but the sums are limited and local authorities have established eligibility guidelines. About 18% of households have been nominated for such subsidies, which come from the State budget.

Financing housing renewal

The costs of urgent work and major repairs for total housing stock are:

- For slab-housing: 11 billion to 25 billion kroon
- For brick housing: 9 billion to 22 billion kroon
- For other types of housing: 4 billion to 8 billion kroon

To rehabilitate the housing stock would require 15 to 20 years, forecasts indicate. Following this schedule, 1.2 billion to 1.8 billion kroon would be invested annually for the slab-housing stock alone from all available sources. Reconstruction is a long-term process, and it is obvious that annual adjustments will be required. These corrections will become more important after 2003, when the actual state of all housing becomes clear, following the filing of information in maintenance manuals. Some houses may have to be demolished, and a rapid program for public housing development initiated.

To improve the technical outlook of houses, the near-term priority will be to accelerate possibilities for favourable reconstruction-targeted loans to be made available to owners of all housing types. Reconstruction loans should cover 12% to 15% of the total sum required annually for the entire national housing stock.

Funding for housing-related needs have come primarily from the following sources: the state budget; funds derived from privatisation, which are channelled into the housing stock; budgets and funds of local municipalities; funds derived from sales of municipal property; and bank loans and residents' own resources.

State budget

Funds are being allocated from the State budget for subsistence aid as well as to administer the loans of the Estonian Housing Foundation for target groups through commercial banks. In the years 1995-98, a total of 75 million kroon was allocated from the state budget for housing loans to the target groups, in particular in loans for young families, young teachers, teachers in rural areas, and for energy-saving projects by associations in blocks of flats.

Funds from privatisation

Funds generated by privatisation have been used through the Estonian Housing Foundation since 1997 to relocate tenants living in restituted spaces. Since then banks have released 2 408 loans totalling 463.5 million kroon to these tenants. The average amount of these much sought-after loans is 190 000 kroon.

Funds for municipalities

Following the Funds Generated by Privatisation Act, 25% of moneys gained when privatising municipal properties have been transferred to local municipality reserve funds and 50% to municipality housing funds. Within their assets, local municipalities have to allocate money to develop social houses and shelters, to solve the problems of "compulsory tenants" and for other housing-related spending.

Development plan for housing

In spring 1998, the Estonian Government appointed a committee of housing experts to compile a long-range housing development plan, submitting the appropriate proposals for the amendment of legal acts, and justifying the relevant programs and expenses from the State budget for 1999. The development plan for Estonian housing up to 2010 was discussed for the first time within the Estonian Government in November 1998. The document was presented for adoption in August 2000 (the lag was caused by a cabinet change in spring 1999). The document was not adopted by the Government, but was taken under consideration. The new document is expected to be ready for action in autumn 2001.

Housing finance market

On the national financial market, loan policies and conditions for housing loans have been changed several times over recent years. The Estonian market for loans can be best characterised by rapid growth in loan volumes in 1996-97, followed by stabilisation and stagnation in 1998, and then by new growth in 1999-2000.

Figure 2: Growth in Loan Capacity

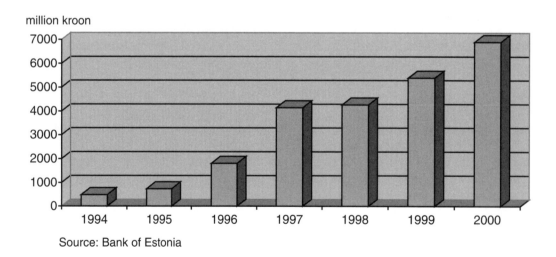

Source: Bank of Estonia

Financial-sector growth stopped in the second half of 1998, and a considerable decline ensued. Banks' balance sheets were reduced, the volume of loan portfolio decreased, the growth of leasing companies was inhibited, the activities of investment funds almost stopped, and insurance companies faced their first problems. In summer 1998 considerable change took place among banks as several of them were merged and others disappeared from the market. Swedish banks and other investors from the Nordic countries entered the Estonian market, a positive development as it strengthened the financial sector and created long-term optimism.

The second half of 1998 was the most complicated period for the financial sector -- the interest rates of housing loans increased by two to three percentage points (from 11%-13% to 13%-15%) and the share of self-funding increased from 30% to 40%. In addition, rather strict requirements were imposed on borrowers. But since the beginning of 1999, loan conditions have become more advantageous, and the interest rate for housing loans has dropped.

Table 11: Interest Rates of Housing Loans
(%)

Housing loans denominated in:	31/12/97	31/12/98	31/12/99	31/03/00	30/06/00	30/09/00	31/12/00
EEK	12.3	12.7	11.8	11.5	11.7	11.7	11.8
DEM	12.8	12.7	10.4	10.9	11.2	10.2	13.1
EUR			9.8	10.0	10.3	10.2	10.3

Three key factors have influenced the growth of loans to individuals, mortgage loans in particular. First, increasing incomes have led to a growth in private loan capacity and the trustworthiness of private individuals. Income growth of households has enabled them to save both for self-financing and to service loans. Second, Estonian banks were able to use West European long-term credit limits permitting their use for long-term mortgage loans. Last, interest rates fell due to the factors listed above.

Table 12: Mortgage Volumes

	12/97	12/98	12/99	06/00	12/00
Mortgage balance (million kroon)	2 125.0	2 892.6	3 360.5	3 759.1	4 478.9
Mortgage balance (% of GDP)	2.66	3.27	3.85	-	-
Monthly turnover (million kroon)	80.5	63.1	152.8	183.4	150.3

Source: The Estonian Statistical Office

Table 13: Mortgages and Total Assets of Banks

	12/97	12/98	12/99	12/00
Balance of mortgages (million kroon)	2 125.3	2 892.6	3 360.5	4 478.9
Balance of total assets (million kroon)	38 767.9	40 997.9	47 071.0	57 825.3
Share of mortgages in total assets (%)	5.48	7.06	7.14	7.75

Source: The Estonian Statistical Office

NOTES

1. Data by Estonian Statistical Office

2. Estonian Human Development Report 1997

3. The numbers are based on estimates from the Tenants Association and the municipalities.

4. Data on notarised purchase-sale contracts of dwellings have been collected since 1995.

5. Real Estate Market Review, Kinnisvaraekspert, Spring 1999

HOUSING FINANCE IN HUNGARY

by
Katalin Szilágyi[*]

Macroeconomic developments and future prospects

After a shock period associated with transition (from 1990 to 1993 the GDP contracted by 17%) the Hungarian economy began to grow in 1994. Growth in the real gross domestic product (GDP) of nearly 3% was supported by the expansion of gross fixed capital formation at a rate of 12.5%. While positive microeconomic trends were observed, the weak external balance produced a strong distrust among international investors. Therefore, the current account deficit (then equal to 9.5% of GDP) could not be financed, particularly in an unfavourable international climate such as prevailed after the Mexican crisis.

In March 1995, a stabilisation program (referred to as the Bokros Package, named after the Minister of Finance) was introduced. The program included structural reforms, immediate currency devaluation, a new exchange-rate regime (crawling peg), a tight wage policy in the public sector and fiscal measures to enhance revenues and expenditures. Stabilisation measures led to a strong decrease of all domestic demand components (private and public consumption as well as investments). The annual average consumer price index reached nearly 30%, and net real earnings declined by 12.2%, which led to a 7.1% contraction in household consumption expenditures. The considerable devaluation of the Hungarian currency (HUF) resulted in strong export growth, while weakening domestic demand and robust gains in competitiveness in the domestic enterprise sector on the domestic market led to a decrease in imports. The deficit-of-trade balance as well as the current account deficit decreased considerably.

The restrictive macroeconomic policy was maintained in 1996: only gross fixed capital formation increased among domestic demand components of GDP. Public consumption and household consumption decreased further. Average net monthly earnings were 5% less than the previous year and 16.6% less than two years earlier. Both the industrial production price index and the consumer price index fell significantly. The announced crawling peg of HUF produced substantial results by eliminating unexpected devaluationary expectations that eventually helped to slow inflation. Meanwhile, the external trade and current account balances improved further; the current account deficit fell below 4% of GDP in 1996. Notably, even in the hardest period of the stabilisation program, real GDP did not decrease. Although the domestic demand components fell strongly, better foreign trade performance and improved labour productivity compensated for that. Consequently, there was positive, if moderate, real GDP growth in 1995-96 as well. The economy seems to have set out on a sustainable path of export-driven growth with decreasing inflation.

---

*   Research Economist, Kopint-Datorg Institute for Economic Research.

Table 1. Main Macroeconomic Indicators, 1994-99, Forecast for 2000-01

	1994	1995	1996	1997	1998	1999	2000	2001[1]
Real gross domestic product, 1995 prices[2]	2.9	1.5	1.3	4.6	4.9	4.4	5.3	4.8
Real household final consumption expenditure, 1995 prices[2]	-0.2	-7.1	-2.7	2.0	5.0	4.6	3.7	4.4
Real total gross fixed capital formation, 1995 prices[2]	12.5	-4.3	6.7	8.8	13.3	5.9	6.5	8.0
Real total industrial production[2]	9.6	4.6	3.4	11.1	12.6	10.4	18.3	12.0
Industrial production price index[2]	11.3	28.9	21.8	20.4	11.3	5.1	11.7	6.8
Consumer price index[2]	18.8	28.2	23.6	18.3	14.3	10.0	9.8	9.0
Average net real monthly earnings[2]	5.2	-12.2	-5.0	4.9	3.6	2.5	1.5	4.3
Exports (goods and services from GDP-statistics) [2]	13.7	13.4	7.4	26.4	16.7	13.2	20.8	13.0
Imports (goods and services from GDP-statistics) [2]	8.8	-0.7	5.7	25.5	22.8	12.3	19.2	13.5
Current account balance (USD bn)	-3.9	-2.5	-1.7	-1.0	-2.3	-2.1	-2.0	-2.5
Current account balance (% of GDP)	-9.5	-5.6	-3.8	-2.2	-4.8	-4.4	-3.8	-4.7
General government budget balance (% of GDP)	-8.1	-6.5	-3.0	-4.6	-4.6	-3.9	-3.5	-3.4

Note: 1) Forecast 2) Denotes annual average % change on previous year.
Sources: Hungarian Central Statistical Office, National Bank of Hungary, Kopint-Datorg, Consensus Economics.

Hungarian economic growth stabilised in 1997: GDP increased by 4.6%, promoted mainly by the 8.8% growth of investments. Due to an increase of nearly 5% in net real earnings, the trend in household consumption changed. The 2% growth, while moderate, represents a marked change from the 10% decline of the two previous years. Production figures point to a clear recovery of the industrial sector: industrial production increased by 11.1%. The restarting of the privatisation program and the consequent large-scale inflow of foreign direct investment (FDI) were key to the foreign trade boom. Both exports and imports increased by more than 25%, while the current account balance deficit fell to its lowest point in the 1990s. For the third consecutive year, net FDI was greater than the current account deficit, resulting in a significant decrease in net external debt.

The expansion continued in 1998, despite the negative impacts of the Russian crisis on the Hungarian economy. Some industrial enterprises (especially in the food-processing industry) remained strongly dependent on the export market of the CIS countries (mainly Russia and Ukraine); import growth thus again exceeded the increase in exports. Moreover, in a generally distrustful international investment climate toward emerging markets, the negative balance of net profit remittances increased strongly. Fortunately, these new challenges to the small, open economy only slowed growth and the expansion continued: the growth rate of real GDP approached 5%. External imbalances increased only moderately, and the current account deficit remained below 5% of GDP. Further, domestic components of GDP increased more strongly than in previous years: investments grew by 13.3%, and private consumption growth reached 5% (net real earnings increased by 3.6%).

In 1999, the effects of the Kosovo crisis and flood damages exacerbated the impacts of the Russian crisis. After a temporary deterioration in the general government budget position and the current account balance, dynamic growth resumed without causing major external imbalances or serious budget problems. Indeed, the general government deficit fell below 4% of GDP, while the current account deficit reached only USD 2.1 billion. Several public investment programs were delayed, but private sector investments and household consumption growth remained dynamic: the growth rate of gross fixed capital formation was 6.6%, and real household expenditures increased by 4.6%. It is noteworthy that as in 1998, household consumption moderately surpassed the growth of net real earnings (+2.5% on average).

Economic developments in 2000 were, unsurprisingly, highly influenced by the buoyant international economy. The upturn in EU activity resulted in dynamic export volume growth exceeding 20%. The favourable conditions on major export markets more than offset the significant drop in the terms of trade, such that despite the steep rise of import prices the current account could improve further. However, the oil price shock held back the disinflationary process, and CPI inflation remained around 10%. Net real earnings slowed to 1.5%, and private consumption lagged behind GDP growth.

The perspectives for the Hungarian economy are generally promising for 2001 and for coming years. The higher growth rate of the domestic components could compensate for the less favourable external outlook. Real wages are expected to increase considerably because of the coming general elections. Presumably, foreign trade will continue to expand, and the current account deficit will remain stable around 4.5% of GDP. On the expenditure side, the most dynamic component of GDP growth will be gross fixed capital formation. Household consumption expenditure will likely increase by 4.4%-4.7%; which probably will develop in line with GDP.

Housing sector overview

Housing sector in Hungary

In sharp contrast with the present state and past trends of other typical welfare indicators, the Hungarian population is relatively well-provided with dwellings. Statistical data seem to support the consensual view of experts that the volume of dwellings is still too high compared to the country's economic performance. The quality of the housing sector, however, still needs to improve.

Table 2: Housing Statistics

	Number of dwellings (thousands)				Inhabitants per 1 000 dwellings	Dwellings per 1 000 inhabitants
	Total	1 room	2 rooms	3 rooms or more		
1960	2 758	1 729	900	129	343	292
1970	3 122	1 440	1 348	334	331	302
1980	3 542	973	1 720	849	302	331
1990	3 853	645	1 681	1 527	269	372
1998	4 032	639	1 730	1 664	251	398
1999	4 048	638	1 734	1 676	249	402

Source: Hungarian Central Statistical Office

The centrally managed housing policy of the past had a significant negative impact on the housing sector. Necessary renovations were generally delayed or ignored by local councils. The relatively high proportion of small flats originated partly with the nationalisation process after World War II, when large and valuable flats or houses typically were converted into several smaller flats. Moreover, in the socialist era housing construction was predominantly carried out by state enterprises, on a massive scale. This approach, considered economical in the short run, yielded a large number of suburban blocks of flats and a sharp deterioration of the quality of new dwellings. The average size of new flats remained below 70 square meters until the early 1980s. The structure of the housing market has been in line with the conditions of an acute shortage of flats and poor economic performance. Nonetheless, rising living standards and the evolution of a better-off middle class have increased demand for larger and more comfortable housing, a trend that is likely to continue.

Private construction gained momentum in the early 1980s. This boom in construction activity reflects both the development of a "quasi-bourgeois" mentality and the still low level of interest rates for construction loans (despite growing inflation). The main feature of these constructions is that they were realised on a reciprocal basis, with no money involved, relying on the physical help of relatives and friends. The favourable income dynamics at the time and gains from "cheap" labour costs for builders have considerably increased the average size of houses. However, by dispensing with skilled professionals on construction sites, new houses have proved to be highly prone to defects, most importantly in the unsatisfactory state of heat insulation systems.

Privatisation of dwellings began in 1989. Tenants of publicly owned flats were offered very attractive conditions in terms of interest payments and the appraised value of rented flats. The prices were set at about 10% of real market value. The great majority of dwellings have been privatised, leading to an unusual ownership structure in which almost 90% of total dwellings are privately owned. A major drawback of this development is that the prospects for long-delayed renovations are now much limited by the owners' budget constraints.

Table 3: Privatisation of Dwellings

	Dwellings sold by local governments	Market value of sold dwellings	Actual sales price of sold dwellings	Market value of sold dwellings	Actual sales price of sold dwellings
	unit	thousand HUF/m^2		USD/m^2	
1990	54 023	21.2	5.0	335.4	14.9
1991	82 118	21.8	5.1	291.7	17.5
1992	74 133	23.1	5.3	292.4	18.1
1993	58 391	23.3	5.8	253.4	22.9
1994	91 959	25.1	6.9	238.7	28.9
1995	105 924	27.0	8.4	214.8	39.1
1996	46 774	28.2	8.4	184.7	45.5
1997	19 221	33.5	8.4	179.3	46.8

Source: Hungarian Central Statistical Office

The housing sector in Hungary can be characterised by the following three features: first, construction activity is still dominated by self-made construction. The "unorganised" tradition of private construction, which originated in the latter part of the socialist period, seems to survive. Private construction is still predominantly based on family help and the labour of colleagues and friends. Often, no skilled specialists are called in. In a developed society, increases in efficiency due to specialisation favour professional contractors, and little family-based construction goes on. Specialisation seems to lag in Hungary, partly because of the high share of "gray economy" in the construction sector.

Figure 1: Tenure in ownership in the EU and Hungary

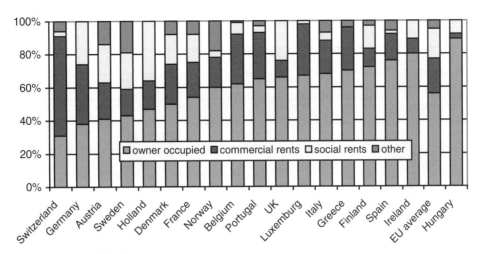

Source: Metropolitan Research Institute

Figure 2: The Distribution of Newly Built Houses by Type of Contractor

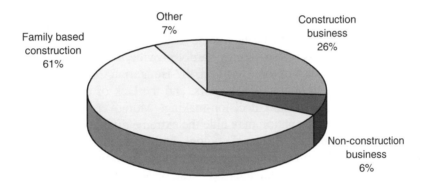

Source: Hungarian Central Statistical Office

Second, mortgage lending and other possible forms of housing loans are underdeveloped. Yet, international experience suggests that the average age at which one buys one's first flat is correlated significantly to the functioning of the mortgage system. Consequently, somewhat as in Italy, young people in Hungary stay longer with their parents while slowly saving resources to purchase a flat, in a long process that usually involves financial help from parents and relatives. As budget constraints are binding (government support is restricted and relatively modest), there is a strong demand for small flats. Thus, this category of flats is quite overpriced.

Third, total spending on housing is low compared to the Western standard. Housing expenses are estimated at 15% of disposable income for an average Hungarian household, while 25%-30% is typical in developed market economies. According to Diamond (1998) the low housing-expense ratio is typical of other Eastern European countries as well, including Poland, the Czech Republic and Slovakia. The gap is even larger when maintenance and enlargement expenses (total expenses without public utility costs) are compared.

Figure 3: Share of Housing Expenditures in CPI in 1999

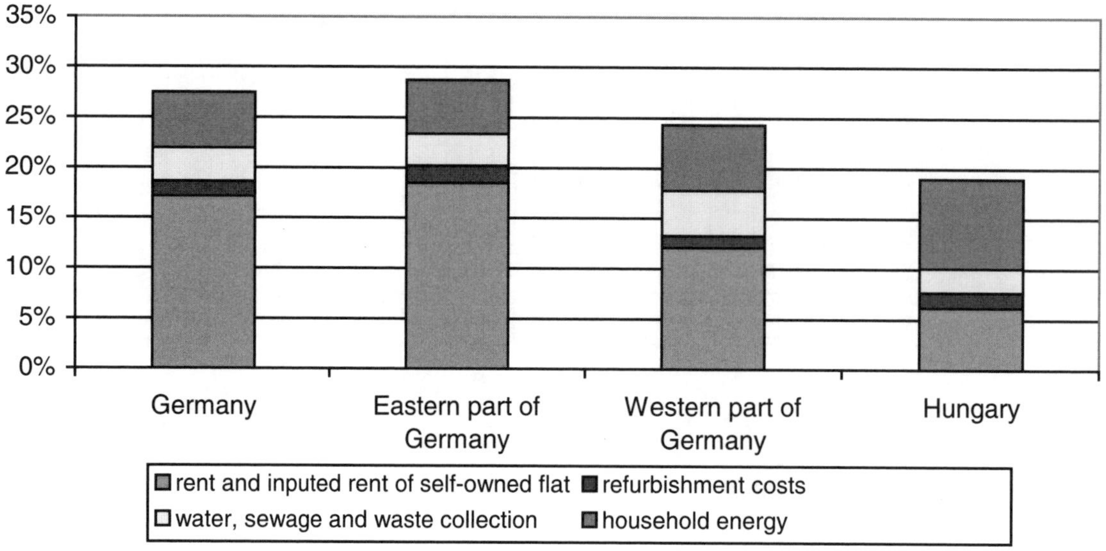

Source: Hungarian Central Statistical Office, Statistisches Bundesamt Deutschland

Reliable data are not available on the evolution of housing prices. Construction (at current prices) figures are available on an aggregate basis for the 1980s, although if one takes into account the socialist system of price-controls, these figures hardly provide a comprehensive and true picture of price developments. Since the start of the transition, the Hungarian Central Statistical Office has been limited, in its data collection, to quantitative factors, and the lack of data measured at market prices seriously constrains both analysis and decision-making. Moreover, the housing market is rather fragmented; aggregated price information may hide the extreme divergence of prices. Real-estate price differences between prosperous and "lagging" regions, and between the larger capital cities and rural areas are very high. Price differentiation became considerable from the early 1990s. The "distribution" of price ratios in housing is still not equivalent to Western observations, though this is not surprising given the relative overpricing of small dwellings and the influence of qualitative factors that are difficult to account for. Prices of units in blocks of flats built in the socialist period are still considered overly high for their quality and supply. This contrasts sharply with the price movements of similar flats in Eastern Germany, where the market for such housing has practically collapsed.

Government housing policy has long favoured new construction; funds of the central government have not been available to buy previously owned flats. The incentive to build may have a significant long-term impact on relative prices: because of the large number of relatively new houses (built to take advantage of government subvention not otherwise available) an excess supply of "second-hand" housing is likely in the longer term.

After the start of the transition, real estate prices lagged far behind inflation for years in all but the luxury category. New construction was motivated by two major factors: first, the provision of high quality suburban houses for the emerging middle class filled an important gap on the market; second, current housing policy, still in favour of new construction, has continued to boost construction activity among better-off families. The dominance of higher quality houses resulted in a significant increase of the average size of newly built houses, which exceeded 100 square meters in the 1990s.

Figure 4: Average Surface of Built Houses (m^2)

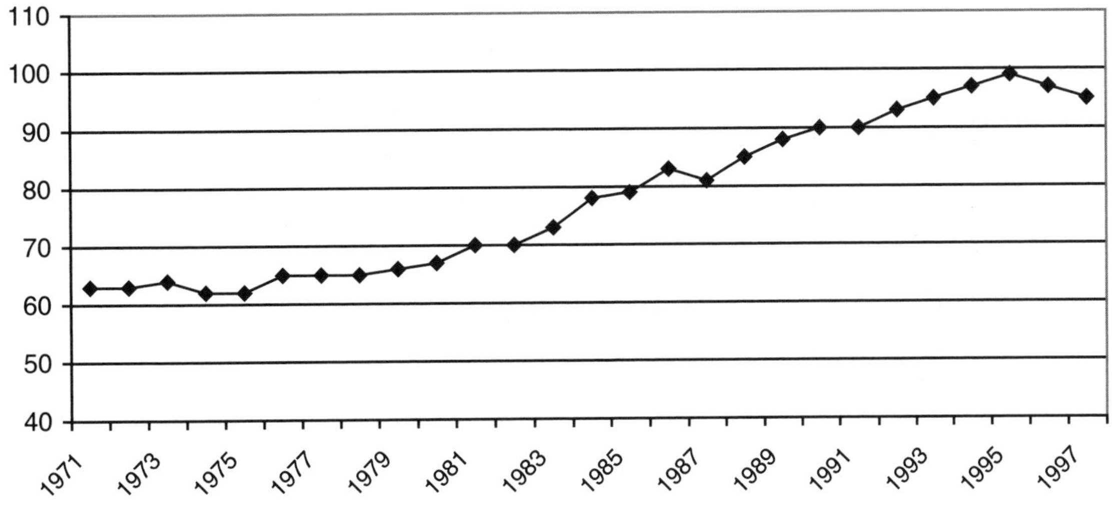

Source: Hungarian Central Statistical Office

The autumn of 1998 was a turning point in the evolution of real estate prices. Following the drastic decline of share prices on the Budapest Stock Exchange (influenced by the Russian financial crisis) the housing market, which had been sluggish, seemed to revive. Anecdotal evidence suggests that many investors turned to the housing market, contributing to a spectacular rise in prices.

Prices began to increase first in the upper categories, but the upswing soon spread to almost all categories. Even the traditionally low prices in "socialist" blocks of flats doubled within a year or so.

In prosperous regions, prices of (non-newly built) real estate now reach or exceed replacement costs. This phenomenon could be the driving force behind a boom in renovations, and is likely to extend the buoyancy of construction activities as well.

Housing policy

Government housing policy has a great impact on the real estate market, in terms both of direct financial support from central and local governments and (from an economic perspective) of taxes evaded in the sector. The latter refers to the very high share of "gray" activities in this sector. If the government increases the volume of direct subsidies while taking effective steps to diminish tax evasion, total government subsidies distributed could actually decrease.

Government involvement in housing policy can be characterised by the ratio of total budgetary spending on housing to GDP. As the following figure demonstrates, with the exception of 1995 the ratio remained below 1% in the 1990s.

Figure 5: Ratio of Total Budgetary Spending on Housing to GDP

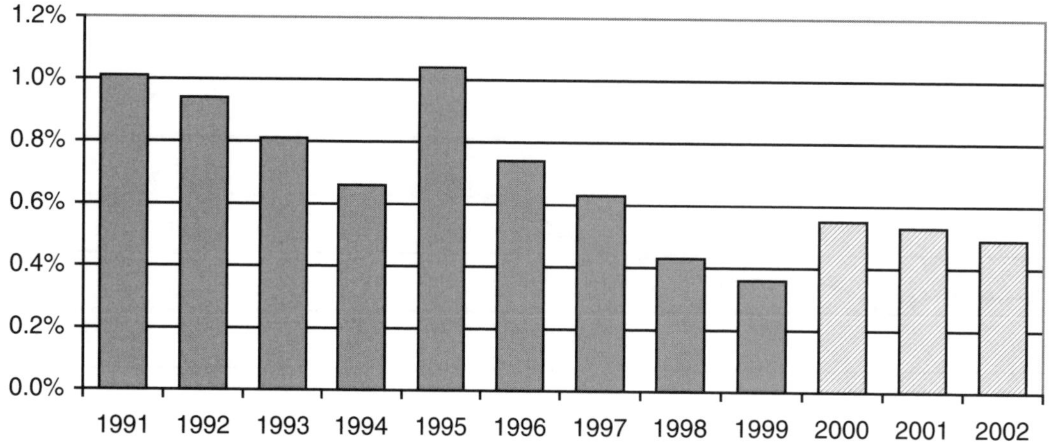

Source: National Bank of Hungary

Modern welfare states are usually involved in housing market developments. Apart from socio-political aims, state intervention can be economically justified based on the theory of "market failure." A widely cited argument for such intervention is that sufficient long-term funds cannot be raised on the market – that is, a privately owned banking system cannot solve the problem of term-structure transformation to reach a socially desired level of financial gearing. This revelation led to the development of several types of market-based solutions, from the German *Bausparkasse* model to the American system of partially state-guaranteed mortgage loans.

Economic argumentation (and the guaranteed volume of long-term resources) aside, state intervention can mean direct financial assistance to selected social groups on a social-policy basis. Finally, active government policy can influence the size and timing of the joint effect by the multiplicative impact of state subsidies.

The Hungarian system of housing policy is rather mixed. A large variety of interventionist aims and tools are in use. The present government, in addition to accepting the "market failure" argument on the housing market, views housing policy as an appropriate instrument to realise social-policy goals and to reach economic objectives. Major instruments of Hungarian housing policy are as follows:

Interest payment subsidies and loan guarantees inherited from the 1980s

During the 1980s, a large amount of construction credits was distributed under very attractive conditions. The procedure was highly atypical, even for the socialist system, as decisions to extend credit were not based on any credibility analysis. Interest rates were nominally fixed at very low levels, and despite gradually growing inflation, the total volume of credits was fully guaranteed by the state. The full guarantee on these credits meant a longer-term implicit debt of the central budget. In the early transitional period the government unilaterally increased interest rates to a level close to the market one. The radical increase in interest payments led to an extremely high level of non-performing debt outstanding. Though the total amount of loss is considerable, the average remaining balance per loan is relatively low (or at least inflated to now). This makes the potential costs of credit supervision very high. Political debates about the possibility of cancelling outstanding debt have emerged periodically but the idea has always been rejected.

72

Housing support scheme (social political support)

This eminent feature of Hungarian housing policy originated in the past. While major characteristics will be discussed in the next section, it is worth note that this subsidy is available only in case of new construction or the purchase of a newly built dwelling. This constraint (compared to the unconstrained base case) has a significant impact on the proportion of assets available on the market. Moreover, by selecting the preferential social groups, housing policy implicitly redistributes social wealth.

VAT refund

As in the case of the construction support scheme, new construction is a prerequisite for a VAT refund. All residents constructing a new dwelling or buying a newly constructed one are eligible. The tax refund can reach 60% of total VAT paid on the invoices for purchase of the flat, or for materials and services used in construction. The normal VAT rate, which applies to nearly all kinds of construction materials and services, is very high, 25% in Hungary. The refund amount is maximised at 400 000 forints (USD 1 380) per dwelling, which corresponds to a relatively low value of investment (USD 11 500).

It should be noted, however, that the government eliminated the VAT refund and the housing support scheme from 1 January 2001.

Preferential interest payment support

This new housing policy tool follows explicit social-policy goals, entitling a well-defined preferential social group (young couples and families with three or more children). Entitlement is constrained to new construction or purchase of a newly constructed dwelling. Major characteristics will be discussed in the next section.

General interest payment support

An outstanding tool of housing policy, it does not necessarily entail new construction, but is available for purchase, renovation or enlargement. There is no preferred group: anyone can apply. The newly founded mortgage banks, including the state-owned Bank for Land Credit and Mortgage Loans, are entitled to a 1.5% + 4% budgetary support on mortgage bonds issued, to provide more favourable funding costs. The amount of support is fixed only for the first five years of the debt, which adds uncertainty to the system, since the typical term is supposed to be significantly higher.

Home Savings and Loan Associations

To save enough for self-financed housing, would-be purchasers can apply for government support through home savings accounts. Home savings account holders or beneficiaries are eligible for state subsidies on the amount deposited on their account in the given year. A prerequisite for receiving the state subsidy is that the interest rate of the mortgage loan, predetermined by the saving scheme, does not exceed 10%.

The state subsidises new deposits on savings accounts by 30%, with a ceiling of 36 000 forints a year, part of a moderate 120 000 forint (USD 414) annual limit on supported savings, that can, however, be consolidated among family members.

State support in this scheme is transferred by the central budget directly to the home savings and loan association. Home savings and loan associations separately manage government support, and interest thereupon, on participants' accounts.

This element of the housing policy clearly imitates the German *Bausparkasse* model. The scheme was launched in 1997.

Modernisation programs

Special, preferential interest-rate credit lines are available for residential societies (*de facto* for those of owners of dwellings in blocks of flats) as an incentive to modernise heating systems.

Other supported programs

These include financial support to the adaptation of housing to the needs of disabled people, as well as reconstruction in regions hit by floods and other natural disasters.

The declared political goal of the government is to get 40 000 houses or flats built yearly (up from 19 200 built in 1999). In the longer term, the concept of housing policy recognises the following important features:

Various forms of housing benefits should replace the dominant housing support schemes. That is, government financial assistance should aim more at providing habitation than flat ownership. Policy tools could include the centrally managed distribution of units in tenements on housing estates, and contributions to rents on a social policy basis.

The construction of council flats should receive greater emphasis. This is expected to modify the housing ownership structure in favour of habitation support.

A decentralisation of housing policy is highly desirable. The current system of central distribution of government support should be replaced by the active involvement of local governments in both decision-making and administration. More authority should be dedicated to lower levels of state administration in this area. This is expected to increase the efficiency of social policy programs.

Housing finance systems

Home Savings and Loan Associations (HSLA)

The Act on Home Savings and Loan Associations was passed in 1996 (CXIII/1996). The concept follows the German *Bausparkasse* model, as it aims to separate the system of housing credits from other elements of the financial architecture. The contract amount to disburse is a function of savings accumulated in the system: new credit placements are covered by the repayments of earlier credits and the accumulation of new savings in such a closed system. A crucial factor is that interest rates on both deposits and credits are nominally fixed in advance. Consequently, the operation of the system requires calculable monetary conditions. Not surprisingly, it has been successful in Germany and Austria.

According to the Act on Home Savings and Loan Associations, an agreement may be concluded with a HSLA by natural persons as well as housing co-operatives or the superintendent of a condominium building. Apart from construction and purchase of new flats, the credit can be used for remodelling, renovation, enlargement or purchase of any dwelling. The agreement is a fixed account and credit contract with a home savings and loan association, and includes provisions requiring the home savings account holder to deposit one lump sum upon opening or to make regular fixed-amount deposits as specified in the payment schedule throughout the savings period. The HSLA assumes the obligation, if the terms and conditions specified in the agreement are fulfilled, to extend a loan -- as prescribed in the operational regulations, that is, not necessarily right away -- for housing purposes.

The agreement is concluded for a specific amount, equal to the aggregate amount to include all deposits made by the home savings account holder, the interests credited to such deposits, state subsidies, interest credited to such subsidies and the home loan to be extended by the HSLA. The deposit and credit interest rates defined in the agreement and the handling charge shall not be changed during the term of the agreement.

HSLAs are to establish a sequence, following the method prescribed in the general contract conditions, among the home savings account holders fulfilling the terms of the agreement. Such a sequence shall be based upon the size of the contract amount, the amount saved, the interest credited and the assumed terms of repayment of the home loan. On the basis of such a sequence, the HSLA is to determine the account holders to whom the contract amount may be disbursed at the specified date.

Figure 6: Home Savings and Loans Associations

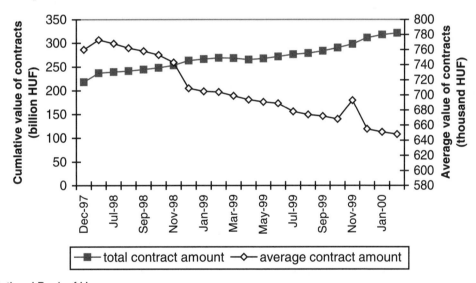

Source: National Bank of Hungary

The appropriate functioning of this system is threatened by two factors. First, Hungary is still far from stable in terms of calculable interest rates and expectations. With highly volatile market rates and expectations, external (i.e. budgetary) smoothing is essential to ensure the continuous accumulation of deposits. While the system, in theory, could operate without budgetary support for a longer term, international experience suggests that HSLAs in practice serve as an instrument of government housing subvention, involving serious budgetary consequences. The established sequence, ranking home savings account holders, adds insecurity to the system -- that is, the capacity of a HSLA to satisfy credit demands and fulfil the terms of an agreement can be limited; several just claims may have to be suspended because of liquidity constraints in the closed system. As the savings period must exceed four years, there is as yet no empirical evidence on the volume of frozen claims.

Housing support schemes

As mentioned, this is a traditionally important element of Hungarian housing policy, also referred to as social-political support. It provides title for residents to apply for housing support in relation to the number of children in the household, calculated according to the table below.

Table 4: Financial Support for Housing

Number of children in the household	Financial support available	
	Forints	USD
1	200 000	690
2	1 200 000	4 140
3	2 200 000	7 590
4	2 400 000	8 275
+1 (over 4 or more)	+200 000 per child	+690 per child

The above amounts (in forints) have not been valorised since 1995, so the original purchasing power of the subsidy (USD18 300 for three children, for example) has been inflated significantly. The entitlement is limited to the purpose of construction or the purchase of new dwellings, and can be used to reduce outstanding debt incurred for that purpose. The support is transferred to the creditor financial institution by the Hungarian State Treasury, once the creditor is certified to have housing debt outstanding. The fulfilment of the personal conditions of the title should be justified by the claimant's local government. The amount of financial support cannot exceed 65% of the purchase price or of construction costs of the new dwelling.

The system has been seriously criticised on various grounds. First, abusive use of the support scheme cannot be excluded and is difficult to audit. Moreover, as the amount of support is relatively low (especially for the needs of a large family) it encourages cheap, low-quality construction. Finally, the efficiency of a social policy providing support for ownership instead of habitation is debatable. A meaningful amount of support can be granted to a preferred social group only at the expense of the whole society.

General interest payment support

The introduction of this new element in government housing policy is a step toward the establishment of an American-style system of state-supported mortgage loans. The new mortgage banks, including the state-owned Bank for Land Credit and Mortgage Loans, are entitled of 1,5 + 4% of budgetary interest rate support after its mortgage bonds. The policy of reducing the costs of funds by state intervention is justified as a needed remedy to the underdeveloped mortgage sector. It also aims to reduce interest rates on mortgage loans. To date, no clear empirical evidence is available on the functioning of the system.

One major advantage, however, is that in contrast with a housing support scheme, there is less likelihood of abuses, given the long-run financial responsibility of the mortgagor. As with preferential interest payment support (see below), such state subventions are widely considered to be market-friendly, having the least distorting effects on the economy.

Preferential interest payment support

This subsidy originally targeted a well-defined social group (young couples purchasing their first flat or families with three or more children), but eligibility was gradually opened to include, from 1 July 2000, all married couples and single parents with no dwellings of their own. The expansion of eligibility, along with the lower than expected success of the facility, seems to suggest that the government is motivated not only by social priorities but by economic objectives (that is, inducing growth by boosting aggregate demand).

A prerequisite is that the interest rate on the housing loan cannot exceed the referential Treasury bond yield by more than 4%. The amount of the support equals the referential yield minus 4%, transferred to the creditor institution on a regular basis. Thus, the cost of the housing credit to eligible borrowers cannot exceed 8%. The contracted value has a maximum of 10 million forints (USD 34 500).

The major drawback of this program, as with housing support schemes, is that it involves forced construction.

Employers' loans

This element of the housing finance system is not (directly) supported from budgetary sources. Below a certain level of contracted value, an employer loan can even be free of interest payments, and highly preferential otherwise. As public burdens are high, this sort of fringe benefit is quite popular in higher-income categories.

Market-based housing loans of commercial banks

Housing loans from commercial banks are very expensive. Given their high interest rates, the effective duration is relatively short. Moreover, the contracted amount is often repaid before maturity, having provided an interim solution (for example, before getting a housing support scheme loan).

Table 5: Weight of Mortgage Loans in the Portfolio of the Banking Sector
(billion HUF)

	mortgage-loans	total assets	ratio
1995	168.9	3 693.3	4.6%
1996	149.1	4 489.5	3.3%
1997	135.8	5 662.5	2.4%
1998	127.4	6 526.4	2.0%
1999	129.7	7 304.8	1.8%
2000	204.8	8 381.6	2.4%

Note: Data are year-end figures
Source: National Bank of Hungary

Mortgage loans

Conditions of mortgage loans

Probably the most common measure of the efficiency of mortgage loans is the ratio of the loan to the value of the real estate subject to the loan contract (loan-to-value ratio, LTV). This value typically exceeds 70% in countries with well-developed mortgage loan markets.

In Hungary, typical mortgage products offer a maximum LTV of 30% to 50%. Typical LTV ratios have improved significantly in recent years, however, and further improvements are expected, with new products offering up to 70% of LTV.

Apart from high real interest rates, two factors prevent mortgage loans from becoming common: uncertainty caused by inflationary conditions, and further uncertainty stemming from poor regulation of the mortgage market.

The first set of problems include high interest rates, the banking system's tendency to adjust mortgage rates slowly to a general decline in interest rates, and public distrust of mortgage products. High interest rates make these products unattractive in the eyes of non-expert potential clients, who view their long-term future monetary burdens in nominal terms. Products offering deferred-payment mortgages pose difficult administrative and internal regulatory problems to banks. Experience shows, moreover, that the public is not willing to accept nominal uncertainty.

Long-term uncertainty regarding price levels and nominal incomes makes the usual mortgage contracts with fixed annual repayments nonsensical. In some conditions the risk associated with unpredictable real variables makes it expensive to modify loan periods, and that favours demand for shorter-term loans. Short-term loans are, thus, less credit-rationed.

Currently, a person approaching the mortgage market with a net demand is capable of spending a much smaller share of his or her income on such an investment than would be the case in an efficient mortgage market. This weakens demand. Consequently, a short-term improvement in the efficiency of a mortgage market with a naturally inelastic supply would incite a steep price rise on the real estate market.

Interestingly, despite the very low level of stock of mortgage debt outstanding, the turnover of mortgage loans is considerable, owing to the typically short loan period set out in the contract. The longest loan period offered by OTP (Hungary's biggest commercial bank, which dominates the mortgage market with a share exceeding 80%) is 10 years, and the typical loan period is five years. Due to high (real) interest rates, however, most loans are repaid before the redemption time. Under Hungarian law, banks cannot rule out prepayment in the mortgage contract.

Housing investments by the population (purchases, refurbishment and new construction) are financed, government support aside, by private savings and by selling property. Because real interest rates are high, under typical loan terms Hungarians borrow only to solve very short-term liquidity problems. This reduces the efficiency of the market, as liquidity constraint helps preserve a less-than-optimal allocation of capital stock (housing). The desire to bring forward housing investment, and for debtors to repay loans as soon as possible, makes actual savings higher than what would be produced by intertemporal optimisation *cum "ideal"* financial market.

Institutions on the mortgage market

The other group of problems concerns the legal infrastructure that should guarantee the safety of mortgage loans. A prudent mortgage loan business, if properly regulated and managed, can generate very safe return on capital. In a sign of Hungary's shortcomings in this area, the OTP, when pricing loans in late 1999, reportedly calculated a 6% premium to counterbalance the risk of nonperforming debts.

The Land and Real Estate Registry could not cope with the wave of cases after the market economy began to develop. Registration of new ownership can take years, and information on ownership and mortgages on an estate, house or flat can be very slow in coming, particularly in the capital, where registries in some districts registries lag by many years.

Adding to the uncertainty are delays in bringing a claim through the courts, where cases often produce unpredicted results. The courts are overburdened, and civil cases can drag on for years. According to a recent study, an average of four years elapses between a default on a mortgage contract and foreclosure on the property. An OTP study suggests that this process take 58 months, two-thirds of it in the courts. By comparison, the US average for such a process is eight months. Even in France, where such procedures are the slowest among countries with well-developed mortgage markets, they take only 18 months.

The problem of credibility

The public attitude toward long-term debt also influences the dynamics of the mortgage market. In the early 1990s, the government several times unilaterally modified the terms of mortgage contracts it guaranteed. These steps might have been justified by the state of the economy at the time. But even if, surprisingly, the Constitutional Court did not deem these steps unconstitutional, they could have a long-term negative impact on the public belief that such long-term loan contracts should be sacred. Government now intends to replace the current support scheme, which pays financial support in cash, by a new system based on mortgage subventions. The public credibility it needs to reach its policy objective may be questionable, given the history of governments often changing the terms of long mortgage contracts.

HOUSING FINANCE IN LATVIA[1]

by
Laura Vecvagare[*]

Macroeconomic characteristics

Latvia has an area of 64 600 square kilometres and a population, according to preliminary results of the 2000 census, of 2.38 million, of which 1.66 million (69%) live in Riga, the capital, and 770 000 (31%) in other areas.

Since regaining independence in 1991, Latvia has carried out numerous reforms to transform the country from a command to a liberal market-driven economy. The first major steps were the liberalisation of prices, currency and the trading system. A national tax system, an independent governmental budget and a national currency were introduced; legal infrastructure for private property was developed and denationalisation and privatisation of state and municipal properties were launched. In 1993, the emphasis of reforms was transferred toward the economy, justice and administration system. In 1994, gross domestic product (GDP) experienced positive growth for the first time since 1991.

The Riga Stock Exchange was established in 1995 and a securities market started to develop. Privatisation of municipal and state-owned housing was launched, when the Law on Privatisation of State and Municipal Dwelling Houses was adopted. In 1995-96 the country's economy survived a banking crisis, and a sound and prudent system of banking supervision was established.

The majority of privatisation has been completed, and at the end of 1998 the private sector accounted for 65% of gross value added (up from 35% in 1994). A few enterprises remain to be privatised, the major ones being the Latvian Shipping Company (currently under privatisation) and Latvenergo (the energy monopoly company).

In recent years a new approach to health protection, culture and education has been sought with the involvement of private financing. Latvia has begun negotiations on accession to the European Union, and the harmonisation of Latvian legislation with EU requirements is continuing. The Latvian Government has adopted a medium-term economic strategy that defines policy priorities. Its goal is to ensure more rapid economic growth, enhance Latvian competitiveness and support its actual and nominal convergence in the EU internal market, as well as to foster environmentally friendly and socially just economic development.[2]

---

[*]   Consultant, Infrastructure Sector Unit, Europe and Central Asia Region, World Bank. The author would like to acknowledge and thank Mrs. Ilze Berzina, Mr. Inesis Feiferis, Mr. Ronalds Fisers, Mrs. Vija Geme, Ms. Ina Jaunite, Mr. Arnis Lagzdins, Mr. Normunds Peterkops, and Mr. Aigars Stokenbergs for their contributions of material and insights in the production of this chapter.

Confidence in the economy is reflected by the large inflows of foreign direct investments (total accumulated foreign direct investments as of September 2000 reached USD 1.95 billion or USD 822 per capita) and by ratings awarded to Latvia by the major international rating agencies.

GDP growth has resumed after the Russian crisis of 1998, and in 2000 it reached 6.6%. GDP growth of around 5% is projected for the following years. Total GDP has increased from USD 4.4 billion in 1995 to USD 7.15 billion at the end of 2000. GDP per capita has increased from USD 1 739 to USD 3 016 in the same period (at purchasing power parity it was USD 4 120 in 1999[3]). The majority of value added in GDP is from the services sector; its share has increased from 49% in 1995 to 68% in 1999.

Table 1: Macroeconomic Indicators

	1994	1995	1996	1997	1998	1999
Population (thousands)	2 566	2 530	2 502	2 480	2 458	2 439
GDP at current prices (USD million)	3 707.00	4 366.59	5 088.37	5 551.62	6 286.34	6 281.82
GDP at 1995 prices (USD million)	4 298.43	4 366.59	4 366.38	4 469.07	4 781.98	N/A
Real GDP growth (%)	0.6	0.8	3.3	8.6	3.9	0.1
GDP per capital at current prices (USD)	1 552	1 529	1 859	2 172	2 522	2 591
GDP per capital at 1995 prices (USD)	1 313	1 529	1 596	1 748	1 825	N/A
Average net wages (% growth over previous year)	47	21	7	12	10	N/A
Real wages (% growth over previous year)	8.2	-2.6	-8.8	3.6	5.3	N/A
Average gross wages (USD)	133.8	166.7	177.6	203.4	234.3	239.0

Source: Central Statistics Bureau of Latvia

The gross savings ratio in 1998 composed 3% of GDP, and it has increased from USD 111 million in 1995 to USD 195 million in 1998. Gross fixed capital formation in 1998 composed 20% of GDP, and it has approximately doubled, from USD 672 million in 1995 (15% of GDP) to USD 1.3 billion in 1998.

Table 2: Gross Capital Formation (Percent of GDP)

	1990	1995	1996	1997	1998
Gross capital formation	40.1	17.6	18.8	22.8	23.0
Of which: Savings	17.1	2.5	0.7	4.0	2.9
Gross fixed capital formation	22.9	15.1	18.1	18.7	20.0

Source: Central Statistics Bureau of Latvia

The budgetary deficit is well controlled by the government. In 1997 and 1998 the state budget had a surplus, while in 1999 it had a deficit of USD 240 million (4% of GDP), and in 2000 it had a deficit of USD 197 million (2.8% of GDP). The target for reduction of the budgetary deficit is 0.5% by 2004.

The local currency -- lats (LVL) -- is pegged to the SDR at a rate of SDR 1 = LVL 0.7997, and the central bank, the Bank of Latvia, has managed to keep this rate unchanged since 1994. The Bank of Latvia pursues a consistent monetary policy in line with IMF requirements, ensuring the stability of the national currency. The LVL/USD exchange rate has been rather stable, varying from an average of 0.51 in 1995 to 0.58 at the end of 1999. However, due to the recent appreciation of the US dollar, the exchange rate had reached 0.61 by the end of 2000 and 0.63 in March 2001.

Annual inflation has stabilised at around 3% (2.6% in 2000) and is expected to remain below 4% in the coming years. Unemployment has stabilised at around 8% of the active population. The average gross monthly salary has increased from USD 154 in the beginning of 1995 to USD 253 at the end of 2000.

Table 3: Inflation

1991	1992	1993	1994	1995	1996	1997	1998	1999
172.2%	951.2%	109.2%	35.9%	25.0%	17.6%	8.4%	4.7%	2.4%

Source: Central Statistics Bureau of Latvia

The foreign trade balance, however, remains negative and at the end of 2000 it reached 18.5% of GDP, or USD 1.3 billion. The foreign trade structure has shifted from being dominated by CIS countries (from 48% of export and 38% of import in 1993 to 9% of export and 17% of import in 2000), to domination by EU countries (from 33% of export and 27% of import in 1993 to 65% of export and 52% of import in 2000). This process was particularly stimulated by the 1998 crisis in Russia.

Housing sector overview

Housing stock and investments

Over the last 10 years the total area of the housing stock has changed little, from 52.9 million square meters in 1990 to 53.6 million square meters at the end of 2000, of which 65% is located in urban areas. The average housing area per capita has increased from 19.8 square meters to 21.8 square meters due mainly to a decrease in population rather than an increase in housing. The majority of apartments have one (25% of total) or two (48%) rooms (that is, sleeping/living area, excluding kitchen and bathroom) and the average area of an apartment is 47.6 square meters. The average area of newly built housing, however, is 90 square meters.

Table 4: Housing Stock

	1990	1995	1996	1997	1998
Total housing stock (million m^2)	52.9	52.7	52.8	53.0	53.2
Average housing area per capita (m^2)	19.8	21.1	21.3	21.5	21.8

Source: Central Statistics Bureau of Latvia

As little to no maintenance was carried out during the Soviet era, buildings suffer from a tremendous level of deterioration. Assuming that 11% (or 3 663 houses) of the total housing stock is uninhabitable, the gross housing area now available is even smaller.

A significant part of existing housing, approximately one-third, consists of multi-apartment block buildings built during the Soviet era. In addition to their rather discouraging outlook and design, their small size and inconvenient floor plans, these buildings are of low-quality construction and are poorly insulated against heat loss. During the Soviet era energy supplies were cheap and abundant, and energy efficiency was not a concern. The concern was with construction costs. With the advent of market conditions, including in the energy sector, energy costs have become an ever larger expenditure for households. Population surveys in 1998 indicated that housing costs composed 21% of total household expenditures, of which more than half (53%) went for utilities. Hence, energy conservation measures become an important concern.

Because the residential sector is a major consumer of heat energy (65%-70% of the total), energy efficiency measures and housing insulation would have a favourable secondary effect on the foreign trade balance of Latvia by reducing fuel imports.

In the Soviet era the State provided the majority of funding for housing construction and maintenance, and only a very small portion was financed by private persons. This situation changed radically with independence. Due to limited resources, housing construction has decreased dramatically since 1990, when five apartments were built per 1 000 inhabitants.[4] In 1998 only 0.5 apartments and 0.5 family houses were built per 1 000 inhabitants, or 1 351 apartments (225 000 square meters) in total.

Table 5: Number of Apartments Constructed

	1994	1995	1996	1997	1998
Total apartments constructed	3 369	1 776	1 483	1 480	1 351
By private persons	798	1 068	1 331	1 332	1 251
By private companies and public organisations	1 512	581	104	115	97
By public enterprises and organisations	1 059	127	48	33	3
New apartments per 1,000 inhabitants	1.31	0.70	0.59	0.60	0.53

Source: Central Statistics Bureau of Latvia

The proportion of private financing of housing construction has increased from 8% in 1990 to almost 100% in 1998, while total investments have decreased eight times, from more than USD 600 million in 1990 to USD 77.7 million, a mere 1.2% of GDP, in 1998.

Another consequence of the termination of public funding for construction was that many buildings remained unfinished. Based on data from the Central Statistics Bureau of Latvia, USD 94 million is needed to complete all unfinished construction, of which USD 17 million is needed for completion of housing.

The need for investment in the housing sector is significant, both for construction of new housing and renovation and upgrading of existing housing stock. The assessment of PriceWaterhouse (in its Market Study on Development of the Mortgage Market in Latvia carried out for the Mortgage and Land Bank of Latvia in 1998) is that 31.2 million square meters of housing stock requires major renovations and fundamental improvements. PriceWaterhouse estimated the total costs of such renovations to be at least USD 2 billion.

Table 6: Capital Investments in Housing Construction

Financed by:	1990	1995	1996	1997	1998
					(USD million at 1998 constant prices)
Private persons	50.3	60.0	70.5	44.4	75.3
Private companies and public organisations	153.1	9.5	0.6	1.0	0.0
State and municipal enterprises	250.1	0.7	2.0	0.0	0.8
Total	627.3	70.2	73.6	75.6	76.8

Source: Central Statistics Bureau of Latvia

Figure 1: Housing Construction

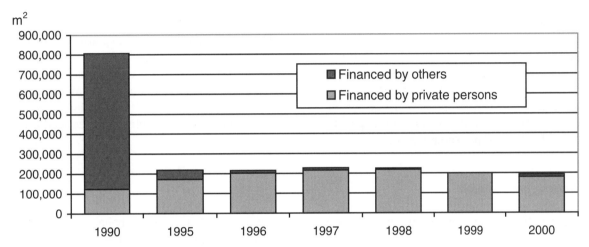

Source: Central Statistics Bureau of Latvia

There are several obstacles, however, to an expansion of housing investments. The major ones are:

- Inefficient housing maintenance and management; the majority of housing stock (even fully privatised buildings) is maintained by municipal housing maintenance organisations.

- Lack of a sense of ownership for common areas.

- Lack of funding.

- Unsettled ownership structure (only 60% of housing has been fully privatised).

Housing market

The housing market in Latvia is mainly dollar-based, for reasons dating to a time when inflation was in three-digit numbers. It is concentrated in Riga, the Riga region and Jurmala. There is some activity in a few other large cities, such as Ventspils, Liepaja, Daugavpils and Ogre. The rural housing market is developing very slowly. This situation arises largely from the high concentration of economic activity in the larger cities, resulting in lower income levels and real estate liquidity in smaller cities and rural areas.

In 1998, real estate transactions and commercial rent composed 6% of gross value added, or USD 337 million at current prices. The annual volume of housing-related transactions assessed by real estate dealers is USD 150 million, most of it in the Riga area. The housing market is dominated by apartment-related transactions composing 85% of the total number of transactions, according to major real estate companies.

Most expensive real estate is located in central Riga. At the end of 1999 the average price for an apartment was USD 850-950 per square meter. Outside the central city, the average price at the end of 1999 was USD 200-375 per square meter, up from an average of USD 100 in 1993.

An average apartment in a multi-apartment block building would cost USD 8 000-15 000, while outside of the major cities, an apartment would cost as little as USD 2 000. Prices, of course, depend on location, condition and type of building.

In recent years Latvia has gone through a period of high demand for high-quality apartments in the centre of Riga, with foreigners as the primary buyers. However, these large and expensive apartments are in oversupply and the market is shifting toward clients in the next decile of income distribution, creating demand for single-family detached and terraced houses. Real estate companies indicate that demand for this type of houses in the USD 60 000-100 000 price range has been increasing in the last few years. Several companies are launching large projects to build small villages of family houses, particularly in the area surrounding Riga. Prices for new single-family detached and terraced houses are USD 400-850 per square meter.

Housing privatisation

The denationalisation or restitution of property, including residential properties, began in 1991. As of the end of 1998, some 9 995 residential properties with 75 000 apartments and a total area of 3.5 million square meters had been returned to their lawful owners.

The privatisation of state and municipal housing was launched in 1995, when the Law on Privatisation of State and Municipal Dwelling Houses was passed. Privatisation is carried out by individual privatisation commissions established in each municipality, and co-ordinated by the Central Apartment Housing Privatisation Commission.

Apartments are privatised using privatisation certificates, which were distributed to individuals based on age, work history, deportation and other factors.[5] Apartments are privatised at a set price of two certificates per square meter (the market price of a certificate with face value of USD 45 has decreased from USD 3.50-5.00 to USD 2.50 per certificate). The certificates expire on 31 December 2001. Any further privatisation of apartments would be carried out for cash.

A major problem has been encountered in the privatisation process when a building itself and the land on which it stands have different owners. While the Civil Code provides for indivisible property of the building and land beneath it, the Law on Privatisation of State and Municipal Dwelling Buildings allowed for separate privatisation of a building and the land. This situation arose because restitution of property to its former lawful owners took place before a privatisation scheme was developed and included the land on which multi-apartment buildings were built during the Soviet era. Therefore, there are cases in which land was restituted to its previous owner, while the municipal apartment building built on it during the Soviet era was being privatised by its tenants. The situation is further complicated when the land under the building consists of several plots belonging to different owners.

A partial solution has been for the land owner(s) and tenants/owners of multi-apartment buildings to sign long-term rental agreements.

There are two types of apartment registration authorities:

- *Land Book* registers real estate title and other legal rights and provides full legal protection.

- *Cadastres* register physical characteristics of an apartment and the persons having signed a rental agreement with the municipality, as well as apartment ownership in the case of accelerated privatisation.

There are two types of housing privatisation:

- Regular or full privatisation: the whole building is privatised and registered in the Land Book and each apartment with assigned respective joint ownership or "ideal part" of the common areas and land is registered as a private property in the Land Book.

- Accelerated privatisation (temporary stage to full privatisation): other apartment is privatised without any assigned "ideal part" of common areas, nor land and ownership of the apartment is registered in the Cadastre only. Once the house has been fully privatised, ownership titles on individual apartments and "ideal parts" of the common areas of the building and land are registered in the Land Book.

The second type of privatisation arose from the slow pace of preparation of housing for privatisation by municipalities due to insufficient capacity and resources. Private individuals were applying to municipalities for privatisation in order to use their privatisation certificates, the initial expiration date for which was 31 December 1999.

There are 505 221 apartments (30 560 houses) eligible for privatisation, 79% (or 391 253) of which have been either privatised via the accelerated process or offered by the municipality for full privatisation. As of the end of 2000, approximately 57% of housing eligible for privatisation had been privatised.[6] As a result of these processes the structure of the housing fund has changed; privately owned housing increased from 30% in 1990 to 53% in 1998 and an estimated 70% in 2000 as based on 2000 census data.

Table 7: Housing Ownership Structure
(million m^2)

	1990	1995	1996	1997	1998
Total Housing Stock	52.9	52.7	52.8	53.0	53.2
Public-owned	36.6	26.2	25.9	25.3	25.2
Co-operative-owned	2.5	2.3	2.4	2.4	2.5
Private-owned	13.8	24.2	25.4	25.2	25.5

Source: Central Statistics Bureau of Latvia

The Central Apartment Housing Privatisation Commission expects that 80% of housing will be privatised by the end of 2001. The remaining 20% not being privatised is expected to be managed by municipalities as rental and social houses.

Before privatisation, maintenance of multi-apartment buildings was carried out either by the local Municipal Housing Administration (MHA) or co-operatives[7] (5% of total housing stock). Housing maintenance and private involvement in this process have become major issues in the housing sector. No mechanism has been developed for promotion or enforcement. The majority of housing, including privatised buildings, is maintained by municipal MHAs rather than privately.

The other reasons for the low pace of establishment of private housing management companies are: low awareness and sense of ownership of common areas; lack of knowledge; lack of incentives; significant differences in welfare and solvency among apartment owners in any one building.

Governmental housing policy

The major emphasis of the government is on development of a mortgage lending system in the country as a source of long-term funding for financing housing investments. For that purpose a special governmental Working Group was established by the Cabinet of Ministers. The main task of the Working Group is to evaluate the current legal and regulatory framework for housing and mortgage-related issues and develop recommendations for improvements.

The key items of governmental housing policy are: alignment and development of legal infrastructure for mortgage lending and housing-related issues; development of market relationships and involvement of the private sector in housing sector; improvement of existing dwelling stock and promotion of new construction of housing; development of mortgage lending; development of subsidies and social guarantees for housing for low-income and socially vulnerable households; improvement of housing legislation; and institutional building in the housing sector.

The needs to establish individual metering systems in apartments, improve energy efficiency of housing, and promote construction of individual family houses are also stated.

The major principles and guidelines are spelled out in several concepts and programs:

- The Concept for Housing Policy was first adopted by the Cabinet of Ministers of Latvia on July 30, 1996.

- The Concept for the Development of Long-Term Crediting for the Construction, Reconstruction and Modernisation of Dwellings was developed and approved by the Cabinet of Ministers on 11 November 1997.

- The Concept for the Establishment of a Mortgage Lending System was approved by the Cabinet of Ministers on 11 November 1997.

- Conceptual Recommendations for the Utilisation of Fiscal Policy in the Development of a Mortgage Lending System, as well as Promotion of Housing Construction, Reconstruction, Renovation and Insulation, were approved by the Cabinet of Ministers on 24 March 1998.

- The National Construction Program for 2000-20 is in the process of preparation.

- The Housing Development Financing Program and Real Estate Financing Project awaits government approval of drafts submitted.

The government is also preparing programs in this area in co-operation with international financial institutions. Separate programs are being developed and implemented by individual municipalities as well.

Housing subsidies

The government provides a general housing subsidy by establishing rental ceilings, which provide a significant hidden housing subsidy to the population. Ceilings for rent or maintenance fees (in the case of privatised housing) are set by each individual municipality based on methodology approved by the Cabinet of Ministers. Current rental ceilings (approximately USD 0.25 per square meter) are two to three times lower than actual maintenance costs, and they vary depending on the level of comfort provided in the apartment -- stove or central district heating, availability of hot water and other factors. Rental ceilings apply to municipal- and state-owned dwellings and for a limited period of time (seven years[8]) to restituted residential buildings for lease agreements signed before restitution.

Social assistance is regulated by the Law on Social Assistance adopted in 1996, which states the minimum guaranteed income per household member, sets requirements for individuals eligible for social assistance, and lays out the main types of assistance. All assistance is provided by local governments. While the law establishes a guaranteed minimum income, each municipality may increase its assistance by broadening types of assistance and amounts, depending on its abilities.

The two major types of social assistance for housing by the municipalities are social housing (individual apartments either in a regular house or in a special dedicated "social house") and housing allowances for rent, heating and fuel.

Figure 2: Structure of Housing Assistance (1998)

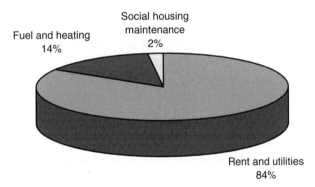

Source: Social Assistance Fund

In 1998, only 32 of 576 municipalities provided social housing services. The total expenditures of municipalities for social housing maintenance were USD 242 000 in 1998. There were 703 social apartments in Latvia in 1998, accommodating 1 409 people. In 1999, the total area of social housing increased by 64% and the number of people accommodated reached 3,026. However, not all people approved as eligible for social housing have been accommodated.

In Riga city there are five social houses with 400 apartments. The city covers 75% of rent and 25% of utility costs in these social houses. Additional 25 social houses are to be established over the next five years. At the end of 1999, 250 people were still on a waiting list for social housing in Riga. While social houses are dedicated mainly to the low-income elderly, assistance to households in temporary difficulty is provided in the form of allowances and temporary settlement in social apartments in regular residential buildings until the household's situation has improved.

89

Housing-related assistance (excluding social housing) composes more than 40% of the total municipal budget for social assistance (up to 56% in the seven 7 largest cities).[9] In 1998, the municipalities spent USD 10 million on assistance for housing, utilities and fuel expenses for 192,903 people.[10] In 1999, this assistance increased to USD 12 million. Of the total, 85% goes to rent and utilities and 15% to fuel expenditures.

No subsidies or assistance are provided or envisaged for improvement, construction or purchase of housing. There are very limited tax advantages and/or allowances related to housing investments (current legislation allows for a double depreciation rate reducing annual taxable income) or mortgage loans.

The major concern remains the implicit housing subsidies provided in the form of rent ceilings, which have a broader secondary effect by imposing pressure and setting "ceilings" on maintenance fees. That hinders private sector's involvement in housing management and maintenance and prevents the housing sector from developing more rapidly. Since these costs are not explicitly accounted for or assessed, there is little awareness of the effects and consequences of such a policy.

Sources of housing financing

Real estate companies indicate that the majority of housing is financed by buyers' own funds (i.e. savings) or borrowings from relatives rather than bank loans. The amount of outstanding mortgage loans during the first nine months of 2000 increased by almost 70%, from USD 92 million at the beginning of the year to USD 154 million at the end of September.[11]

While the mortgage loan portfolio of banks is growing rapidly, it is still very small relative to GDP, primarily because of the low borrowing capacity of the population. Current income of households and the available terms of mortgage loans (high interest rates and currency risk) allow only the 10% to 20% of the population atop the income distribution to obtain bank loans. Historic reasons also play a role: In the Soviet era, borrowing was very limited and almost all investments of private persons were financed from savings. That has created some resistance towards borrowing and being in debt.

While borrowing for the purchase or renovation of individual houses or apartments is available, there are limited possibilities (but no precedents yet) for borrowing for renovation of the common areas of multi-apartment buildings. It would require development of good legal infrastructure to increase the borrowing capacity of these buildings and ensure banks about their repayment capacity as well as efficient foreclosure procedures.

The current structure of housing ownership provides that a building belongs to many owners -- individual owners of apartments -- but maintenance is provided either by a municipal HMO, a private maintenance company (HMC) under an agreement signed with individual apartment owners, or by an association of apartment owners (AAO).

Because banks will lend only against tangible real estate collateral, to borrow for the renovation or insulation of a multi-apartment building requires pledging the individual apartments. That significantly increases transaction costs while creating a "moral hazard" problem (some apartment owners may not be willing to pledge their apartments, and others would have to assume all the obligations, which may reduce the incentives of the others to contribute their share to repaying the loan).

A law on condominiums or another appropriate structure is being developed. Improvement of lending capacity for multi-apartment buildings is a major issue to be addressed. One alternative under consideration is to provide for the legal rights of housing maintenance companies or associations of apartment owners to utilise mortgage rights on individual apartments in the case of default by individual apartment owners. That would strengthen creditworthiness of HMCs and AAOs.

Housing finance

Mortgage lending and housing finance in Latvia

Mortgage lending (residential and commercial) has been developing in Latvia for several years. While the mortgage loan portfolio of banks has nearly doubled each of the last two years, it remains rather small, and at the end of 2000 composed USD 191 million -- 4% of the total assets of the banking sector or 11% of the total loan portfolio. The figure for mortgage loans in relation to GDP is also very low and was about 2.7% at the end of September 2000.

Figure 3: Mortgage Loans Outstanding

USD million

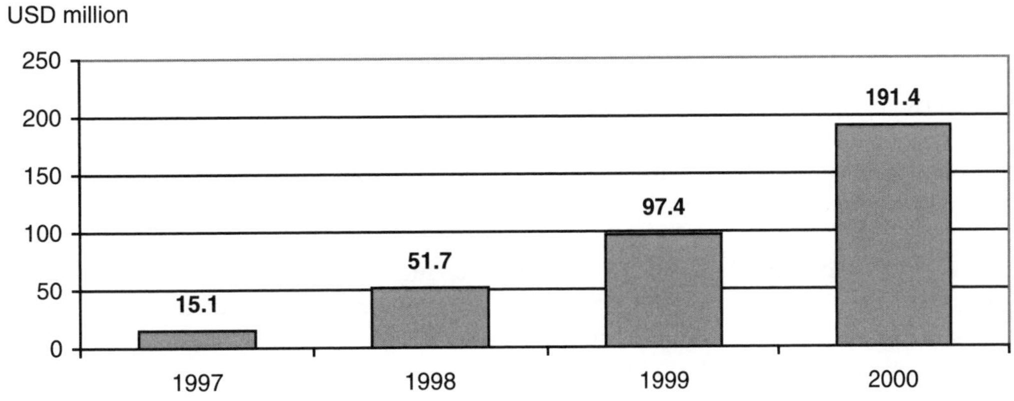

Note: Year-end
Source: Mortgage and Land Bank of Latvia

Table 8: Development of Mortgage Loans

(Year-end)	1998	1999	2000
Mortgage loans outstanding/GDP	0.8%	1.6%	2.7%
Mortgage loans outstanding/total assets of banks	2%	3%	4%
Mortgage loans outstanding/total loan portfolio	5.2%[1]	7.2%	11.0%

Note: 1) Loans issued to domestic enterprises
Source: Bank of Latvia, Central Statistics, and Mortgage and Land Bank of Latvia

Several banks project a rapid increase in mortgage lending in the near future and expect that the mortgage loan portfolio of the whole banking sector may reach USD 300 million to 500 million in the next few years.

Public surveys indicate that people are interested either in small loans of up to USD 2 000 with maturity of up to three years for minor refurbishment, or longer-term loans (10 to 20 years) of up to USD 35 000 to 50 000.[12]

The majority of mortgage loans are issued in OECD currencies -- USD and Euro -- rather than lats. This approach exposes borrowers to an exchange-rate risk, which is particularly problematic for average households borrowing for housing-related purposes, which they may not be able to properly evaluate or assume in time.

The term of mortgage loans was originally quite short, but it has increased rapidly, particularly during the last six months, when several banks began to offer 20- to 40-year mortgage loans. However, the average term of mortgage loans is five to 10 years. The average repayment period of mortgage loans is as short as 3.5 years, some banks have indicated. The main reasons cited for this are low public expectations of the future and the emotional discomfort toward indebtedness, which makes loan repayment a top priority for the use of any extra funds.

In March 2000, interest rates on mortgage loans in Euro were 9% to 13%, in USD 11% to 15% and in LVL 14% to 18%. Interest rates have been decreasing, and at the end of 2000 the average interest rate on loans in lats was 9.53% and in OECD currencies, 10.4%.

Most loans are issued with floating rates based on 3- or 6-month LIBOR (for USD and Euro) or local interbank rates such as RIGIBOR/UNIBOR. Usual margins above these rates are 4% to 8%. Some banks have started to offer fixed interest rates for a period of up to 2 years, which corresponds to the term of lats/currency swaps offered by the Bank of Latvia.

Mortgage loans are usually issued with a loan-to-value ratio of 60% to 70%. The requirement for payment-to-income ratio is 30% to 35%.

The major obstacles for rapid growth of mortgage lending in Latvia, other than the legal issues discussed earlier, are: the low borrowing capacity of the population; high interest rates and currency risk; the lack of personal savings or other funds for down-payments (30% to 40% of real estate value); a resistance to borrowing that has developed for historic reasons; low expectations and high uncertainty among the general public as to future economic development and personal income.

Legal framework for mortgage lending

There is no specific legislation regarding mortgage lending in Latvia, unless the loans are to be refinanced via the issuance of mortgage bonds. Such issuance and related mortgage lending are regulated by the Law on Mortgage Bonds adopted in April 1998 and revised in September 1998.

The law stipulates requirements for banks issuing mortgage bonds, for mortgage loans to be included in the mortgage bond coverage register, for evaluation of property, and for supervision and other related issues.

The law does not require establishment of a specialised mortgage bank for performing mortgage operations (issuing both mortgage loans and mortgage bonds). Universal banks that comply with a set of requirements, such as minimum (own) capital of USD 8.2 million, compliance with banking legislation and Bank of Latvia regulations and internal separation of mortgage operations, may issue mortgage bonds. The main reason for this is that the very small financial market of Latvia (the banking sector had total assets at the end of 1999 of USD 3 billion), which may not justify the establishment of specialised mortgage banks. However, the law requires full separation of mortgage operations from general banking business within a bank, with separate accounting for the mortgage bond coverage register and for its administration. The law provides for priority claim rights for the mortgage bond holders to assets included in the bond coverage register. A special procedure for separation of banking assets in the event of a bank's bankruptcy still needs to be developed. Procedures for management and administration of the mortgage bond coverage register are set in the special regulations of the Securities Market Commission.

The Law on Mortgage Bonds requires that evaluation of the real estate included in the mortgage bonds collateral register is performed by a Latvian certified evaluator. The certification procedure is specified in the Regulations of the Cabinet of Ministers No. 60 of 15 February 2000.

Requirements for mortgage bond issuance and the content of the prospectus are set in the Law on Securities and the Regulations of the Securities Market Commission on Mortgage Bond Emission Prospectus.

Legislation on bank capital adequacy provides a 50% risk weight for loans secured by real estate collateral and a 50% risk weight for mortgage bonds, both of which comply with EU Directives.

Mortgage-related issues are regulated by the Law on Land Books as well as the Civil Law and the Civil Procedures Law (foreclosure procedures, etc.). For full legal protection of real estate related rights, the mortgage has to be registered in the Land Book. The Land Book system has been fully computerised and is expected to be accessible on-line in 2001.

A special interministerial Working Group has been established by the Cabinet of Ministers, which is working continuously on the development and improvement of legal infrastructure for mortgage lending operations. The Working Group has identified several areas that require improvement, such as housing management and maintenance (a law on condominiums or other appropriate structure), information disclosure for mortgage bond investors (Law on Securities and Regulations on Mortgage Bond Emission Prospectus), foreclosure procedures (Civil Procedures Law). Special sub-groups have been established to analyse these areas of legislation and develop recommendations for amendments in co-operation with local and international experts.

Housing finance system

Banking sector

Mortgage loans are issued by general-purpose non-specialised banks and financed mainly from deposits, foreign borrowings and equity, which determines the current terms.

The structure of funding sources creates a significant maturity mismatch between assets and liabilities. At the end of the third quarter of 2000 the majority of deposits were demand (61%) or short-term deposits (up to 1 year; 32%) and only 7.4% were term deposits for 1 year or longer. Of all loans, 76% have a term longer than 1 year, including 20% with a term longer than 5 years.

Limited amounts are financed by the issuance of mortgage bonds. As of the end of September 2000 three mortgage bond issues in the total amount of USD 8.2 million had been registered with the Securities Market Commission, USD 4.7 million of which are in circulation. All three issues were made by the Mortgage and Land Bank of Latvia, the only fully state-owned bank remaining. The following are the key parameters of these bonds:

Table 9: Issuance of Mortgage Bonds

Issued	Maturity	Coupon	Registered	In circulation
February 1999	February 2002	8.50%	USD 1.6 million	USD 1.6 million
May 2000	August 2003	8.00%	USD 5 million	USD 2.1 million
May 2000	February 2005	8.50%	USD 1.6 million	USD 0.98 million

Note: As of September 2000.
Source: Mortgage and Land Bank of Latvia, Securities Market Commission

Mortgage bonds are issued in lats and yield varies from 8% to 8.6%, approximately 1% above government securities issue.

Development of long-term lats funding is essential for affordable mortgage loans to develop in Latvia, and mortgage bonds are a key instrument in this process. There is generally a shortage of long-term financial instruments in the financial market, as indicated by a very high demand for mortgage bonds. Mortgage bonds will be essential for the implementation of pension reform and the future development of private pension funds and life insurance in Latvia.

Other lenders

Contract saving schemes and building societies are at the earliest stage of development in Latvia and have limited penetration in the housing financing market. The largest savings and loan company in Latvia is Dzelzcelnieks KS (Railway Workers S&L) and its assets compose 80% of total assets in the sector. Total loans worth USD 2.1 million were granted in 1999, of which 38%, or USD 0.8 million, were housing-related.

Mortgage loans are also issued by life insurance companies. At the end of 1999 their mortgage loan portfolio composed 3% of the total technical reserves of the industry, or USD 2.6 million.[13]

Government policy

Development of mortgage bonds and mortgage lending is an important issue for the Government of Latvia due to its impact on the development of the national economy, as well for the reasons mentioned above. It is also a major task of the interministerial Working Group. The Working Group's interests cover both the legal framework and related private structures such as the Stock Exchange and Central Depository. Through the initiative of the Working Group and the Mortgage and Land Bank of Latvia, several fees have been restructured and reduced to lower barriers to mortgage bond development.

Due to the Working Group initiative, the Bank of Latvia approved a reduction of risk weighing for mortgage loans and indicated its willingness to accept mortgage bonds among other private-sector securities (subject to recommendation of supervisory authorities and approval of the Bank's management) for its repurchase transactions and Lombard credits as well as direct investments in the implementation of its monetary policy.

NOTES

1. This chapter was prepared in the Ministry of Finance/the World Bank Technical Unit as an aide-memoire for the OECD Workshop on Housing Finance in Transition Economies. It presents an unofficial summary of housing and related finance in the country. The data and information presented have been gathered from a variety of sources and attempt to offer a brief insight into this complex subject and situation. The goal has been to present a readable, comprehensive overview. The material should be viewed as an introduction only, however, and recognised as an unofficial briefing paper.

2. Welcome to Latvia; EBRD Annual Meeting May 21-22, 2000

3. Facts and Figures about the Baltic Sea Region

4. Housing Development Financing Program by the Ministry of Finance of the Republic of Latvia (draft)

5. Privatisation certificate is dematerialised security granted by the state, which can be used as a means of payment in privatisation of state or municipal property (Ministry of Environment and Regional Development).

6. Central Apartment Building Privatisation Commission

7. The building was owned by the co-operative and each of the apartment owners had a share in the co-operative respectively to the share of his or her apartment in the building. These co-operative apartments are currently being privatised as well and the co-operative remains only as a maintenance company for the building.

8. At the beginning of 2001 prolongation of this term has been under consideration by the Parliament.

9. Implementation of Social Assistance Policy in Municipalities in 1998

10. Social Assistance Fund

11. Including both housing and commercial mortgage loans.

12. Housing Development Financing Program of the Ministry of Finance (draft)

13. State Insurance Supervision Inspectorate

FRAMEWORK FOR THE HOUSING SECTOR OF LITHUANIA

by
Dalia Jurgaityte[*]

Demographic and macroeconomic characteristics

Population

Some 40% of the population lives in the six largest municipalities (Vilnius, Kaunas, Klaipeda, šiauliai, Panevezys and Alytus). The average population density has grown from 39.5 inhabitants per square kilometre in 1950 to 56.8 in 1998, while the country's population increased by 48% over the period, from 2.5 million to 3.7 million. One can identify three distinct clusters of counties with different population densities (Figure 1). At the lower end, Utena and Taurage counties have population densities of 30 inhabitants per square kilometre. The highest densities are in Vilnius, Kaunas and Klaipeda counties, with values three times higher. The other five counties form a cluster with an average population density of 45 inhabitants per square kilometre.

Rapid urbanisation has taken place in Lithuania in the last 30 years. The urban population has grown almost 3.5 times since 1950, while the rural population has decreased by 36%. Migration to urban centres came largely before 1990. Since 1993, despite the overall population decline, rural areas have gained new residents, reversing long-standing migration trends. Emigration from Lithuania has also increased, but less than one might have expected given the domestic economic difficulties (Table 1).

An indicator of potential demand for dwellings is the population growth rate. Currently, the country is experiencing a natural population decrease (Table 1, 2). The highest population increase was in the 1970s, followed by moderate growth in the 1980s. Since 1990, birth rates have declined, while death rates have increased. Birth rates fell particularly sharply in urban areas. Overall, Lithuania is experiencing an alarming decline in population, reflecting social and housing problems.

The 1989 population census identified 1 million households in Lithuania. The number of households increased by 10 000 to 11 000 a year in the 1980s, while in 1992-94 there was a decline of 10 000. The relative proportion of single-person households is growing, and women account for two-thirds of these households. While the divorce rate increased dramatically -- from 35.1 per 100 new marriages in 1990 to 60.5 per 100 -- marriages decreased from 9.8 to 5.1 per thousand inhabitants over the same period. Women outnumber men in the population, particularly in the post-retirement age group. Experts estimate the number of households at 1.3 million in 1999.

---

*   Housing and Urban Development Foundation, Lithuania

Figure 1: Lithuanian Population Density by County, January 1999

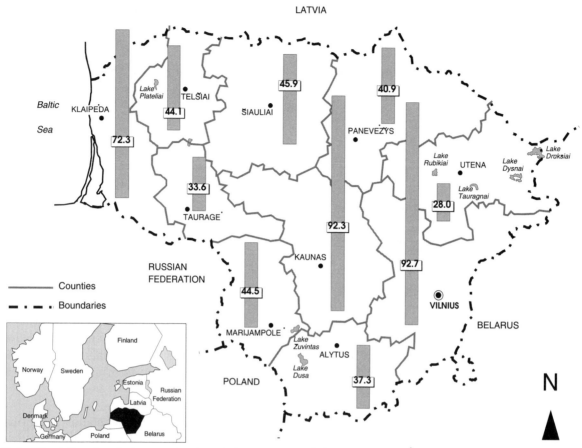

Note: Population density is a number in each bar per county (inhabitants per km^2)
Source: Districts of Lithuania, Economic and Social Development, Department of Statistics, Vilnius 1999

Table 1: Population Migration, 1980-2000

							(1 000 inhabitants)
	1980	1990	1996	1997	1998	1999	2000
Net urban migration	29.6	14.4	-10.0	-6.5	-1.8	N/A	N/A
-- Immigration	116.0	87.1	47.2	47.2	39.5	N/A	N/A
-- Emigration	86.4	72.7	57.2	53.7	41.3	N/A	N/A
Net rural migration	-20.7	-2.8	9.1	6.6	2.4	N/A	N/A
-- Immigration	59.1	45.8	36.6	34.5	25.9	N/A	N/A
-- Emigration	79.8	48.6	27.5	27.9	23.5	N/A	N/A
Net foreign migration	N/A	-8.8	-0.9	0.1	0.6	1.3	-1.1
-- Immigration	N/A	14.7	3.0	2.6	2.7	2.7	1.5
-- Emigration	N/A	23.6	3.9	2.5	2.1	1.4	2.6
Total migration	N/A	292.5	175.5	168.3	135.1	N/A	N/A
-- % of population	N/A	7.9%	4.7%	4.5%	3.6%	N/A	N/A
Total population	3 404.2	3 708.2	3 711.9	3 707.2	3 704.0	3 700.8	3 698.5
-- Urban	2 074.4	2 526.9	2 518.5	2 534.5	2 525.2	2 523.2	2 522.2
-- Rural	1 329.8	1 181.3	1 193.5	1 172.7	1 178.8	1 177.6	1 176.3

Source: Demographic Yearbooks, Department of Statistics, Vilnius, 1994-2000

Table 2: Natural Population Increase, 1960-2000

	1960	1970	1980	1990	2000
Natural increase	14.7	8.8	4.7	4.6	-1.2
-- Birth rate	18.1	17.7	15.2	15.3	9.3
-- Death rate	7.9	8.9	10.5	10.7	10.5

Source: Statistical Yearbooks, Department of Statistics, Vilnius, 1997-2000

Figure 2: GDP, Inflation and Unemployment Rates

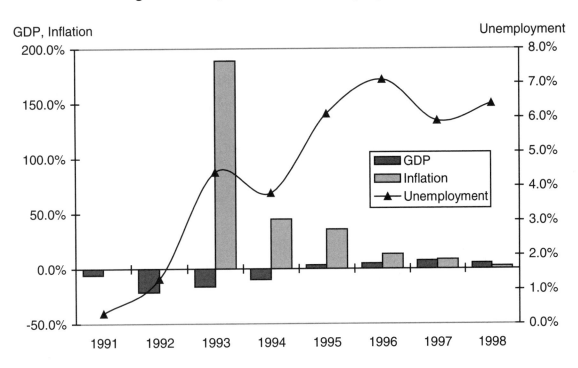

Source: Economic and Social Development in Lithuania, Department of Statistics, Vilnius 1998-99

Macroeconomic developments

The Lithuanian economy, as measured by gross domestic product (GDP), is some USD 10 billion. In 1998, according to revised estimates[1], GDP increased by 5.1% (Figure 2). The Central Bank expected GDP to grow by 3% in 1999. However, GDP shrank 4.8% over the first part of the year. The downward revisions are more realistic. The current recession was preceded by economic growth ranging from 3.3% to 7.3% in 1995-1997 due to prudent monetary and fiscal policies.

Until 1991, industry accounted for 44.4% of GDP (Table 3), followed by agriculture (16.4%) and construction (5.4%). During the first years of independence, Lithuanian industry suffered the steepest decline in the Baltic region, with production down by 51.6% in 1992. Due to industrial restructuring, industry grew by 5.4% in 1997 and by 7% in 1998. Services have increased their share of GDP, reflecting typical transformations to a market-oriented, service-based economy.

99

Table 3: Major Sectors' Share of Total Output, 1991-98

(% of value added GDP, current price)

	1991	1992	1993	1994	1995	1996	1997	1998[1]
Industry	44.4	37.5	34.2	27.0	26.1	25.8	25.2	22.5
Agriculture	16.4	13.8	14.2	10.7	11.7	12.2	11.7	12.3
Construction	5.4	3.9	5.1	7.2	7.1	7.1	7.7	9.0
Real estate and financial services			11.5	11.7	10.5	10.5	9.6	10.7
Other services	33.9[2]	44.8[2]	35.0	43.4	44.5	44.4	35.8	35.4

Note: 1) January-September. 2) Including real estate and financial services.
Source: UN\ECE Economic Survey of Europe, Issues: 1996-97, 1998 No. 1, and 1999 No. 1.

The main manufacturing sectors in Lithuania are food processing, light industry, machine building, metalworking, electronics, electrical appliances, chemicals, building materials and energy industries. Manufacturing depends on imports of raw materials. Light industry's modern technology and qualified work force have given it a comparative advantage over other sectors. The electronics and electrical appliances industries have accessed successfully the European markets. The energy sector is undergoing privatisation and structural changes.[2] Lithuania is the largest electricity producer in the Baltic region, with 16.8 billion kWh generated in 1996 (Ministry of Economy data). The construction industry, mostly privatised, experienced recovery in the mid-1990s with 6.6% growth in 1997. The construction sector contributed some 9% to GDP in 1998, as indicated in Table 3.

Inflation soared into triple digits in 1991-93, as the economy felt the combined effects of price liberalisation and wage increases aimed at compensating for inflation. In 1998, inflation fell for the fifth consecutive year (from 35.7% in 1995 to 2.4% in 1998[3]). In 1999, the inflation rate decreased to 0.3%, and in 2000 it was 1.4%. The current macroeconomic climate, with low inflation rates, might lead to increased investment in housing activities; however, other factors also affect the interest rates for commercial loans. Unemployment reached 8.4% in 1999. However, in 2000, it reached 11.5%. Those estimates are based on labour exchange numbers. The labour force survey estimates unemployment to be 4.5% above the labour exchange figure.

Foreign trade, investment and financing

To promote trade, custom tariffs for all imported goods averaged 10% in 1995. A free-trade agreement with the European Union came into force in January 1995. In 1996, a free-trade agreement on agricultural products with the Baltic states became effective. In spite of trade liberalisation, foreign trade data indicated a significant redirection of trade only in January 1999. Germany, Latvia and Belarus became the leading export destinations, while the Russian Federation fell to fourth place. The trade deficit stood at 7.1 billion litas in 1997 and 8.3 billion litas in 1998, 19.4% of GDP.[4] In 1994-96, foreign direct investment (FDI) amounted to USD 700 million, and in 1997 it surged to USD 1.05 billion. FDI reached a record high of USD 582 million in 1998. 62% of FDI capital is of EU origin. In 1996, two important bills were passed to promote foreign investment. First, the land reform bill was enacted in July 1996. It allows foreign enterprises to buy land, thereby removing a major obstacle to Lithuanian accession to the EU. The second bill allowed foreign banks to operate through branch offices. It facilitates foreign investment operations and meets EU requirements for banking laws.

The economy has been experiencing a shortage of capital to finance investment. Access to international financial markets has improved considerably. Lithuania has an international credit rating of BBB from Standard and Poor's (September 1998) and a sub-investment Ba1 rating from Moody's. In March 1999, Lithuania raised Euro 200 million through CS First Boston and Dresdner banks. As a member of the European Bank for Reconstruction and Development, International Monetary Fund and the World Bank, Lithuania receives loans for currency stabilisation, structural reforms in banking, agriculture, energy and social security. The country also receives grants under the European Union Phare programs. Domestic financial and capital markets are critical to structural reforms and to financing economic growth. To raise funds for investment, enterprises turn either to the capital market or to commercial banks for loans. Much has been achieved in pushing down interest rates for loans. However, the interest rate on loans still remains relatively high. In 1996, interest rates dropped to 16% for loans in litas and to 14.73% in hard currency. In 1997-98, rates plummeted further but remained within the 11% to 13% range. Low inflation rates no doubt account for these trends. Therefore, in September 1999, the average commercial interest rate stood at 12.68% on hard-currency loans and 11.17% in litas, which does not stimulate mortgage markets. The high margin reflects various commercial risks.

Sweeping measures were taken to reform the banking sector and to liberalise financial services following the banking crisis in 1995.[5] In June 1996, a law introducing recapitalisation securities was enacted, a condition imposed by the IMF in return for a loan to overcome effects of the banking crisis. Confidence in banks has been partially restored after the State increased mandatory bank deposit insurance from 4 000 to 25 000 litas in 1997. The capital market is functioning but volumes are not big; investment funds and private pension funds are just starting to operate. A large portion of stocks is traded on direct deals, indicating poor liquidity. Enterprises have experienced difficulty in raising capital. The public still has not acquired a culture of following, understanding and using capital markets as a vehicle of diversified savings. The Government introduced saving bonds in 1999.

Economic policies and privatisation

Economic reform was initiated as early as 1987 with the establishment of collective and personal enterprises. The transition to a market economy started after independence, when the Law on Initial Privatisation of State Property was adopted in February 1991. Prices were liberalised in November of that year, triggering inflationary pressures.

Lithuania introduced a national currency, the litas, and established a Currency Board in April 1994. Since then, the litas has been pegged to the US dollar at an exchange rate of 4 to 1. Tight financial discipline and an absence of exchange-rate volatility brought relative stabilisation to export-driven recovery. Commercial banks comply with the ratios set by the Central Bank (capital adequacy, solvency, and maximum open exposure in foreign currency and to a single customer). The Government borrows abroad and on domestic markets, issuing Treasury notes. Two shortcomings of the monetary policy have emerged. First, the country's financial dependency on international capital markets has increased. Second, a strengthening US dollar (and consequently litas) against European currencies has hurt exports. It became more profitable to import goods than to produce them domestically. Thus, incentives weakened for savings and investment. A fixed-rate exchange policy contributed to delays in restructuring. Consensus was reached to transfer monetary functions from the Currency Board to the Central Bank by dismantling the board in 2000. The litas is to be pegged to a basket of the Euro and the US dollar, while a fixed exchange rate will be kept during the transition period.

The major priorities in Lithuanian fiscal policy are to restructure the tax system, to minimise budgetary arrears and to improve tax administration. The Government strengthened tax administration by establishing the Tax Police Department and reorganising the State Tax Inspection Office. Lithuania currently has an individual income tax rate of 33% on personal income and 29% on corporate income. The value-added tax is levied at a rate of 18%; excise taxes are applied to gasoline, tobacco, alcohol and spirits. Trade taxes play a small role in the tax system with minor exceptions for agricultural produce. The tax system is not used to protect domestic industry or the housing sector. In 1994-96, a budget deficit existed mainly due to two problems: corporate tax arrears and overestimated revenues (including the collapse of commercial banks in 1995-96). In 1999, the Government struggled to balance the State budget as revenues fell short of projections. Fiscal policy was supplemented with austerity measures and the phasing out of various hidden subsidies. The 1994 budget earmarked 224 million litas for subsidies. Large amounts were allocated to compensate heating and gas enterprises for preferential tariffs granted to households.

The Government's economic development strategy aims at developing market institutions, and upgrading the technological potential and infrastructure of the economy. It also aims to integrate Lithuania into EU political and economic structures. The Government expects to trigger economic recovery by promoting exports and foreign direct investment, while it attempts to increase domestic demand. For instance, revenues from Telecom privatisation were used to compensate bank depositors who lost savings in the 1990-91 hyperinflationary period. The aim was to increase the monetary purchasing power of the population to balance an increased supply of goods and services redirected to domestic markets from export markets. If a demand increase is absorbed by the effects of recession, the unexpected repercussion will be a serious strain on fiscal deficit.

As an integral part of Lithuania's economic reforms, the privatisation process was launched in September 1991. The entire privatisation process may be divided into three major stages.

The first stage, a mass privatisation for vouchers with some elements of cash sales, covers the period of September 1991 to July 1995. State-owned enterprises, land, agriculture companies and apartments were offered in exchange for privatisation vouchers (issued in dematerialised form by opening voucher accounts). More than 2.6 million voucher accounts were opened in the banks. Housing privatisation has accounted for 19% of vouchers, while about 65% of vouchers were exchanged for shares in state enterprises. The remaining vouchers were used to acquire agricultural enterprises and land.[6] Land not subjected to restitution claims was offered for privatisation. Country-dwellers willing to undertake farming activities had priority in the privatisation of the land, while owners of single-family housing were given the same privileges in purchasing built-up residential land, in rural and urban areas. The mass privatisation carried out in 1 160 state companies, formerly known as *kolchozes*, resulted in a transfer of 97% of agricultural assets into private hands. This phase of privatisation included the sale of apartments to tenants. Privatisation vouchers were accepted as payment for 80% of the price. Some 95% of the formerly state-owned flats became private by 1995.

The second stage, a privatisation for cash sales, covers the period July 1995 to 1997. Privatisation under the 1995 Privatisation Law excludes voucher privatisation. The methods of privatisation are public subscriptions of shares (for small and medium-sized enterprises), auctions (for small enterprises), public tenders (for medium-sized and large enterprises), and leases with an option to purchase. In 1996, 47 entities were privatised for 3.2 million litas, and in 1997, 272 entities were privatised for 80.9 million litas.

The third stage, a tender privatisation, covers the period from 1998 to date. Governmental resolution on 11 February 1997 slotted for privatisation the large-scale state-controlled enterprises of the transport, energy and telecommunications sectors. The Law on Privatisation entrusted the State Property Fund (SPF) to hold, use, dispose and privatise state-owned property.[7] In 1998, 344 enterprises were privatised, generating 2.3 billion litas. Among the biggest deals are Lithuanian Telecom, Hotel Lietuva and a third of the oil industry. SPF expected privatisation sales to amount to 1 billion litas in 1999.

Housing sector overview

Trends and challenges for urban and rural development

Land restitution and administration

Government land policy has the following objectives:

- To restitute land and to implement land reform;

- To stimulate the development of a land market by developing a land registration system and a mortgage system;

- To levy a real property tax based on market values;

- To create a land information system that will serve both the State administration and the general public for the purposes of land use, physical planning and environmental monitoring;

- To revise the institutional set-up of land administration.

The restitution of ownership rights (or compensation) is at the centre of Lithuanian land reform. Some 2.5 million to 3 million parcels have to be surveyed, privatised or leased. The three major types of land being privatised are:

- Agricultural and forest land in rural areas (more than 690 000 people have applied to have their ownership rights in agricultural land restored);

- Allotments of members of gardeners associations (there are 218 500 such members, cultivating a total area of 21 100 hectares), and

- Parcels with housing units and other buildings, mainly in urban areas (multi-flat houses cannot own the land).

Land privatisation has accelerated due to improvements in the cadastre and land registration systems. Still, the biggest challenge for real-estate registration is the legacy of separated property rights of land and buildings.

Settlements network

Before World War II, Lithuania had only two big cities, Vilnius (186 000 inhabitants) and Kaunas (154 000), and one medium-sized town, Klaipeda (51 000). Now Vilnius and Kaunas each has more than 400 000 people; Klaipeda, šiauliai and Panevezys have more than 100 000 each. Other large urban centres are Alytus and Marijampole, with more than 50 000; and 13 towns fall into the medium-size category of 20 000 to 50 000. There are also 72 small towns and urban-type settlements in rural areas.

Lithuania has a well-balanced network of human settlements that has resulted from the distribution of different functions among urban centres. Vilnius is the historical and cultural centre and the administrative capital. Klaipeda is the country's main port, while Kaunas is the educational, business and trading centre. In rural areas, the system of farmsteads (120 000) that existed before World War II was reorganised into collective farms. After 1990, the system of human settlements started to change. Many rural centres started to lose their economic and social importance. Job opportunities in rural areas are rare, and some 70% of all unemployed young people live in small rural centres. Consequently, living conditions in rural settlements have worsened considerably. The regional differentiation has been addressed by promoting the development of small and medium enterprises. As regards housing provision, much lower growth rates in rural areas reflect the lack of demand and employment opportunities in these localities (Table 4).

Table 4: Dwellings Completed (thousands)

	1990	1991	1992	1993	1994	1995	1996	1997
Total Dwellings	1 159	1 166	1 111	1 204	1 226	1 247	1 270	1 278
-- Annual change of dwellings	14.1	6.5	-55.2	93.3	22.0	20.8	23.1	8.0
-- Growth rate		0.6%	-4.7%	8.4%	1.8%	1.7%	1.9%	0.6%
Newly completed buildings	22.1	15.3	12.7	8.2	6.9	5.6	5.6	5.6
-- Urban	17.5	12.8	11.2	7.4	6.1	4.6	4.4	4.4
-- Rural	4.6	2.5	1.5	0.8	0.8	1.0	1.2	1.1

Note: Data on housing supply in 1993 show a higher growth rate due to a new definition applied in housing statistics.
Source: Statistical Yearbooks, Department of Statistics, Vilnius, 1998

National policies and objectives for spatial development

In 1995, the former Ministry of Construction and Urban Development drafted a new national comprehensive plan for the period up to 2010. The document, currently under discussion, defines spatial development priorities, conditions and instruments for territorial management, and actions to implement the plan. Spatial development policy was outlined more generally in the national action plan for 1996-2000 prepared for the United Nations Conference on Human Settlements (Habitat II) in 1996.

In the area of regional planning, the Government's goal is to minimise growing regional disparities. The Government, together with the counties and municipalities, plans to assess the development potential of rural areas and small towns. On this basis, action plans to balance and regulate development will be prepared. Within the framework of the Agricultural Program for Rural Development and Employment (1995), measures are proposed to develop rural infrastructure, increase employment, develop agro-tourism, and promote small and medium-size enterprises. Lithuania has many old towns and well-preserved architectural and historic monuments. The Government intends to prepare programs to mobilise financial resources for renovation and modernisation. In urban development, attention is given to the conservation and rehabilitation of the historical and cultural heritage. The Government intends to develop programs and measures to preserve existing green areas, retain residential functions and restrict traffic in old town centres. Special efforts have been successfully initiated in Vilnius, which joined the UNESCO list of World Heritage Sites in 1995.

Housing reforms

Restitution of property rights to dwellings

Privatisation and restitution are considered the hallmark of the housing reform process. The law on Procedure and Terms of Restitution of Property Rights of Citizens to Existing Real Estate (June 1991) is the legal framework for compensating or returning real estate to former owners. Since 1991, 8 500 applications have been submitted for restitution of property rights to dwellings. Property rights have been restored to 4 600 owners (53%). Only 978 claimants (one in five of those approved) have received compensation in kind (payment in cash, forest, another dwelling or land). As of January 1999, about 28% of applications submitted were still awaiting property-rights resolution (Figure 3).

Figure 3: Geographical Distribution of Total Claims and Claims to be Resolved for Property Restitution, January 1999

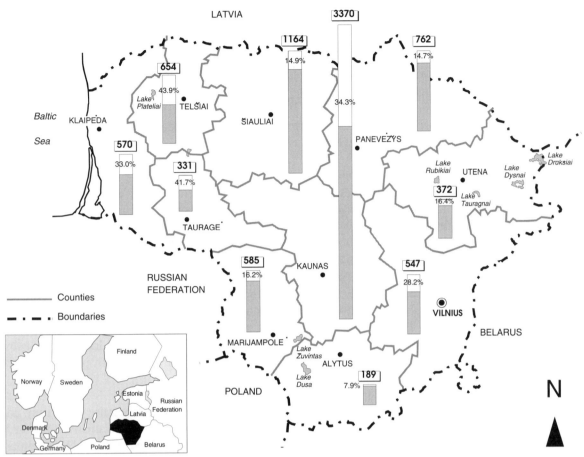

Note: The legend in bars is the following: The above figure stands for total restitution claims; a percentage in the bar specifies restitution claims to be satisfied, and the shadowed area represents a share of settled claims to date.

Source: Economic and Social Development in Lithuania, Department of Statistics, Issues 3/1998 and 2/1999.

National housing policies

In 1992, the Parliament established the basis of a housing policy for the transition period when it approved the *Bustas* governmental program. The program formulated the following objectives:

- Gradually move from State housing provision to housing purchase;

- Shift away from uniform housing to individual choice, with the State remaining responsible for providing housing only to socially and economically vulnerable population groups;

- Create favourable conditions for the provision of long-term loans for housing construction;

- Promote housing construction by different types of developers: public, private, joint-stock companies and housing associations; and

- Create legal and economic conditions for the public housing stock privatisation.

105

Under the *Bustas* program, the Government set a goal of building 12 000 to 14 000 housing units annually. In practice, new construction is well below that target range. Mass privatisation of public housing has eliminated the opportunity to provide shelter to socially disadvantaged households. The overall outcome has been controversial.

Currently, the Government's goals in housing are to:

- Encourage new construction where individuals finance their housing;

- Direct financial markets to provide long-term financing;

- Encourage individuals, homeowner associations and public enterprises to save energy by renovating and insulating dwellings.

Most housing policy measures have focused on the development of effective instruments to make long-term housing loans available to the majority of the population. Such a universal approach requires strengthening of the banking sector and of mortgage institutions. The purchasing power of the population in the large urban housing markets in particular remains limited and needs to be enhanced. This objective appears to be complex and its achievement must be a long-term goal. At present, long-term soft loans for housing construction and renovation are supported by the State and allocated to households without housing or which have less than 10 square meters per person or which are classified as socially supportable. Some 100 000 households are eligible for state support and are officially registered with local municipalities. Experts recognise that the State is unable to respond to the volume of applications. To this end, Parliament is considering a new version of the Law on Provision of Citizens with Dwellings (1992). The Ministry of Environment has drafted a Housing Policy Strategy to assist the debate. The Government passed Resolution 794 to appropriate funds for municipal housing for 1999-2000.

Another major problem in the housing sector is associated with the dramatic increase of heating and hot water charges, which has created a considerable burden for housing occupants and wide dissatisfaction with Government policies. According to the Housing and Urban Development Foundation (HUDF), the average household spends about 14% of its income on energy costs. In response to this problem, the Government has established two instruments. First, since May 1997, homeowners and homeowners associations have been able to obtain technical assistance and loans for the preparation and implementation of energy efficiency projects from HUDF.[8]

The foundation facilitates and supports market development in Lithuania with an ultimate objective of establishing sustainable market-based systems.

The objectives of the Energy Efficiency Housing Pilot Project (EEHPP) are to:

- Support private initiatives to improve residential energy efficiency;

- Support public initiatives in improving energy efficiency in schools; and

- Support the privatisation of housing, enabling increased private initiatives in housing maintenance.

The World Bank extended a USD 10 million loan for the project. USD 5.2 million was allocated for homeowners to improve energy efficiency in residential buildings. USD 4.7 million was allocated for municipalities to invest in energy efficiency measures and renovation of public schools. The Lithuanian Government agreed to provide 30% matching funds for the project. The Danish Ministry of Housing and Urban Affairs and the Dutch Ministry of Economics agreed to provide the main technical assistance for the project.

As of January 2001, 217 homeowners associations and 26 single-family house owners signed loan agreements for more than USD 9 million. Energy efficiency measures were implemented in almost 200 multi- or single-family buildings.

The project significantly advanced awareness within Lithuanian society regarding building maintenance and energy efficiency issues and demonstrated that joint efforts of private businesses, municipalities and homeowners can lead to the successful renovation of residential and public buildings. Successful implementation of public school renovation projects generated significant demand from the municipalities for additional loans. Affordable financing, extensive support networks and enhanced awareness boosted demand for housing improvement loans.

Energy efficiency measures have resulted in 10% to 50% energy savings and improved the longevity of renovated buildings. The project provided a boost to numerous local energy consultants, manufacturers of energy efficiency equipment and building-renovation contractors. Social monitoring of project participants highlighted the significance of the "first-try" experience and indicated a need for wide-ranging assistance for homeowners associations undertaking energy efficiency improvements. Most participants surveyed (members of homeowners associations) were satisfied with their renovations, and premature loan repayments reflected the substantial cost-effectiveness of the projects.

Subsidy and support schemes for heat and hot water were also introduced. Low-income households are eligible for subsidies if heating bills exceed 25% of their income, or hot-water bills exceed 5%. The Social and Labour Ministry estimates that 30% of urban households are eligible for these subsidies.

Municipal housing policy initiatives

The *Bustas* program was the first national response to the State's political determination to withdraw from housing supply. While one goal of the program was to facilitate housing privatisation, it failed to restrict conversion of residential into commercial properties or to define maintenance responsibilities for common ownership areas. Currently, common elements are maintained in most cases by municipal Housing Maintenance Enterprises (HMEs). Municipalities are concerned with these problems but have failed to address the issue systematically.

A municipal housing policy has been developed only for Vilnius. It has four strategic objectives: to maintain and improve existing housing stock; to help people who cannot afford adequate housing; to provide support to meet new housing demand; and to redefine housing roles and responsibilities. Each objective has its own goals. To maintain and improve the existing housing stock, for example, the municipality aims to privatise its Housing Maintenance Enterprise, to support Homeowners Associations, to maintain city housing, to implement housing renovation and energy-saving programs, and to set and enforce minimum housing standards, as well as health and safety regulations. Its action plan envisaged a first phase for 1998-99 and a second for 2000-05. The policy document recognises that the State, Homeowners Associations, individual owners, tenants and private-sector actors must be involved to solve housing problems in Vilnius. A Housing Division with 20 staff members in the city administration and the subcommittee on Housing Issues, which is being established with the Council, indicate a commitment to institutionalise and implement these objectives.

Framework for housing finance

Lithuania's housing sector is well into the transition process: The housing stock is largely privatised, some new types of housing organisations and intermediaries have developed, and there are arrangements for trading and mortgaging residential property. However, new housing construction is in the doldrums and arrangements for housing capital reinvestment and maintenance (not least to improve energy efficiency) are patchy.

This section covers housing investment and financing of housing provision. Special emphasis is placed on the development of mortgage infrastructure and mortgage products for the housing market. The chapter also explores changes in housing demand, focusing on housing costs, affordability, housing subsidies and allowances.

Housing investment and financing of new housing construction

Housing investment

In 1993-98, total investment in housing almost doubled, as private individuals became the main contributors to the investment process, particularly after privatisation and the elimination of restrictions on private construction. However, housing investment decreased within the portfolio of total investment from 23% to 7.4% in the 1993-98 period, as in most countries in transition, due to the collapse of public investment in housing (Table 5).

Private individuals' investment in housing almost tripled in 1993-97. Yet, recent data reveal warning signs that should be addressed. First, absolute private and other investment began to decrease in 1997. Second, private individuals made 90% of total housing investment in 1997, indicating that housing is not considered attractive by institutional investors. During the reforms, conditions have not been secure enough to attract institutional investors. The housing market remains in the hands of owner-occupiers, which makes it difficult to raise the capital needed to increase housing production, especially when average household income remains low. The data confirm that the significant increase in individual housing investment has been unable to compensate for the shortage of other sources. Consequently, housing's share in total investment has fallen nearly by half.

Table 5: Housing investment, 1993-1998
(in current million litai)

	1993	1994	1995	1996	1997	1998
Total capital investment	1 160	2 311	3 163	4 380	5 488	6 834
Total investment in housing or residential buildings	266.2	465.3	503.0	570.3	560.5	507.5
(Share in total capital investment)	*22.9%*	*20.1%*	*15.9%*	*13.0%*	*10.2%*	*7.4%*
Public sector investment	79.1	74.0	44.8	36.9	44.6	86.6
(Share in total investment in housing)	*29.7%*	*15.9%*	*8.9%*	*6.5%*	*8.0%*	*17.1%*
Private sector investment	187.1	391.3	458.2	533.4	515.9	420.9
Occupiers' assets	175.5	361.1	429.0	511.1	505.9	394.4
(Share in total investment in housing)	*65.9%*	*77.6%*	*85.3%*	*89.6%*	*90.2%*	*77.7%*
Other sources of investment in housing	11.6	30.2	29.2	22.3	10.0	26.5
(Share in total investment in housing)	*4.4%*	*6.5%*	*5.8%*	*3.9%*	*1.8%*	*5.2%*

Sources: Statistical Yearbook 1999 (Vilnius, 1999), Institute of Architecture and Construction, Kaunas, May 1999.

In the period 1990-94, new housing construction decreased by 70%. Such drops have been common to all countries in transition (50% on average), but in Lithuania the change was more dramatic. Construction output grew by 6.6% in 1997, mostly due to the state investment, but its share of GDP remains relatively low. Forecasts by the Institute of Economics and Privatisation show construction increasing to between 7.8% and 8.2% of GDP by 2002. The housing sector is not viewed as a major economic force in the Lithuanian economy.

Financing land development and housing construction

Although not in physical short supply, the housing land market is developed. Land transactions after privatisation doubled in 1997, but sales of land parcels account for only 1.3% of total transactions (building sales represent 14%).[9] Complexities arise from local, county and state involvement in the disposal of public land. The process of land acquisition by legal entities is not clear and transparent, although the tender procedure is used for these purposes. There are further complexities in developing leased land. Nevertheless, the active privatisation of the housing stock and the state-run industries means that attention is now focused on State-owned land. The State is about to privatise much of its land holdings and this offers a number of opportunities.

Only limited financing is available for housing land acquisition and development. There is no bank lending system for the process, although land can be pledged (with future modifications). The major reason is that banks do not consider undeveloped land as being sufficiently liquid collateral. At the same time, few commercial enterprises specialise in financing land development, and the demand for such loans is very limited.

Municipalities are currently responsible for infrastructure development, but budget restrictions impose severe constraints. Local governments depend heavily on central government transfers with limited opportunity to generate revenues of their own. Overall, the lack of adequate land development financing has produced a significant shortage of land parcels with developed infrastructure available for sale. In 1998, the Ministry of Finance proposed the Lithuanian Municipal Development Program to assist in the development of a system of municipal investments in infrastructure and municipal services and thereby support the reform of local government finance. The program seeks to provide training, technical assistance and investment support to about 40 of the 56 municipalities by 2002 using credit lines provided by foreign and international financial institutions. Subprojects funded through the Municipal Development Program will focus on infrastructure loans that can be repaid through user fees. In most cases the municipal enterprise will be the final borrower, and the municipality will guarantee the loan (in accordance with the Law on Municipal Borrowing).

The Law on Municipal Borrowing specifies the following conditions:

- Outstanding debt principal cannot exceed 20% of annual revenues (in exceptional cases the Ministry of Finance may allow up to 50%).

- Annual borrowing limit of a municipality is 10% of annual revenues, including a 5% limit on short–term borrowing.

- Annual debt service related to borrowing cannot exceed 10% of annual revenues.

- The municipality or its enterprise should contribute at least 10% of the total cost of the investment and project preparation costs.

Shortages of affordable and accessible housing construction finance have been manifested in recent trends in new-housing sales, escalating construction prices, reduced housing production, and an increasing number of uncompleted dwellings. Existing arrangements for new construction finance are still far from efficient, and new construction finance continues to be a problem. Significant changes have taken place in the financing of residential construction during the transition period. Government policy focused on redefining its role from that of a major developer and supplier of new housing to that of an enabler, providing state support for new construction financed through personal savings. Housing finance reforms centred mainly on:

- Re-allocating responsibilities from the state in housing construction finance;

- Establishing extrabudgetary state and self-government support funds for construction; and

- Reducing significantly the direct finance of construction through both the state and municipal budgets.

The reduction in direct State financing was supplemented with the *Bustas* governmental program for subsidised construction financing. Housing construction associations (co-operatives) and individuals on waiting lists could apply for a 5% interest-rate construction loan over 25 years, interest-free for 3 years and with an 80% to 90% loan-to-value ratio. The subsidies are paid from the General Support Fund raised from revenues from housing privatisation, land sales and the State budget. Municipalities also created construction funds, of which 10% comes from State fund resources. This program is expensive to the Government, amounting in 1996 to approximately 3.4% of the central Government budget.[10]

The availability of cheap financing from State funds and tax privileges made the provision of new housing through construction associations (co-operatives) particularly attractive until 1995. Most of the funding designated for low-interest loans was assigned to these organisations. During 1993-95, they received 129 billion litai in low-interest credit. After that, existing co-operatives were re-registered as housing construction associations to complete the construction process. Subsidised construction finance is no longer available to housing construction associations and supports only the completion of housing.

Lithuania's current system for construction finance has the following basic characteristics:

- Informal financing of construction by private individuals is the predominant form. It relies on small, personal savings, sometimes organised into mutual forms of finance, such as construction associations. This leads to an unprofessional approach to financing in which owners become "self-developers" with little opportunity effectively to manage the risks associated with development.

- Development companies sometimes organise future buyers into associations, supplying them with building and developer services, which allows tax advantages and easier access to public funding.

- Limited direct State financing is available for the construction of public housing and for target groups, with plans that municipal financing should make up not less than 15% to 20% of construction investment.

- Low levels of commercial construction finance are available to those able to manage effectively both development and construction risks, to improve construction technology, and to develop the construction industry through competition.

Table 6: Loans for Construction
(thousands of litai, %)

	All loans	Loans for construction	Share
2000/Q4	5,062,669	177,338	3.5
2000/Q3	4,862,008	183,247	3.8
2000/Q2	4,838,879	180,016	3.7
2000/Q1	4,739,217	173,355	3.7
1999/Q4	4,986,297	172,435	3.5
1999/Q3	5,097,243	180,880	3.5
1999/Q2	4,968,634	188,913	3.8
1999/Q1	4,577,258	149,344	3.3
1998/Q4	3,993,875	140,387	3.5
1998/Q3	3,671,283	140,533	3.8
1998/Q2	3,455,029	129,447	3.7
1998/Q1	3,338,776	100,112	3.0
1995/Q4	3,107,937	387,072	12.5
1995/Q3	3,676,331	380,761	10.4
1995/Q2	3,643,122	351,192	9.6
1995/Q1	3,639,296	328,847	9.0

Note: Data refer to end of period.
Source: Bank of Lithuania

The last point is illustrated by Table 6 above. The value of total housing loans to the value of all outstanding loans in both commercial and government financial institutions in the fourth quarter of 1995 was 12.5%. In December 2000 it decreased to 3.5%. A network of temporary subsidiary companies also handles some of this activity.

In summary, Lithuania has a limited capitalised and institutionally backed development sector with little support for entry-level firms. Housing development remains fragmented.

Factors affecting housing demand

Savings

Like other countries in transition, Lithuania began its economic reforms without sufficient local financial resources or savings. At the end of 1997, bank deposits totalled 5.9 billion litai, of which private account deposits stood at 2.2 billion litai. Foreign currency deposits equalled 2.3 billion litai and stood at 39% of local and foreign currency deposits. The banking sector has not accrued sufficient savings, especially for long-term lending. With a predominance of short-term deposits, bank deposits comprise only 15.4% of GDP. In more successful economies in transition they stand at 30%.[11]

During the transition the Government has failed to develop efficient tools to prompt growth in national and private-sector savings, which remain low (Figure 4).

Figure 4: National Savings

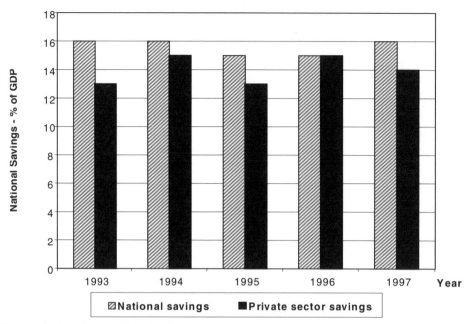

Source: United Nations Development Program, *Lithuanian Human Development Report 1998*, (Vilnius, 1998).

The situation with respect to household savings is similar, though it might be considered better in terms of total savings and investments' share of household income according to data in Table 7.[12] Policies are needed to attract private savings and investments into the housing sector. There are no financial instruments, such as housing, municipal or private developer government-guaranteed bonds, notes or other housing-related securities, which could become an attractive savings instrument for channelling funds into housing construction or purchase. Investment funds designed for equity investment do not appear to operate due to an inadequate legal base and unfavourable tax treatment. Credit unions (or savings and loan financial institutions) do not yet play a significant role in the financial market.

Table 7: Monthly Household Income, 1999
(Litas, %)

	City		Town		Rural	
Household income	2 215	100%	1 544	100%	789	100%
Household savings and investments	600	29.7%	405	26.3%	183	23.2%
-- Household savings	329	14.8%	211	13.7%	96	12.2%
-- Household investments	331	14.9%	194	12.6%	87	11.0%

Source: Lithuanian Free Market Institute, *A Survey of Macroeconomic Variables in Lithuania 1999/2000*

Incomes and affordability

Following a dramatic decline at the start of the transition, personal income experienced positive growth and adjustment. Monthly disposable income began to increase, reaching 415.4 litas per household member in 2000. Household income has also increased, although salaries vary significantly and roughly 8% of employees in 1997 had a monthly salary exceeding 1,500 litai.[13] Income inequalities remain relatively high. The Gini index, which reflects the extent to which income distribution among individuals within an economy deviates from perfectly equal distribution, was 0.31 for Lithuania in 1997. In East European countries and the Baltic countries, the index fluctuates from 0.25 to 0.34.[14] Consumption inequality in Lithuania is increasing as well. According to the 1998 Lithuanian Human Development Report, up to 37.2% of households with three children or more are poor; and more than a quarter of the rural population is impoverished. The incidence of poverty is six to seven times higher among those with primary and secondary education than among those with a tertiary education.

Despite positive trends in income growth, house purchase remains unaffordable for a large number of Lithuanian households. Calculations based on household income and savings data in Table 7 and house price data show that it takes 10 to 14 years of saving to become a flat owner in Vilnius.[15] As data suggest, the maximum and minimum prices of units of different sizes vary significantly (Figure 5), but ratios of house price to income remain high. Most new households will not be able to purchase housing without mortgage or other support. It should be noted that house purchase assistance must be carefully targeted. Given the mass privatisation of the housing stock, most households wishing to move will have an asset to sell or rent out to generate income. This needs to be factored into any assessment of affordability.

While new households face problems affording home ownership, housing costs in the public rental sector appear to be modest. According to time-series data, rental housing is more affordable, and average housing costs -- rent plus utilities (fuel, electricity and gas) -- have fallen, constituting 14.4% of total household expenditures. In 1998 these costs were higher for urban households (15.0%), and relatively lower (12.4%) for rural households. Local experts indicate that housing costs are as high as 30% for some groups, mostly due to increasing utility prices. Fees for hot and cold water and sewerage increased 14-fold in 1993-98; heating costs rose by 6.8 times; gas and electricity by 2.6 times. An estimated 20% of Vilnius households have difficulty covering utility costs, and if adequate maintenance were carried out up to 40% of homeowners might have financial difficulties sustaining them.[16] It has been suggested that official statistics related to income are not reliable and should be interpreted with caution.

Figure 5: Prices of Standard Flats in Vilnius, 1998

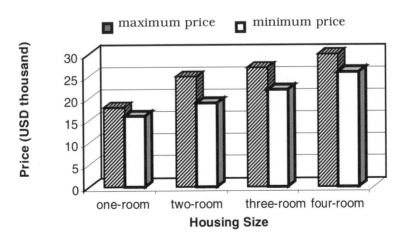

Source: State Land Cadastre and Register, May 1999

The Lithuanian Government is under pressure to balance its budget and reduce public spending. Public financial support for housing is limited, although different types of direct and indirect governmental support have been introduced during the transition period (Table 8). Governmental Resolution 794 of June 1999 indicates a commitment to distribute funds from the General Fund for Housing Construction and Acquisition for the period 1999-2000 and to establish municipal housing funds. These funds are designed to: promote the construction of residential buildings; facilitate the modernisation of existing municipal housing; and assist the purchase of dwellings at market prices.

Though rents in public-sector housing remain low, rental subsidies are slowly shifting from general support (available irrespective of income) toward personal, means-tested support. According to a draft law, 135 litai per person is the basis for calculating monthly rent allowances. For households earning less than twice this amount per person, rent allowances are paid irrespective of the rental sector. However, rent allowance schemes are complex and have perverse incentives (including unemployment and poverty traps, the need to encourage households to find the lowest rents and the need to integrate with other welfare benefits). Similar observations can be made concerning energy-cost allowances (especially the need to encourage households to use energy more efficiently) -- a much larger subsidy in Lithuania, as energy costs have risen much faster than rents and are reaching world-market levels.

Property taxes can have a number of aims, including the raising of revenue (possibly earmarked for particular uses), the promotion or reduction of demand, and the promotion of equity. In Lithuania, the main taxes affecting housing include a tax on developed land, a value-added tax (VAT) on construction, a capital gains tax, and corporate taxes on developers, private landlords and homeowners associations. These, and relief when offered, have a significant impact on the housing market, but this appears uncoordinated by the Government. For example, the VAT is not levied on construction renovation or insulation work or on the design of houses and flats funded from State or municipal budgets. Further, VAT may be reimbursed, but only to those entities registered as VAT payers with the State Tax Agency. Usually, physical persons or construction associations are not on the register of VAT payers and may not be reimbursed.

Table 8: Main Support Schemes, 1997

	Type of support	Financial source	Allocated amount (million litai)
BUSTAS	Subsidy element of soft loans	Extrabudgetary fund	17.7
Heat and hot water	Subsidy	National budget	230
Energy saving	Subsidy element of soft loans	World Bank loan and domestic counterpart funding	Approximately 1
Support for Municipal housing acquisition	Grant	National budget	10[1]

Note: 1) 1998
Source: Danish Ministry of Housing and Lithuanian Ministry of Construction and Urban Development, *Study on Government Assistance Programs to the Housing Sector*, (Vilnius, August 1998).

Financial institutions and mortgage market infrastructure

One condition of mortgage market development -- macroeconomic stability -- has been met. In addition, Lithuania has economic growth, strict control over public expenditure, low inflation and short-term currency stability. In this environment, real interest rates are becoming positive while nominal interest rates are falling to levels where it becomes possible for potential mortgagers to afford mortgage instruments and to service the mortgage with their incomes (Table 9).

Table 9: Average Nominal Interest Rates and Inflation
(%)

	1993	1994	1995	1996	1997	1998	1999	2000
Inflation	N/A	N/A	35.7	13.1	8.4	2.4	0.3	1.4
General government securities	N/A	21.43	27.48	20.46	8.90	11.18	11.87	9.29
Time deposits in Litas[1]	90.40	48.43	20.05	13.95	9.01	7.44	8.07	6.35
Time deposits in foreign currency[1]	23.58	24.91	15.97	9.36	6.43	5.05	6.38	5.15
Loans in Litas[2]	91.82	62.30	27.08	21.56	14.39	12.21	9.92	11.89
Loans in foreign currency[2]	68.70	51.98	26.93	21.63	12.39	10.28	11.11	10.62

Note: 1) Data for 1997 and onward refer to time deposits for two and more years. Data before 1997 refer to shorter maturity time deposits. 2) Data for 1999 refer to housing loans while the rates for other loans were slightly higher: 13.09% in litas and 11.46% in foreign currency.
Source: Lithuanian National Bank, January 2001

A second important condition of mortgage market development -- strong financial institutions -- is in its infancy in Lithuania. The structure of credit institutions has developed (Table 10). At the same time the State has increased bank deposit insurance from 4 000 to 25 000 litai. Total borrowing from foreign financial institutions recently doubled.

Table 10: Credit Institutions, January 2001

Type	Number
Deposit money banks	10
Other banks	1
Foreign bank branches	4
Foreign bank representative offices	4
Credit unions	38

Source: The National Bank of Lithuania

The financial system is slowly becoming stronger. The banking sector started to recover in 1997 after the 1995-96 crisis. Commercial bank assets by the end of 1997 comprised 8.3 billion litai, having increased by 40% over the year. In 2000, the consolidated assets of banking institutions including commercial banks, foreign bank branches and credit unions reached 14 billion litas. Services rendered grew by 18%. The volume of loans grew by a factor of 2.1. However, relatively weak and inefficient private commercial banks continue to operate. The Bank of Lithuania has not taken adequate action to speed recapitalisation of these banks. They do not have sufficient funds to grow. Only two commercial banks have significant funds. The largest has assets worth some 2.5 billion litas, but is still oriented toward commercial lending. Commercial banks operate on a very short-term deposit base.

Time deposits exceeding six months constitute only 12% of total deposits. The majority of terms-of-deposit agreements vary from less than one to three months.[17] There are no specific housing savings banks/mortgagees, and interbank lending is insignificant.

In 2000, banks began extending long-term (up to 25 years) loans to purchase or build a dwelling. The main conditions for receiving such loans are: the initial contribution is 30% of the value of the dwelling being purchased, the annual interest rate on the loans extended in US dollars is approximately 10% to 11%, and loan durations are up to 25 years. Housing loans are extended in US dollars, Euro or litas. The major requirements set for loan recipients are: monthly contributions to the bank cannot exceed 40% of total family income; and after paying the contribution to the bank, the family must have at least USD 120 per member.

As of today the total loan portfolio of housing loans of all banks amounts to USD 72.5 million. Each month, banks in Lithuania extend about 260 loans for a total of USD 2.5 million. The average single loan is for USD 20 000, and the average duration is 15 years. Conditions for loan recipients in Lithuania are more favourable than they are in neighbouring countries. The interest rate is lower (in Latvia and Estonia it is 11% to 12% in US dollars, or 12% to 13% in the national currency). Moreover, in Lithuania there is a possibility of decreasing the initial contribution to 5 per cent by insuring it. According to the Lithuanian banks, housing-loans risk accounts for 3.5%.

The development of the banking sector has been slowed by the fact that most banking assets belong to the State. By the end of 1997, close to 50% of all banking assets were State-owned. During the reforms, three State banks were poorly managed and funds from the State budget (loans received on behalf of the State and privatisation revenues) were used to cover their losses. Despite political approval, the privatisation of the State banks was postponed.

Traditional long-term investors in the mortgage market, such as private pension funds and life insurance companies, are also poorly developed, thus limiting the availability of long-term resources. A law on pension funds is under discussion in the Seimas, or Parliament. Its adoption may stimulate the development of long-term financial instruments. The major sources of long-term money are the State budget, an extrabudgetary supporting fund and governmental external debt. Long-term private sector debt does not play a significant role; in 1997 it was only 4.6% of total external debt. Investment funds, which usually play a major role in financial markets, are non-existent in Lithuania. Several joint-stock investment companies were reorganised into controlling investment companies, but they are small, declining in number, and limited in investment policy.

The weakness of the banking and capital markets has hindered the development of a secondary mortgage market. Such a market can encourage the operations of the primary mortgage market by improving liquidity and diversifying risk. A stronger, more widely based set of financial institutions is likely to allow longer-term and more varied (for example, fixed rate, capped and discounted) mortgage products to be developed. However, a mortgage securitisation system is being proposed. The basic objective is to assist the Lithuanian financial sector and capital markets to adopt European Union legislation and to support integration into the EU single market. Within this context, Government policy relating to mortgage market development should be refined.

The third condition of mortgage market development -- its infrastructure elements – is taking shape in Lithuania. With the privatisation of the nation's housing stock, a real estate market has developed with the sale, resale and purchase of housing. The liquidity of the real estate market increased with the growth of new players such as real-estate agents and certified independent surveyors. Lithuania has a Central Real Estate Register and 15 regional offices. From April 1998 to March 1999, 28 000 real-estate objects were registered as collateral valued at 7.5 billion litai, while loans valued at 5.5 billion litai were granted.

In summary, many of the foundations of a mortgage market are in place -- strengthening economic fundamentals, an improving banking sector and a real-estate market. Further, the Lithuanian Government has indicated its intention to expand mortgage lending. An agreement between the Danish Minister of Economic Affairs and the Lithuanian Finance Minister has been concluded with the aim of strengthening the mortgage lending system.

Mortgage products

The Lithuanian Government is directly involved in retail mortgage activity offering subsidised mortgage products. This practice prevents the development of commercial mortgage lending and restricts its efficiency in terms of all-in costs and affordability to consumers. The Government continues to finance mortgages while commercial mortgage lending is just emerging. In short, the presence of the former may be hindering the development of the latter. So the existing mortgage lending system consists of two separate subsystems operating on different principles. The first is through State support programs based on non-market principles and the second is from commercial banks based on commercial principles. A hybrid system, using Government guarantees, is in the offing.

In 1992, the Law on State Support for the Provision of Dwellings for Citizens was adopted. Residents can apply for a subsidised loan for the acquisition or construction of a house or flat. The main characteristics of the loans offered through the State programs are presented in Table 11. As discussed in Section B (housing subsidies), these loans have highly subsidised interest rates and the Government pays part of the principal. They are available only to a limited number of people within the target groups. The General Fund for Housing Construction and Acquisition has approximately 300 million litai and does not make a profit.

Table 11: Terms of Mortgages through the *Bustas* Program

Commercial banks	Savings Bank (former State bank)	Vilnius Bank
Interest rate	5% annual rate. The difference with the market interest rate charged by the commercial bank is covered by the Support Fund.	
Other terms	No interest for families on social benefits; 20% discount on principal for orphans; 10% discount on principal for families with disabled members; Interest and discounted part of principal are covered by the General Support Fund.	
Maturity	Up to 10 years for the purchase of a dwelling; Up to 12 years for the construction of a dwelling	Up to 10 years for the purchase of a dwelling.
Currency	US dollars and Litas	US dollars
Loan-to-value ratio	Banks grant a loan up to 90% of the pledged property market value. The down payment varies from 10% to 30% of the dwelling value.	
Required income level	Monthly mortgage payments shall not exceed 40% of family's net income, and 500 litai per family member shall remain after monthly payment	Monthly mortgage payments shall not exceed 40% of family's net income
Repayment	Dwelling purchase loan: up to one year's grace period; Construction loan: 3 years' grace period for principal with quarterly payments; Interest on both products are paid monthly the month after the loan is granted	Monthly annuity repayment, Monthly grace period.
Collateral and insurance	The dwelling shall be pledged and insured; life insurance for 30% of the mortgage.	

In 1997, only 1 380 households were granted privileged loans through the State program. Yet, nearly 8% of all residents (some 90 000 households in urban areas) are registered for State support and it takes six to ten years to receive a loan. There is also a high dropout rate between initial expressions of interest and mortgaging. Funds allocated for this purpose from the State budget were insufficient even to meet the needs of those on benefit. The program envisaged the construction of 65 000 flats from 1995 to 2000, or 13 000 per year. Meanwhile, during 1996-97, only approximately 11 000 flats were built.

A government-guaranteed mortgage insurance system is being developed. In 1999, the Housing Loan Insurance Company was registered with 7 million litai of capital and 95 million litai allocated for eligible loans insurance. Mortgage insurance will be provided if the following conditions are met:

- Loans must be for house purchase, construction or renovation;

- Down payments of 5% to 10% are required;

- Loans have maturity of 10 to 25 years; insurance premiums are paid up-front by the Government, with the insurance fund taking 90% risk and the bank 10%;

- Principal and interest payments cannot exceed 40% of household income.

The authorised capital of the company currently totals 17 million litas (USD 4.25 million). The company aims to carry out insurance and more effectively resolve the problem of providing dwellings for Lithuanian residents, while obtaining the maximum profit.

Insured housing loans have several essential advantages over uninsured loans. First, the recipient of an insured loan needs an initial contribution equalling only 5%. In addition, some banks apply a discount of 1 percentage point interest rate to insured loans. Other banks grant additional privileges to recipients of insured housing loans when loans are repaid prior to the established term; no taxes are to be paid in repaying a loan before its term.

The company has co-operative agreements with five major banks of Lithuania: Vilniaus Bank, Agricultural Bank of Lithuania, Savings Bank of Lithuania, "Snoras" Bank and the public company bank Hansabank.

The housing loan insurance contract stipulates that the recipient shall be the insured – a citizen of Lithuania who, at the end of the term of the loan contract shall not be older than 65 and who meets other requirements set by the company and the bank. The contract further stipulates that the bank which grants the loan and which is registered in Lithuania, and which has signed the agreement on co-operation with the company, shall be the covered party.

The housing loan being insured cannot exceed 95% of the value of the dwelling being purchased or mortgaged. That is, the loan recipient must have an initial contribution amounting to at least 5% of the value of the dwelling being purchased. The loan being insured cannot exceed USD 75 000.

The insured must mortgage the immovable property, which has been purchased, is under construction or is undergoing reconstruction for the means of the loan to the bank.

Further, the insured must insure his or her life for the term of the loan by a sum not less than the amount of the loan that has not been paid back. The property that has been purchased, is under construction or is undergoing reconstruction must be insured for the term of the loan at a value not less than the market value determined by the licensed valuators at the sum insured, which is not less than the part of the loan that has not been paid pack.

By means of the housing loan insurance contract the company shall ensure 95% or 100% repayment of the unrecovered housing loan. In the event the recipient of the loan fails to pay back the housing loan or a part thereof, under certain terms established in the insurance contract, the bank would cancel the housing loan contract and appeal to the insurance company for the payment of the insurance benefit. After the company has paid the insurance benefit, the bank shall transfer to it all the rights of claim to the recipient of the loan, including the rights to the property mortgaged. The company shall meet its requirements from the amount recovered within the limits of the insurance benefit, and shall transfer the remaining amount to the bank. The latter can cover interest, fines, forfeit and sanctions that the recipient of the loan failed to pay and which do not constitute the object of the housing loan insurance contract.

The average tariff of the housing loan insurance premium is 4% to 5% of the sum insured, its amount depending on the terms of the housing loan contract. However, it is noteworthy that the great majority of loan recipients make use of loan insurance services free of charge. This is due to the fact that state funds pay for the whole insurance premium of citizens entitled to the state's support in providing them with dwellings.

Thus far the whole insurance premium of such individuals has been covered by state funds. This year, however, it is planned to gradually phase out this privilege. A procedure is being developed under which only 70% of the insurance premium will be paid for citizens entitled to state support; they themselves will have to pay the remaining part of the premium.

Also, restrictions are being planned on the sum insured -- the whole insurance premium will be paid from state funds for loan recipients who take their loans under commercial conditions and whose loan does not exceed USD 37 500. The recipient will have to pay the part of the insurance premium exceeding that amount. About 25% of the insured now pay the premium themselves, while others receive compensation for it. We suppose that in 2001 the rules will be co-ordinated with the bank to allow borrowing the insurance premium from the bank. This would significantly increase the number of customers for whom the insurance premium is not compensated.

The company, which began activity in July 2000, is successfully carrying out its objectives. On 10 January this year the hundredth insurance contract was concluded; the number of preliminary consents given to insure housing loans exceeds 130. According to the insurance contracts concluded and preliminary consents given, the total sum insured stands at USD 2.25 million. Insurance premiums collected total USD 110 000.

At present several problems hinder the development of the housing loans market in Lithuania:

- A substantial number of Lithuanian residents derive unofficial income.

- There is no sufficiently comprehensive new-dwelling crediting scheme.

- The advantages of housing loans are being insufficiently marketed.

- The state position on the housing loans market is vague.

- Non-participation of immovable property agencies in working with housing loans is a problem (with the exception of assessing enterprises).

In short, if households meet the eligibility criteria of the scheme and of the bank, then Government-backed insurance will be forthcoming. Households on the waiting lists will be eligible for

Government-guaranteed mortgage insurance. The scheme is a welcome development, but a number of issues need to be monitored:

- Whether cost-to-value differences impede applicants.

- Whether Government, particularly the Ministry of Finance, is content to have an open-ended scheme, not cash-limited.

- Whether relatively low down payments impede the development of savings, sound credit histories, and wider mortgage market development.

- How far the availability of Government insurance impedes the commercial (including risk appraisal) approach of the banks.

There may be other means to stimulate the effective demand for mortgages. Part-buy, part-rent schemes and/or equity share schemes may allow some middle-income households to purchase housing at a modest cost to the public purse. However, they are inherently complex and may require further legislative change.

Commercial mortgage lending is not well developed. Only three commercial banks offer residential mortgages, although other commercial banks occasionally offer limited mortgage funds, often to their own employees. One foreign financial institution (the Baltic-American Enterprise Fund) has started a mortgage program, lending USD 5 million in residential mortgage.

As in many countries in transition, the mortgage instruments offered by commercial banks are expensive in terms of high interest rates and short maturity. They are affordable only to high-income groups (Table 12). Usually the loan is denominated in a foreign currency because the local currency is considered to be overvalued. This currency risk further increases the borrower's risk and correspondingly leads to a low volume of mortgage operations in the private banking sector. Long-term residential mortgage lending is still considered by the private banking sector as particularly risky. To compensate, the banks have significantly increased their margins over the cost of funds they use to finance mortgages. The margin between the interest charged and one-year deposit interest rates varies between 5% and 8%. In a well-functioning housing market, the value of this indicator should be positive, but with the housing loan rate only modestly higher than the cost of the funds (on average 1.5% to 2%).

Table 12: Commercial Mortgage Financing Offered by Major Banks

Interest rate	9.5-13.5%
Term	Up to 25 years
Currency	In USD, Euro, Litas
Size of a loan	70% of a dwelling's market price
Required income level	Monthly mortgage payments shall not exceed 40% of borrower's income
Required income for mortgage: Loan size – 100,000 litas Interest rate – 11%	Net family income should exceed 3,500 litai

Source: Data by the Housing and Urban Development Foundation, Vilnius, 2001.

In summary, the risks associated with mortgage lending remain high and the private banking sector remains a reluctant mortgagee, preferring to lend to larger legal entities. Although housing has been largely privatised in Lithuania, housing finance has not.

Financing of maintenance and renewal

Maintenance and renewal of multi-family housing

Much of the previous analysis concentrates on increasing the development and financing of new housing production. However, even in periods of rapid expansion of the housing stock, the management, repair and improvement of existing units remains central. Three factors compound this importance in Lithuania:

- Lithuania's housing stock expanded rapidly at times in the 1960s, 1970s and 1980s using particular building forms and methods. These properties will age and suffer the same elemental failures at the same time.

- Multi-family blocks of flats requiring special management and maintenance arrangements for common parts and common services (compared to single-family dwellings), dominate the housing stock.

- Mass privatisation of the stock in the early 1990s was undertaken without a robust legal and regulatory framework. Tenant/landlord relationships have to be replaced by client/contractor relationships with related organisational and financial changes.

First, there is a need for accurate information on the conditions of the housing stock. An accurate sample survey is a first step toward assessing conditions and disrepair, the timing and the extent of future repair and improvement requirements and costs.

Second, there is a need to examine ways of increasing the funding for house repair and improvement. Specifically, the following might be explored: provision of "sinking funds" built up over time to cope with future major repair expenditure; development of home improvement equity loans; and development of some form of home improvement subsidy arrangements for the most intractable cost-over-value cases, particularly for low-income households.

Third, given the number of owners in individual multi-family blocks, there is a need to bring them together as single purchasing "clients." There has been some success in promoting homeowners associations. These offer a range of benefits in the management, maintenance and improvement of multi-family housing. However, only 4 500 have emerged. There appear to be a number of financial and other means to further expand coverage:

- Proposed legislative changes which do not require homeowners association membership but do require all households to abide by the decisions of properly constituted homeowners associations.

- Tax incentives for homeowners associations, perhaps through tax relief to individual households for sinking fund or other maintenance contributions.

- Making energy efficiency or other home improvement grants and subsidies dependent on the existence of a properly constituted homeowners association. The Energy Efficiency Housing Pilot Project of the World Bank offers grants and loans via homeowners associations for energy efficiency improvements. Some 30 homeowners associations have been sponsored in an 18-month period.

- Making the payment of fuel subsidies dependent on the presence of a properly constituted homeowners association.

- Making property maintenance subsidies, now available through municipalities and municipal maintenance companies, payable directly to homeowners associations.

Maintenance and renewal of public housing

There are no available data on income and expenditure in public housing. However, following mass privatisation the stock clearly contains older and often substandard units, scattered through different multi-family buildings. Low monthly rents -- from 0.2 to 1.7 litas per square meter -- do not allow cost recovery of management and maintenance work. The deficit between actual income and required expenditure is being managed by simply not carrying out needed long-term maintenance work. The backlog of repairs and improvements in public housing is increasing. While public-sector rent adjustment appears to be long overdue, one can question whether current tenants of public housing should have to bear all the costs of past mistakes, and their willingness and ability to do so are unclear.

A broad way to address the gap between current income and required maintenance and renewal expenditures is to gradually liberalise rents. Basic rent fees should take into account the depreciation from the updated procurement price of the flat, repair work and maintenance, and management overheads. Simultaneously with the first rental adjustments, subsidies would have to be provided to low-income households.

Expanding rental housing

A number of new households will continue to be unable to become owner-occupiers. Intervention, through some form of subsidy, will be required. This subsidy could be provided to increase what already are extremely high levels of owner-occupation. However, such an approach imposes high repair costs on low-income households, and may prevent reinvestment in the existing stock reaching sustainable levels.

An expanded and more vibrant rental sector is required. Any successful rental housing system should offer choices to households, provide a coherent rent structure, and be regulated. This would allow landlords to be properly capitalised. The rental system needs to have revenue streams, covering at least operating costs: management, maintenance and insurance costs. A number of models, or more likely a number of combinations of models, are possible: the continuation and re-expansion of municipal rental housing; the design and promotion of non-profit (or non-profit-distributing) housing for the rent sector (community-based and/or aligned with expanded homeownership associations and/or municipal maintenance companies, once outside the municipal sector); the expansion, and where necessary the licensing and regulation, of the private, profit-making, rental sector.

In relation to these options the State will need to examine: the form of subsidy (capital or revenue; to producer or consumer, that is, whether in the form of general "bricks and mortar" subsidies or personal subsidies); the extent to which subsidies go to bodies outside public finance controls, which can leverage private finance; the transfer of risk from State to private and independent sectors; and the degree it wishes to regulate organisations operating in a subsidised market.

It is not possible to fully consider all these options in this report. However, they do need the attention of policy-makers, landlords and financial institutions if the sector is to play its full role.

NOTES

1.　　26 April 1999, Department of Statistics.

2.　　Mazheikiai refinery (the only refinery in the Baltic countries), Butinge oil terminal and oil pipelines have been merged for privatisation. The oil terminal started to operate in 1999, marking an important economic restructuring benchmark. Lithuania exports electricity to Belarus, Latvia and the Kaliningrad region of the Russian Federation. Electricity export to Western Europe would highlight integration into EU efforts.

3.　　Inflation in 1998 was 6.5% in Estonia and 2.8% in Latvia.

4.　　The current account deficit deteriorated to 12.1% of GDP (5.2 billion litas) in 1998. In 1997, it was at 10.2% of GDP or 1.3 billion litas less than the last year. The current account deterioration is associated with two major factors: First, exports to the Russian Federation and CIS steeply declined because of increased financial risks there. Second, considerable inflows of foreign capital were attracted for large-scale privatisation, particularly in 1998.

5.　　In 1995, when the Central Bank imposed tighter control for compliance with the Law on Commercial Banks (January 1995), several major banks collapsed and the country faced a general banking crisis. In May 1996, of the 27 banks licensed in Lithuania, 16 were under suspension or facing bankruptcy proceedings. Today, Hermis and Vilnius banks, out of 11 banks operating, have significant credit resources on hand while others emerged weaker after the crisis.

6.　　About 93% of investment vouchers valued at approximately 10.5 billion litas (USD 2.4 billion) have been used in this privatisation stage. The remaining 7% of vouchers (litas 726 million) were deposited into private investment accounts to purchase apartments (not yet privatised), agricultural land (but no more than 80 hectares), land for private use, and land plots of collective gardens.

7.　　The SPF co-ordinates the privatisation process. It organises privatisation of the largest state-controlled enterprises in industry and infrastructure. Privatisation of these enterprises is carried out through a competitive procedure of international tenders prepared and executed by international consultants. Specially appointed Public Tender Commissions carry out international tenders for privatisation of strategic energy, transport and telecommunications enterprises. The commissions determine criteria to prepare privatisation programs reflecting the governmental policy and experience of other countries.

8.　　Five advisory centres were established. via the Energy Efficiency and Housing Pilot Project. The project started in 1996 with the World Bank (USD 10 million) loan and the assistance of two Dutch ministries (Ministry of Housing and Urban Development and Ministry of Economics).

9.　　Data provided by the State Cadastre and Register, Vilnius, May 1999.

10.　　Staff Appraisal Report Republic of Lithuania Energy Efficiency/Housing Pilot Project, The World Bank, 1996.

11.　　See United Nations Development Programme, *Lithuanian Human Development Report 1998* (Vilnius, 1998).

12.   The data provided in Table 7 are not official and are used for illustration only. To collect data, the Institute uses expert opinions instead of a household budget survey. It should be interpreted with care. The author preferred the data for two reasons. First, the shadow economy exists, only part of the population declares its income and consumption expenditure exceeded disposable income per capita in 1997-98. Second, the official statistics do not yet show income from savings and investments.

13.   According to the Housing Credit Foundation, Vilnius, May 1999.

14.   See United Nations Development Programme, *Lithuanian Human Development Report 1998* (Vilnius, 1998).

15.   The estimate reflects first-half 1998 figures for an average household with average income purchasing a standard two-room flat in Vilnius

16.   Vilnius Municipality, *A Housing Policy for the City of Vilnius*. Proposal, P. 6

17.   Housing and Urban Development Foundation, Vilnius, 1999

HOUSING FINANCE IN POLAND

by
Marek Zawislak[*]

Macroeconomic characteristics

The population of Poland increased slightly in the 1990s and reached 38.6 million in 2000.

For most of the 1990s, Poland enjoyed fairly rapid economic growth and steadily falling inflation rates. The deep recession of the first transition years has been overcome. In 1999, per-capita GDP was higher than that of 1989. Inflation has been curbed, declining from levels exceeding 300% in the early 1990s to single-digit levels in 1999. However, interest rates on loans remain fairly high. The 1998 crisis had no serious impact on the Polish economy, as measured by the major economic indicators.

Table 1: Macroeconomic Indicators

	1993	1994	1995	1996	1997	1998	1999	2000
Population (year-end, 1 000)	38 505	38 581	38 609	38 639	38 660	38 667	38 654	38 644
Exchange rate (zloty/USD, year-end)	1.81	2.27	2.42	2.70	3.28	3.49	3.97	4,34
Gross GDP (USD mil.)	86 066	92 690	126 577	142 759	143 101	157 440	154 049	
GDP per capita (USD)	2 238	2 405	3 280	3 697	3 702	4 072	3 985	
Real GDP growth (%)	3.8	5.2	7.0	6.0	6.8	4.8	4.1	4.1
Gross fixed capital formation (% of GDP)		16.2	18.7	20.8	23.6	26.0	26.5	
Inflation (%, year/year)		32.2	27.8	19.9	14.9	11.8	7.3	10.1
Inflation (%, Dec/Dec)		29.5	21.6	18.5	13.2	8.6	9.8	8.5
Lombard credit rate (%)	33	31	30	25	27	20	20.5	23
Average monthly gross wage (zloty)		525.0	690.9	874.3	1 065.8	1 232.7	1 290.6	1 324.2
Average monthly gross wage: real growth (%)		1.7	2.8	5.5	5.9	3.3	4.7	2.6

Source: National Statistics Office, National Bank of Poland, Author's calculation

Future prospects are favourable, though a return to the growth rates of the mid-1990s is considered unlikely. The inflation rate was lower in 1999 than in the previous year, but in 2000 it turned slightly upward.

---

[*]   Director, Housing Finance Systems Department, State Office for Housing and Urban Development, Poland

Housing sector overview

Legal and institutional issues

During the 1990s, the housing sector in Poland experienced a shift from arrangements typical of centrally planned economies to a market-driven environment. This is visible both in new housing construction and maintenance of existing stock. Before the "change," state-controlled housing co-operatives and state-owned management companies dominated the housing sector. Most of the housing stock consisted of public rentals or co-operative rentals.[1] Most new construction was developed by co-operatives that relied heavily on government subsidies. Construction companies were state-owned as well.

One of the first transition changes directly affecting housing was the ownership transfer of land and rental housing stock within the public sector. The state granted ownership of much of its real estate assets to newly formed local authorities (municipalities).

Another important decision was the adoption of the Act of 1994 on Ownership of Premises, which restored the institutional and legal framework for condominiums. The new regulations greatly facilitated the privatisation of the public stock and enabled efficient management of multi-family buildings.

The Act of 1994 on Transfer of Company-Owned Dwellings by State-Owned Companies, in order to accelerate the privatisation of state-owned enterprises and separate their usual business from the burden of maintaining housing stock (which often was occupied by persons who had lost any connection with the owner company), enabled the transfer of employers' rental buildings to municipalities or housing co-operatives. Local authorities were obliged to accept the tenants, and co-operatives to grant them membership rights.

As a result of the Act of 1994 on Residential Rental and Housing Allowances, the letting of dwellings has become a domain of the Civil Code, wherein the contracting parties can decide freely upon the terms of agreements, including rent rates (previously set by Government ordinance). Only in publicly owned rental stock have permanent limits on rental rates been imposed. Municipalities are authorised to raise rents in their stock only within the limit of 3% of the replacement value of the flat (the average is now around 1%). The regulated rent (up to the same replacement-value percentage ceiling) has been retained in private rental stock inhabited by tenants who moved in before the reform, based on decisions by relevant authorities. The law stipulates that rents in the private stock will be freed completely in 2005. The rent rate limitations do not apply to apartments larger than 80 square meters. Municipalities have also been obliged to deliver social housing to the poorest households or to those given the right to rent a social dwelling by court decision. At the same time, the law allows the eviction of those lacking judicial recognition of the right to a social dwelling.

Present conditions

Housing construction output fell from about 130 000 units in 1990 to about 87 600 in 2000, mostly due to the withdrawal of the state from extensive subsidy programs for inexpensive co-operative

---

1   There are principally two types of tenure in co-operative stock: **co-operative rental**, where the tenant has covered only a fraction of the construction costs (the rest was covered by subsidy) and the tenant's title to the dwelling is similar to rental arrangements (cannot be sold), and **co-operative owner-occupancy**, where the tenant has covered the full costs of construction and the title to dwelling is very much like ownership (can be sold or used as collateral – co-operative owner-occupancy title is usually valued the same as ownership proper).

housing (Figure 1). The decrease was followed by the improvement of standards among newly built dwellings (Table 2, 3).

The new output is dominated by single-family housing developed by future occupiers. The co-operatives' output has fallen considerably and remains on a downward trend. Municipal housing output has been low across the decade (around 3 000 units per year). New investors, commercial developers and social housing associations (social rental housing), are gaining momentum. Most units built in 1998 were owner-occupied.

Figure 1: Housing Construction Output, 1990-2000

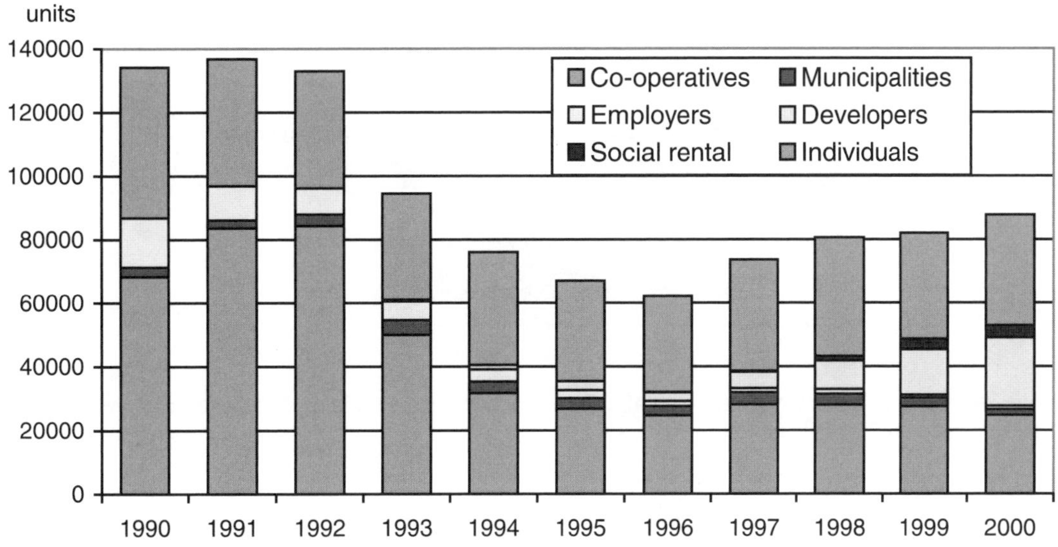

Note: Data or 2000 are preliminary.
Source: National Statistics Office

Table 2: Useful Floor Area of Newly Constructed Dwellings (m^2)

	1981-90	1991-95	1995	1996	1997	1998	1999
Average per dwelling	70.4	80.1	89.6	92.1	93.3	93.4	87.3
Of which: Urban area	63.4	72.3	80.5	82.4	84.4	83.9	78.4
Rural area	90.9	105.1	112.9	118.1	120.2	124.0	122.9
Of which: Multi-family	N/A	N/A	61.3	61.0	60.6	61.4	57,6
Single-family	N/A	N/A	122.0	126.5	130.5	132.6	130.7

Source: National Statistics Office

Table 3: Useful Floor Area of Newly Constructed Dwellings by Type of Developer (m^2)

	1991-95	1995	1996	1997	1998	1999	2000
Co-operatives	61.1	61.3	61.0	60.6	61.4	58.3	62,9
Municipalities	51.6	50.0	44.6	49.3	49.1	46.7	48.0
Employers	60.8	61.8	65.9	68.2	58.3	64.8	64.9
Developers on profit basis	68.9	64.5	61.2	60.4	58.9	59.3	62.9
Social rental	N/A	N/A	50.0	51.8	51.6	50.5	54.4
Individuals (single family)	116.1	122.0	126.5	130.5	132.6	130.6	133.2

Source: National Statistics Office

The rental sector in Poland diminished over the past decade (Figure 2). There are several factors shaping the process. New construction is dominated by owner-occupancies, whether individual, co-operative or provided by developers on a for-profit basis. The tenure structure is also affected by the privatisation of existing units (sale to sitting tenants) (Table 4-6). The relatively high dynamic of privatisation is due to considerable discounts offered to buyers -- typically 80% of the market value and higher. The third factor is the shift of titles within the housing co-operatives. Rental co-operative titles to existing units have frequently been transformed into ownership co-operative titles.[1] The preferential conditions for transforming the titles provide an incentive to faster repayment of the loans granted to co-operatives before the transition. In addition, new co-operative flats are almost exclusively co-operative owner-occupancies. It is notable, however, that the pace at which the public rental stock has been transformed into owner-occupied stock is much slower than in many other transition countries.

Figure 2: Tenure Structure

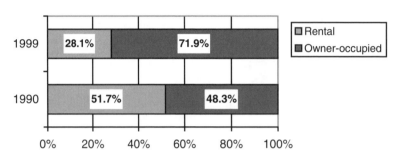

Note: "Rental" includes co-operative rental. "Owner-occupied" includes co-operative owner-occupied.
Source: National Statistics Office

Table 4: Housing Stock by Landlord

	1990	1994	1996	1998	1999
Co-operative	24.9%	27.7%	27.7%	28.5%	28.7%
Private	43.8%	43.5%	49.7%	52.4%	53.5%
Public	31.3%	28.8%	22.5%	19.1%	17.8%
-- Municipal	18.0%	17.8%	14.6%	13.3%	12.5%
-- Employer provided	13.3%	11.0%	7.9%	5.8%	5.3%

Note: "Co-operative" includes co-operative owner-occupied.
Source: National Statistics Office

Table 5: Sales of Public Dwellings to Sitting Tenants
(thousand units)

	1992	1999	Total sold: 1992-1999
Municipal dwellings	2 028.0	1 458.3	569.7
Employer provided dwellings	1 480.1	617.0	863.1
Total	3 508.1	2 075.3	1 432.8

Source: National Statistics Office

---

1   Based on the new Law on housing co-operatives there will be three possible types of tenure in co-operative stock: co-operative rental, co-operative owner-occupancy, and ownership. Starting 24th April 2001, co-operative titles holders will be given the right to apply for transforming their existing tenures into ownership.

Table 6: Privatised Dwellings in Buildings Owned by Municipalities or Employers
(thousand units)

	1995	1999
Dwellings in buildings owned or co-owned by municipalities	2 035.3	1 999.9
(Share of privatised dwellings)	14.8%	27.1%
Dwellings in buildings owned or co-owned by employers	1 155.3	754.2
(Share of privatised dwellings)	6.2%	18.2%

Source: National Statistics Office

Table 7: Co-operative Rental and Co-operative Owner-Occupied Dwellings
(thousand units)

	1988	1994	1996	1998	1999
Co-operative dwellings total	2 800	3 170.3	3 204.6	3 329.3	3 350.2
-- Co-operative rental	2 333	1 545.4	1 416.6	1 285.7	1 185.1
(share)	83.3%	48.7%	44.2%	38.6%	35.4%
-- Co-operative owner-occupied	467	1 624.9	1 788.0	2 043.6	2 165.1
(share)	16.7%	51.3%	55.8%	61.4%	64.6%

Source: Bogusz J., Kierunki prywatyzacji zasobu mieszkaniowego w krajach Europy środkowej i wschodniej, Warszawa 1993; Country Profiles on the Housing Sector: Poland, UN/ECE, 1998; National Statistics Office

Table 8: Housing Stock

	1980	1990	1993	1994	1995	1996	1997	1998	1999
Total dwellings (1000)	9 794	11 022	11 366	11 434	11 491	11 547	11 613	11 688	11 763
Dwellings per 1000 population	274.1	288.7	295.2	296.4	297.6	298.8	300.4	302.3	304.3
Persons per dwelling	3.55	3.4	3.32	3.31	3.29	3.28	3.26	3.24	3.22

Source: National Statistics Office

The low output of the 1990s added to the severe housing deficit. The number of households exceeds the number of dwellings by about 1.5 million. Poland, with about 300 dwellings per 1 000 inhabitants, ranks far below most European countries (Table 8). The problem will grow even more acute as members of the Baby Boom generation of the early 1980s leave their parents' homes.

The demand for new housing is fairly restricted at present. The ratio of average monthly income to the price of 1 square meter varies from 0.6 to 0.8 depending on the region. Few people can afford to rent or buy a new dwelling at market prices. The cost of credit, and fairly high transaction costs, aggravate the problem. Two non-income related factors further inhibit demand: consumption models (little is saved, consumer durables and cars are bought with loans); and regulated rents and tenant's rights keep sitting tenants in.

On the supply side, there is a problem of serviced land for housing. Infrastructure is a municipal responsibility, but municipalities lack budgetary resources for necessary investment. As a result, overall cost of residential development is higher (either final tender prices for serviced land are higher or cost of construction is transferred to investors).

Renovation is also a pressing need, concerning both the old stock and the panel-block buildings built in the 1970s and 1980s. The Housing Research Institute estimated the repair backlog at zlotys 30 billion in 1996 (some 8% of GDP).

During the transition period, different types of direct and indirect financial support for the housing sector have been introduced. State budget expenses allocated for housing purposes do not fully reflect the scale of state assistance, much of which comes in indirect forms. Including the overall impact of housing tax relief and a preferential VAT rate on construction materials and services, the total value of the government support should at least be doubled.

Table 9: Tax Deductions of Housing Expenses
(thousands zloty)

	Deduction from taxable income		Deduction from tax
	Total	By tax rate	
1993	4 099 491	N/A	
1994	4 923 207	N/A	
1995	7 207 728	N/A	
1996	11 817 264	N/A	
1997	1 722 019	20%: 1 280 127 32%: 325 767 44%: 116 125	2 374 875
1998	3 983 452	19%: 2 095 165 30%: 785 166 40%: 1 103 121	2 249 969
1999	3 986 260	19%: 1 998 879 30%: 882 959 40%: 1 104 422	3 380 235

Note: Until the end o 1996, no tax deduction of housing expenses was available.
Source: Ministry of Finance

The Government's tax reform proposals in 1999 presupposed the abolition of most forms of tax relief in the personal income tax, including those providing incentives for home-purchase and renovation (a taxpayer can deduct part of the cost of building, buying or renovating a house or unit). A presidential veto of the reform proposals left the housing tax-relief system substantially unchanged. The system of housing tax deductions is simple to administer but primarily targets the wealthiest citizens. Financial support through tax deductions is granted to every taxpayer, regardless of income. The sole limit is on the amount of available support (19% of the average price of construction of 70 square meters). High-income taxpayers who purchase expensive houses usually receive as much or more support than the less affluent, whose purchases of less-expensive dwellings does not allow them to reach the support limit.

Recent housing policy initiatives are designed to consolidate progress toward a better-targeted housing subsidy system that is more consistent with market-based housing finance. New proposals are outlined in Assumptions for State Housing Policy for the Years 1999-2003, the official document approved by the Government in July 1999. The principal policies aimed at stimulating housing investment are summarised below.

Interest rate subsidies to mortgage loans (the "Own Apartment" program) are designed to support the system of tax deductions as a tool to stimulate housing demand. The target group comprises households which, due to insufficient cash resources to buy a housing unit, have to resort to bank credit. The state will finance the repayment of 50% of interest on mortgage loans. The beneficiaries of the program will consist of households: of which annual income does not exceed an annually published income level (zlotys 72 000 in 2000); which did not benefit from housing-expense tax deductions; and which will be granted a mortgage loan of up to 20 years to purchase, build, adapt or redevelop a housing unit.

Table 10: Execution of Central Budget Allocations for Housing
(millions zloty)

Type of allocation	1991	1992	1993	1994	1995	1996	1997	1998	1999	2000
Total	**1 226.7**	**2 349.9**	**1 923.5**	**2 760.3**	**2 816.6**	**3 397.6**	**3 392.2**	**3 297.0**	**2 103.5**	**2 590.4**
Co-operative loans interest buy-down	67.2	699.1	975.0	751.1	829.5	1 415.6	1 111.3	1 055.3	609.2	414.0
Co-operative loans payments	422.3	702.6	0.2		0.1			0.9		
Guaranteed payments to housing savings booklets' owners	121.7	264.3	261.7	1 404.6	1 125.7	817.7	908.0	1 213.0	911.4	1 368.4
Mortgage Fund			12.1	1.1	5.9	13.1	15.2	8.7	8.9	
National Housing Fund					58.7	342.0	220.0	332.3	150.0	242.5
Thermal Modernisation Fund									5.0	12.0
Thermal modernisation subsidies to co-operatives					10.0	39.9	49.8			
Subsidies to municipalities for housing allowances payments				38.9	229.7	265.3	324.3	456.2	416.9	550.0
Refunds to housing co-operative candidates				25.1	31.7	44.8	274.3	2.3		
Subsidies to municipalities for housing infrastructure construction				89.9	89.6	55.0	90.0	39.9		
Subsidies to heat providers in housing sector								54.0		
Subsidies to housing co-operatives	615.5	683.9	530.4	449.6	435.7	404.2	399.3	134.4		
Share of housing expenditures:										
To Gross Domestic Product	1.5%	2.0%	1.2%	1.3%	1.0%	0.9%	0.8%	0.6%	0.4%	0.4%
To Central budget	5.1%	6.1%	3.8%	4.0%	3.1%	3.1%	2.7%	2.4%	1.5%	1.7%

Source: State Office for Housing and Urban Development

Subsidy will cover loans with a loan-to value ratio of up to 70% and not exceeding the value of 50 square meters of a unit (interest on excessive loan amounts will not be subsidised). Assistance is given for five years with a renewal option upon borrower's application, provided that an eligibility income ceiling is not exceeded in the year the application is submitted. The price per square meter must not exceed a certain limit, which varies by region. Another requirement is that the unit financed should not be sold for at least five years after the loan disbursement. In the event of an earlier sale, any assistance received will have to be repaid.

The state is also involved in supporting rental co-operative and social rental construction. The National Housing Fund, which depends for its resources on the central budget, is used to co-finance rental construction. Long-term indexed mortgages at preferential interest rates (half of market levels) can be granted to housing co-operatives and social housing associations (non-profit developers) for building dwellings for income-eligible households. Rents in social housing associations' stock cannot exceed 4% of the replacement value of the rented flat yearly.

State-supported credit arrangements are also available for housing renovation. Thermal modernisation loans are offered to investors whose projects meet certain thermal and economic efficiency criteria. The support is transferred at the end in the form of the lump-sum repayment of the remaining 25% of the loan principal. The grants come from the Thermal Modernisation Fund, which draws those moneys from the central budget.

The report Assumptions for State Housing Policy for the Years 1999-2003 also envisages subsidised loans for general repair purposes. The beneficiaries are mostly owners of multi-family housing (housing co-operatives, condominium owners associations, and municipalities). The state will cover 50% of interest on commercial loans granted for renovation purposes. Maximum repayment periods for such loans will be 10 years.

Mortgage loans

Before the transition, housing-related loans came from selected state-owned or state-controlled banks, notably PKO BP (a state savings bank). Loan terms were stipulated in Government ordinances. The last such ordinance was adopted in 1988. The most popular product under this ordinance was a construction loan for housing co-operatives. Its term was 40 years and the interest rate was fixed at 3% or 6% (depending on type of tenure). No down payment was required (10% or 20% of the loan value had to be repaid in a lump sum, and 30% was paid by the budget). Yearly repayments were set at 1% or 2% of the value of the unit. The budget covered the difference between the costs to banks (plus some margin) and interest due.

The Act of 1989 on Restructuring Loan Agreements came shortly after the transition. It repealed administrative restrictions on loan agreements, especially regarding interest rates. When inflation rates were high, banks instantly applied adjustable rates to existing agreements. To make these loans repayable, the state provided a mechanism to buy down part of the interest on housing loans from budgetary resources. Such support continues, constituting a considerable burden within the housing budget.

The model of subsidised lending was not repealed completely. Government ordinances of the early 1990s introduced a support system in which the budget covered part of the interest on newly granted loans. This time, however, loans had to be collateralised by a mortgage; the loan amount could not exceed 80% of the property value; and the borrower's effort ratio could not be less than 25% of household income. This policy was finally given up in 1995.

The transition brought great change in the way the banking sector operated. Banks were transformed into commercial institutions, and several new banks were established. More than 30 have entered the mortgage market, though a few banks dominate the market.

The first mortgage loans granted on a fully commercial basis (at market rates without state support to the borrower) appeared in 1994. These were mostly dual-indexed mortgages disbursed under the Mortgage Fund program. In 1992, the Government of Poland and institutions such as the World Bank and the US Agency for International Development concluded a series of agreements concerning support for the Polish housing sector. One outcome was the establishment of the Mortgage Fund as a liquidity facility to fund inflation-proof mortgage loans. The Mortgage Fund was designed to encourage the development of a market-based housing finance system in Poland by implementing suitable mortgage products, training loan officers, establishing a network of banks offering mortgage loans, and providing the banks with loan financing. The basic type of mortgage offered was a so-called dual-indexed mortgage (DIM), a product designed for inflationary economies. DIM is an adjustable mortgage built around two variable indexes; the interest due on the remaining loan balance moves with shifts in market interest rates, and the borrower's monthly payment fluctuates with wage changes. DIM is rather hard to administer and requires professional bank personnel. It carries considerable risk for the lender, as its amortisation period is not known at the moment of origination. It may prove much more expensive to the borrower than other mortgage types. The Mortgage Fund program successfully promoted mortgage loans (especially DIMs, which dominated in the market for most of the 1990s) and helped the banking sector with training its personnel.

Figure 3: Housing Loans Outstanding

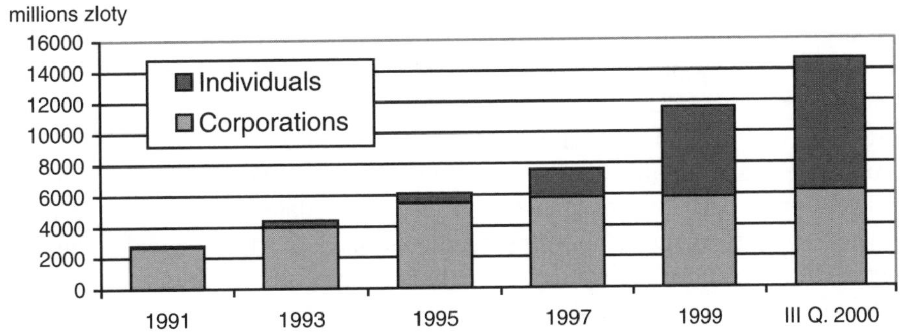

Note: Data as of the end of period. "Corporations" include co-operatives
Source: National Bank of Poland

In 1996, banks' portfolios contained more than zlotys 600 million in market-rate housing loans. The majority (about 85%) were mortgage loans to house-buyers. Since then the sector has experienced dynamic growth – banks' mortgage-loan portfolios have doubled every year. At the end of 1999, outstanding market-rated housing loans totalled about zlotys 7.6 billion. The ratio of mortgages granted to individuals was about the same as in 1996.

Table 11: Housing Loans Outstanding by Type
(millions zloty, as of 30 September 2000)

Granted to:	Individuals	Corporations	Total
Housing loans total	8 427.4	6 171.7	14 644.1
Collateralised by mortgage and state-supported through interest buy-down[1]	69.2	0.1	69.3
Other state-supported through interest buy-down[2]	20.5	3 796.3	3 816.8
Funded from Mortgage Fund	56.3	0.5	56.8
Other	8 325.9	2 375.3	10 701.2
Granted to municipalities	116.9	--	--

Note: 1) Granted in the early 1990s (until March 1995) as government subsidised loans. 2) So-called "old housing loans" granted to individuals and housing co-operatives under government ordinances in 1965-1992.
Source: National Bank of Poland

Mortgages on offer include DIMs, DPMs and conventional ARMs. DIMs were particularly popular until the interest rate decreases of 1999. As PKO BP (the leading bank in affordable DIM loans) charged no prepayment penalties with DIMs, they were regularly prepaid. Loan amounts varied between 30 000 zloty in 1996 and 40 000 zloty in mid-1999, meaning that the typical loan-to-value ratio (LTV) was 40% to 60%. The maximum LTV levels are 70% to 80%, though some products (one is called "Young Professional") require no down payment. Maximum loan terms vary from 15 to 25 years but typical maturity does not exceed 15 years.

In 1996-98, interest rates on mortgage loans remained fairly stable around 25%. They declined significantly in 1999 due to the steep decreases of central bank rates and growing competition in the market. Average rates ranged between 16% and 18%. Last year's 500 basis-point increase of central bank rates pushed mortgage rates up by an average 300 basis points.

In 1997, the Act on Mortgage Bonds and Mortgage Banks was adopted. It introduced a German model of mortgage securitisation known as *Pfandbriefe*. So far, two mortgage banks are operational and a few others are in the licensing process. Mortgage banks are specialised financial institutions with the right to issue mortgage bonds (*Pfandbriefe*) against the mortgages in their portfolio. Mortgage bonds, which are long-term safe capital market instruments, are supposed to provide suitable long-term financing for mortgage loans originated by mortgage banks and have positive impact on their interest and maturity. There have been two mortgage bond issues to date. For some time regulations were unclear as to whether all financial institutions could purchase mortgage bonds. Current regulations, following amendment of financial legislation, make mortgage bonds eligible investments for insurance companies, pension funds and investment funds.

Housing loans currently offered by Polish banks are mostly still funded with short-term deposits. It should be noted, however, that securitisation will not instantly improve the affordability of mortgage financing. The spreads between rates on loans and deposits in commercial banks are still high enough to make alternative funding techniques non-competitive in final price-of-credit terms.

The development of lending for housing purposes is slowly reshaping the pattern of housing financing for individuals. Until recently, housing construction was financed almost exclusively with cash (excluding subsidised loans of pre-transition years and the early 1990s). In 1998, the share of credit in housing financing was about 10%. In 1999, the figure rose to 15%.

Housing finance systems: contract savings schemes

Apart from the above-mentioned depository and mortgage bank models of funding housing loans, a contract savings model also exists in Poland. In fact, two contract savings systems were established by separate legal acts. One is the Act of October 1995, which introduced the institution of *kasa mieszkaniowa* (KM). The other is the Act of June 1997, which regulates the operation of *kasa oszczednosciowo-budowlana* (KOB), modelled on contract savings systems in Germany and Austria (*Bausparkassen*). The KOB system is not yet in operation, due to the Government initiative (supported by the central bank) to stop the licensing process until the Law of 1997 is amended. The KM institutions, which started operations in late 1996 and in 1997, have granted insignificant numbers of loans.

Considering that in the KM system state support to savers is transferred through tax deductions, it would have to be redesigned as well (due to tax system reform). Recently, the Government decided to replace the two systems with one that would be consistent with the latest Government economic policies. Table 12 below compares key features of the two systems with the future system.

The choice of the existing KM model as the base for building the new system seems obvious. KM needs a constant influx of new savers to keep its liquidity, which cannot be done without state incentives for savers. Yet, the experience of other transition countries (the Czech Republic, Slovakia, Hungary) with German-type systems shows that they tend to quickly monopolise housing budgets. Non-profit organisations operating on a smaller scale of the KM type are much more acceptable from the budgetary viewpoint. State support for savers in the new system will rely on interest subsidies in the savings period that will permit savings at market rates. The subsidies will be transferred to the savings account until the amount of savings exceeds the average value of 25 square meters. The system avoids the danger inherent in the Polish version of *Bausparkasse*: The rate of return is biggest for relatively small yearly savings, which discourages the large savings volumes necessary for house or apartment purchase.

Table 12: Contract Savings Schemes

Feature	KM	KOB	New system
Organisation	Non-profit division of universal bank	Specialised financial institution	Non-profit division of universal bank
Interest rate on savings	Adjustable with cap – at least 0.25% of central bank's bill rediscount rate[1] but not less than 2%	Fixed	Saver rate (including subsidy) – 0.8 bill rediscount rate Bank rate (excluding subsidy) – same as KM
Interest rate on loans	Adjustable with caps – not more than 0.5% of bill rediscount rate but not less than 4%	Fixed – cannot exceed interest rate on savings by more than 3 percentage points	Same as KM
Maximum loan to savings ratio	Up to 150%	Up to 100%	Up to 100%
Type of state support	Tax deduction of up to 30% of yearly savings	Grant equal to up to 30% of yearly savings	Interest rate subsidy in the saving period – covers difference between bank rate and saver rate
Limit on state support	6% of the average price of construction of 70 square meters	Grant calculation base limited – yearly savings not bigger than average price of construction of 3 square meters	Interest rate subsidised until savings total exceed average price of construction of 25 square meters
Minimum/maximum saving period	3/-	2/-	4/7
Number of banks	3	4 (not operational)	-
Number of savers	ca. 70,000	-	Will take over the KM savers

Note: 1) Currently 19.50%

FUNDING THE HOUSING CONSTRUCTION IN THE SLOVAK REPUBLIC

by

Viera Hlavaèova[*]

Macroeconomic characteristics

From its establishment in 1993, the Slovak Republic began building a functioning market economy. Table 1 reflects developments in macroeconomic indicators in 1993-99, as well as perspectives for 2000-2003.

After curbing the economic fall, and following a rise in basic macroeconomic indicators in 1996, a new decline occurred in 1998-99. This was largely because of the adoption of a package of recovery measures, which included radical short-term restrictions on budgetary expenses. While these measures resulted in slower economic growth, they were necessary for the longer-term recovery of economic development.

The anticipated trends were borne out in 1999. Economic growth slowed (in terms of inflation-adjusted GDP), the inflation rate rose, the unemployment rate increased, real wages dropped, and real domestic demand declined (which, however, had a positive effect on the deficit in the payment current account balance). Domestic aggregated demand was influenced by a real drop in gross capital formation and a slight growth of household consumption. The real growth of GDP was supported by a slight growth in exports and a slight real decline of imports of goods and services. The improved export performance and reduced import demands resulted in a decline of the nominal value of the trade deficit.

The rise in average inflation, an interim phenomenon, resulted from the increase in indirect taxes and the implementation of arrangements involving state-regulated prices.

The unemployment rate has increased in part with slower GDP growth and a harsh financial situation in many enterprises; labour productivity, meantime, has been rising.

Monetary policy has benefited from a reduction of domestic demand, a curbing of public expenses and a corresponding decline in pressures on the domestic financial market, as well as an overall improvement in the transparency of cabinet and fiscal policies. These factors contributed to declining interest rates. A new system of monetary policy management has been launched, and it may be further liberalised later. Overall, better conditions have been established for economic growth.

---

[*]   Ministry Adviser, Economy Housing Department, the Ministry of Construction and Regional Development, Slovak Republic

Table 1: Economic Development: Referential Scenario

	1993	1994	1995	1996	1997	1998	1999	2000	2001	2002	2003
GDP and its use											
Gross domestic product (SKK million)	369.1	440.5	516.8	575.5	653.9	717.4	779.3	850.0	930.0	1020.0	1117.0
--- Growth rate (%)	11.1	19.3	17.3	11.4	13.6	9.7	8.6	9.1	9.4	9.7	9.5
Consumption in totall	288.5	315.8	360.8	420.6	471.2	517.7	555.5	605.0	663.1	731.0	804.4
Consumption of households	196.2	221.9	252.7	286.1	322.3	360.1	395.4	438.4	488.9	548.3	613.7
Consumption of non-profit institutions				2.4	2.7	2.9	3.0	3.1	3.1	3.2	3.3
Consumption of state administration	92.3	93.9	108.1	132.1	146.2	154.7	157.1	163.5	171.1	179.5	187.4
Gross capital formation	101.0	101.8	146.6	226.7	252.9	282.7	263.3	272.8	292.2	312.1	333.7
Gross fixed capital formation	120.7	129.4	141.5	212.7	252.7	292.4	257.3	246.7	262.7	286.2	313.9
Changes in materials inventory	-19.7	-27.6	5.1	14.0	0.2	-9.7	6.0	26.2	29.5	25.9	19.9
Net export	-20.4	22.9	9.4	-69.2	-67.5	-80.1	-39.5	-27.9	-25.3	-23.0	-21.1
Export of products and services	227.8	286.6	325.8	334.0	396.9	456.8	504.9	553.3	608.0	671.4	738.4
Import of products and services	248.2	263.7	316.4	403.2	464.4	536.9	544.4	581.2	633.4	694.4	759.5
Domestic demand	389.5	417.6	507.4	647.3	724.1	800.4	818.8	874.0	944.6	1023.1	1110.9
Gross domestic savings	80.6	124.7	156.0	155.1	182.7	199.7	223.8	243.9	263.9	283.4	305.1
GDP constant prices (SKK billion)	460.8	483.4	516.8	550.8	586.8	612.7	624.5	640.0	660.1	683.0	710.7
--- Growth rate (%)	-3.7	4.9	6.9	6.6	6.5	4.4	1.9	2.5	3.1	3.5	4.0
Prices											
Inflation rate (%)	25.1	11.7	7.2	5.4	6.4	5.6	14.2	10.6	8.1	7.0	6.4
Inflation - average for the year (%)	23.2	13.4	9.9	5.8	6.1	6.7	10.6	11.9	8.5	7.2	6.5
Labour market											
Average monthly nominal wage (SKK)	5,372	6,285	7,195	8,154	9,226	10,003	10,744	11,566	12,486	13,539	14,715
--- Growth rate (%)	18.4	17.0	14.5	13.3	13.1	8.4	7.4	7.6	8.0	8.4	8.7
Unemployment rate (%)			12.8	11.1	11.8	12.5	16.1	19.0	17.5	17.2	16.1
Exchange rate											
SKK/USD average		30.790	32.040	29.740	30.650	33.620	35.240	42.250	43.303	43.700	44.151 44.599

Source: Mid-term Financial Forecast for 2000-2003, Draft, March 2000

From 2001-03, the reforms undertaken should produce an acceleration of economic growth. A gradual recovery is anticipated in GDP growth (by an estimated 5%, with a concurrent increase in GDP per capita) and all its components. The inflation rate should fall to an estimated 4.6%-5 % by 2004, and economic growth and pro-active policies in the labour market should lead to a decline in unemployment of an estimated 13.6%-16.8%.

GDP growth will be based largely on export growth, but also on increasing household consumption (as real wages and employment rise) and on gross fixed-capital formation. Real growth of the economy and of employment will depend on how rapidly and completely economic restructuring measures are implemented, and on direct foreign investments expected after 2000. Successful implementation of alterations will lead to greater competitiveness, labour productivity, capital investments and exports.

Table 2 provides demographic developments in population and the number of census households. Natural population growth has moved to a declining trend. The number of census households has not developed in parallel to population developments; it is assumed that the number of households should grow faster than the population. In terms of apartment demand, the level of apartment availability for the population is crucial.

Table 2: Demographic Developments

Year	Population	Household in census
1991	5 283 404	1 827 575
1993	5 324 632	N/A
1994	5 347 413	N/A
1995	5 363 676	N/A
1996	5 373 810	N/A
1997	5 383 214	N/A
2000	5 400 637	1 931 441
2005	5 420 227	1 964 507

Note: Figures for 2005 are forecasts.
Source: Statistical Office of the Slovak Republic

Housing sector overview

Housing construction and its funding methods have undergone a series of changes in the recent past, as reflected in both the scope and structure of construction. In 1990, the state was heavily involved in housing construction, in the systematic planning of housing construction, and through the direct system of subsidies or low-interest loans. These factors directly influenced the number of apartments completed – a total of 1 352 779 apartments from 1948 to 1990 (with the most intense period of construction coming from 1971-80, when 442 112 apartments were completed). In this period, however, housing stock declined significantly, by about 465 000 apartments. The structure of housing types constructed changed significantly as well. From 1948-60, private housing construction represented 52.2% of total construction, while communal housing construction represented 46.3% of the total. From 1981-90, private housing construction formed 31.1% of the total; communal housing construction, 19.4%; and co-operative housing construction, 47.5%.

With the transformation of the national economy from a centrally ruled to a market economy, the housing data also reflect social changes in financing practices after 1990. During 1991-2000, housing construction declined, with only 109 417 apartments completed. In 1993, the Czechoslovak Federal Republic was split into two independent successor states: the Czech Republic and the Slovak Republic. This, too, was reflected in the transformation process.

Role of the state as defined by the State Housing Concept

Through changes in social conditions in 1989, housing policy experienced essential alterations. As the state ended its support for the funding of housing construction, such construction came to a near-complete halt. In response, the cabinet in 1995 adopted its Concept of State Housing Policy by the Year 2000, setting out housing policy goals. This document defined the roles of citizens, of municipalities and of the state in providing housing. In a market economy, the responsibility for procuring housing is shifted to the citizen. The state and the municipalities should prepare suitable conditions to allow citizens to obtain housing.

The municipalities' tasks include land-use planning and preparation, assessing availability of building plots for housing construction, co-ordinating and participating in the development of housing and related technical infrastructure, and providing conditions to make housing available to socially dependent population groups.

The state's tasks include the passage of legislation governing the economic instruments to support housing development, and the establishment of legal regulations and standards to remove all barriers to development and all non-systematic regulations, with the ultimate goal of harmonisation with EU legislation.

Figure 1: Development in the Number of Started and Completed Apartments

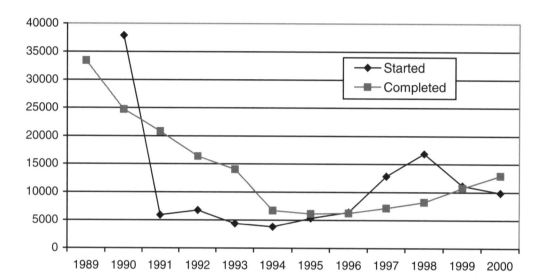

The system of economic instruments to support housing development vested in legislation is gradually becoming established. These instruments helped produce a recovery of housing construction, although housing supply remains short of the population's demands. After an initial start in 1996-98, housing construction entered a recession in 1999 due to the lack of available financial sources and to the broader economic situation in the Slovak Republic.

The structure of ownership forms and the numbers of started and completed apartments make it clear that the largest share of apartments is built under private ownership. In 1998, 80.6% of apartments started and 74.4% of apartments completed were under private ownership. In 1999, 87% of apartments started and 83.1% of those completed were privately owned; and in 2000, 87.6% of apartments started and 92.8% of those completed were in private ownership. This represented an essential change from the pre-1990 period, when individuals owned only about one-third of apartments completed, with the rest owned by housing co-operatives or the state.

In the census of 3 March 1991, the Slovak Republic reported 5 274 335 individual residents, 1 617 828 permanently occupied apartments, and 151 005 others not permanently occupied. Thus, there were 307 permanently occupied apartments per 1 000 individuals (335 apartments when those not permanently occupied are included). Professionals in the sector estimate that there were 312 permanently occupied apartments per 1 000 individuals in 1996; in 2000 the share of permanently occupied apartments was expected to reach 320 per 1 000 individuals.

According to the 3 March 1991 census data, the average apartment had floor surface of 72.8 square meters, and the average dwelling/use surface of an apartment was 47.3 square meters. The average per-capita floor surface was 22.3 square meters and the average per-capita dwelling/use surface was 14.5 square meters. More recent data will have to await a new census of population, houses and apartments, but development in the area has been positive: In 2000, average floor surface of newly completed apartments reached 135 square meters, with average dwelling/use surface of 82.5 square metres. This trend reflected changes in the apartment ownership structure and a higher share of apartments completed as family dwellings.

Apartment availability per 1 000 individuals in the Slovak Republic compares to the levels in other countries in transition, but lags significantly behind the developed countries of Western Europe, where the normal standard is 400 to 460 apartments per 1 000 individuals.

A more accurate picture of developments in the area will become clear only after the results of the March 2001 census of population, houses and apartments become available.

At present, the Slovak Republic appears to lack about 200 000 apartments. Conditions should be established to allow completion of 20 000 apartments a year after 2002, which would eventually allow the Republic to reach the level of developed countries, with a yearly pace of five to six apartments being built per 1 000 individuals.

Privatisation and ownership relations in the housing sector

At the time of the last census, 50.2% of all permanently occupied apartments (811 440) were in family houses and 49.8% (806 388) were in apartment houses. Building co-operatives owned 22.1% of apartments (357 709) and 27.7% (448 679 apartments) were state-owned rentals.

Legislation aimed at privatising the housing stock has changed the apartment ownership structure. In the first stage, state-owned apartments were transferred to municipality ownership free of charge; in the second, apartments were transferred to the ownership of current apartment users (either tenants or housing co-operative members) for payment. By 31 December 1999, about 145 000 apartments (8% of all housing stock) remained in municipality ownership; housing co-operatives owned about 280 000 apartments (16% of all housing stock). This low share of apartments transferred is due to the unlimited period for transferring a co-operative apartment as provided in the act on ownership of apartments and non-residential rooms.

Existing legislative and economic conditions have done little to make housing ownership and management more attractive. Delays in the deregulation of rental fees have made it difficult to recoup investments in apartment construction; owners of apartments built with state funding have faced permanent economic losses. These reasons, along with municipalities' limited resources and above-standard tenant protections (a review of legal regulations began only recently), the construction of rental apartments has been limited, and involved significant state support. Rental-apartment construction of such limited scope cannot satisfy the demand from the lowest-income categories, or from young families.

According to the Concept of State Housing Policy by the Year 2000, liberalisation of rental fees was to begin, in a scheduled series of steps, not long after the Concept's 1995 adoption. However, the prescribed 70% increase in rents was not introduced until 1 January 2000. Other measures -- the regulation of rental fees for apartments owned by "natural persons," provision of free apartments in houses owned by natural persons and legal persons, and apartments in houses built without public funds -- approved after the effect of the measure, were cancelled. Since that date a system for providing housing allowances and mitigating adverse impacts of liberalisation on lower-income households has been introduced. A further 45% increase in rent took effect on 1 February 2001; and in apartments completed with public assistance after that date, cost-based rent each year may not exceed 5% of the acquisition price for the apartment.

Housing construction is affected by the limited funds available to municipalities for rental-apartment construction, for building infrastructure and for construction of rental apartments for lower-income residents.

By providing and approving land-use planning documentation on settlement units and zones, municipalities play an important role in the development of housing construction. However, municipalities have no legal right to influence the use of plots in accordance with already approved plans, or to exercise progressive taxation of such land plots. Legislation will be needed to permit the application of progressive taxation to long-term undeveloped plots so as to establish more favourable conditions for the acquisition of such plots.

Largely for the reasons cited, municipalities now attempt to seek plots suitable for building by expanding the municipality's *intravilan* (own territory) employing a methodology in effect from 1 January 2001.

Building up technical infrastructure is a prerequisite for housing construction. Pursuant to the act on public administration, municipalities have authority for construction and management of local communications and development of administered territory. But in practice, municipalities also co-ordinate the provision of technical infrastructure construction with other legal entities, such as the state monopoly organisations (state enterprises of water and sewerage management, state electricity utilities and state gas utilities as Slovenský plynárenský priemysel, š.p.).

Due to the distorted price regulation of products provided by those state monopoly organisations, such enterprises have no natural economic interest in building up networks within municipalities. Municipalities often must build networks from their own resources, or from loans, with ample state aid; they then regularly transfer completed infrastructure to state ownership, via the state enterprises. Price deregulation is then launched, and the privatisation of such monopoly enterprises is prepared. In the field of water and sewerage management, joint stock companies are established with the participation of municipalities, which are legally accountable for a given part in relation to the population.

Social policy in housing

Social policy in housing is demonstrated through state support/aid for use of the housing stock, and state support/aid for housing construction.

As regards use of housing stock, the Act on Housing Allowances has been approved, but it still reflects a centralised approach to the administration and funding of the state economy. As regards reform plans for public administration and the devolution of powers to regional and self-governing bodies, the act needs to be modified to comply with systems usually applied in the EU countries.

In the field of state support/aid to promote housing construction, several support instruments have been adopted, aiming at all population groups, regardless of income level. Social policy, however, has offered limited opportunities for apartment acquisition by lower-income groups, particularly young families. Apartment construction in this area has been implemented solely with a significant involvement of state subsidies. The near-halt to construction of rental apartments was caused by a strict regulation of rental fees, which led to continued economic losses for holders of housing stock. That deformity was removed only after 1 February 2001. It was impossible to develop construction of specific types of dwelling, particularly young people's first housing units (so-called starter apartments), housing for elderly people in retailer houses with residential care services, and lower-standard housing for non-performers not paying rent or for asocial individuals.

To establish conditions more supportive of the construction of apartments for those with low incomes, legislation was adopted recently.

Funding housing construction

Several economic systems have been established or enhanced to fund housing construction. The state has also supported construction of rental apartments and technical infrastructure for apartments through direct subsidies. As mentioned, the state is taking a gradual approach toward adopting further measures that directly or indirectly support housing construction.

State support in funding housing construction can be divided into the direct and the indirect. The former comprises the establishment of systems of funding housing construction, such as building savings schemes, mortgage loans and the State Fund of Housing Development (ŠFRB), as well as the provision of support for the funding through subsidy programs and bank guarantee program.

Building savings schemes

Building savings schemes are applied for the longest period, yet they represent the most stable instruments for funding housing construction. A building savings scheme involves funding with fixed interest rates, independent of floating market interest rates, plus a state premium to the building savings. Two building societies operate in Slovakia: Prvá stavebná sporiteľňa, A.S. (PSS) and Všeobecná úverová banka Wüstenrot, A.S. (VÚBW). Foreign shareholders have interests in both.

From 1992-2000, the state provided funds in the form of state premiums to building savings totalling SKK 17.41 billion. By 1 January 2000 both building societies had spent funds amounting to SKK 71.93 billion (Table 3).

Table 3: Performance of Building Societies
(SKK million)

	1992 – 2000		
	PSS	VÚBW	Total
1. State premium to building saving	13 588.5	3 822.9	17 411.4
2. Building loans	1 174.6	1 090.0	2 264.6
3. Bridge loans	31 185.9	8 148.2	39 334.1
4. Sub-total (2 + 3)	32 360.4	9 238.2	41 598.6
5. Allocated saved sum to the building loan	2 084.8	1 824.0	3 908.8
6. Other purpose use of saved sum	15 655.3	6 325.0	21 980.3
7. Sub-total (4 + 5 + 6)	50 100.5	17 387.2	67 487.7
8. Building loans for legal entities	1 951.2	636.7	2 587.9
9. Bonds of PKB	400.0	100.0	500.0
10. State bonds for ŠFRB, HZL for VÚB	800.0	555.0	1 355.0
11. Sub-total (8 + 9 + 10)	3 151.2	1 291.7	4 442.9
13. Total – natural persons + others (7+11)	53 251.7	18 678.9	71 930.6

Source: Documents of building societies.

Of a total loan volume for 1992-2000 amounting to SKK 41.59 billion, and to legal entities amounting to SKK 2.57 billion, about SKK 13.67 billion was used for new construction. Moreover, the building societies purchased state bonds for SKK 1 billion for the ŠFRB, bonds of Prvá komunálna banka A.S. for SKK 500 million, and mortgage certificates for SKK 355 million, funds from which were used to support housing construction as well. In total, from 1992 to 2000, building societies supported housing construction with SKK 15.53 billion, representing 21.6% of the societies' total disbursed resources for the period. This indicates that building societies invested approximately 78% of their resources in this period in apartment modernisation.

Mortgage loans

Mortgage loans represent another method of providing financing for housing construction. The Banking Act defines a mortgage loan as a long-term loan with a maturity period of no less than five years, secured by a lien on local real estate, that is extended by a bank to legal entities or natural persons for acquisition, construction, reconstruction or maintenance of local real estate, and financed through the issuance and sale of mortgage certificates. This system was established by legislation enabling mortgage transactions from 28 January 1997. As of 31 December 2000 six banking institutions were licensed to carry out mortgage transactions, five of them providing mortgage loans for housing construction and one providing mortgage loans to implement business plans.

In spite of the established legislation and licenses for providing mortgage transactions, the funding system does not meet the anticipated role. In 1997-98, only Všeobecná úverová banka A.S. Bratislava provided mortgage loans to a non-significant extent. Other banks -- Slovenská sporiteľňa, Istrobanka, Tatra banka and Hypovereinsbank Slovakia – later began providing mortgage loans. Table 4 offers an overview of loans extended for new housing construction in 1999-2000.

Table 4: Mortgage Loans Extended by Banks

	Všeobecná úverová banka, a.s.	Slovenská sporiteľňa, a.s.	Istrobanka, a.s.	Tatra banka, a.s.	Total
Number of loans	1 667	516	58	1	2 242
-- for natural persons	1 580	516	58	1	2 155
-- for legal entities	87	0	0	0	87
Size of loans (SKK million)	1 186.88	328.94	66.98	3.8	1 586.6
-- for natural persons	984.08	328.94	66.98	3.8	1 383.8
-- for legal entities	202.8	0	0	0	202.8

Source: Data provided by banks

That so small an amount of mortgage loans has been provided reflects the economic inability of individuals to meet the conditions for such loans (proving the capability to repay the loan, and pledging collateral). For natural persons, annual interest rates are 10% to 12.5% and average maturity is 13.8 years; loan amounts average only SKK 625 000. The development of mortgage loans and transactions has been hampered further by the lack of stimulation instruments, non-adjusted legislation, underdeveloped capital markets and standard forms of accumulation of long-term resources. The provision on state contributions to reduce interest rates on mortgage loans for housing construction took effect 11 October 1999. In 1999-2000, the state contribution represented 6 percentage points.

State Fund of Housing Development

The State Fund of Housing Development (ŠFRB) was established by a law setting out the conditions for providing state support for extension and advancing the housing stock. Table 5 offers data on fund volumes provided from the ŠFRB by 1996.

Table 5: Overview of ŠFRB Support for Expanding and Advancing the Housing Stock
(SKK million)

	1996	1997	1998	1999	2000	Total
Support for expansion and advancing the housing stock	349.06	1 678.21	3 530.74	1 645.42	3 411.48	10 614.92
-- Loans	335.57	1 374.48	2 794.45	1 276.11	2 956.15	8 736.77
-- Contributions non-returnable	13.49	303.73	736.29	339.31	455.33	1 878.15

From 1996 to 2000, ŠFRB concluded 20 451 contracts and provided a total of SKK 10.61 billion, of which SKK 8.73 billion was in loans and SKK 1.88 billion in non-returnable contributions. Support aimed predominantly at apartment construction. Overall, the ŠFRB has supported construction of 20 484 apartments. From 1996-2000, the state allocated SKK 10.38 billion to the system in the form of indirect subventions, revenues from the sale of government bonds, and non-budgetary resources. The amendment of the Act on ŠFRB in effect since 1 April 2000 cancelled the provision of non-returnable contributions, establishing the conditions for the ŠFRB to become revolving and eventually separate from the state budget.

Subsidy programs for housing construction

In addition to funding support for housing construction, state support for housing construction comes through annual allocations of subsidies from the state budget and allocations of funds acquired through privatisation for the construction of infrastructure, rental apartments and apartments for those in need, and to renovate apartments included on the UNESCO World Heritage List. Additional forms of support were provided to municipalities within the Programs of Housing Development, annually approved by the Slovak Republic cabinet. A total of SKK 6.20 billion was allocated from public funds (the state budget and the National Property Fund) from 1996 to 2000.

Bank guarantee program

The state program to support housing construction by providing state guarantees on construction loans established conditions to allow the use of private finance in the housing sector. This program enabled the Government to support legal entities by pledging to back loans for housing construction. The program gives priority to guarantees on loans for the construction of rental apartments for lower-income groups. The program, adopted in 1999, took effect in 2000 with the allocation of SKK 200 million from the state budget. This form of support will be provided in accordance with the state aid act, which is fully compatible with EU Directives.

Indirect support

The area of indirect support by the state for housing construction, which includes tax relief and tax stimulation, lags significantly behind the measures of direct support adopted within the Concept of State Housing Policy.

In fiscal policy, only partial measures have been implemented, such as:

- The exemption from the taxation on real estate as apartments, family houses and blocks of flats for a period of five to 15 years (by 1 January 1993).

- The exemption for housing co-operatives from tax on incomes made from rental fees for co-operative apartments, garages and payment for operations related to their use (by 1 January 1993).

- The exemption on income tax for natural persons on interest from deposits in building savings schemes (since 1 April 1994).

- The exemption on incomes from interest revenues on mortgage certificates of natural persons and legal entities (since 1 April 1999).

- An option for legal entities to deduct the value of a donation to the ŠFRB aimed at the construction of rental apartments (since 1 January 2000).

These fiscal measures have not motivated investors to participate significantly in housing construction. To stimulate housing construction, fiscal instruments will be needed that provide real incentives to investors in the field.

Prospect for the funding of housing construction

In 1999, the cabinet adopted the Concept on Developing Housing Construction. According to this document, the efficient exploitation of financial sources requires improving certain systems to better direct their effects to individual population groups and strata of certain income levels.

State economic instruments used to support housing growth will reflect the Concept's goal of encouraging construction funded largely from private resources, while public funds, both state and local, will be directed to support housing for the weakest groups in society. Indirect support will be provided through tax relief.

In the 2000-2010 period, all existing funding systems for housing construction should participate in financing such construction, including investors' own resources. Banking resources should play a significant role through mortgage loans using resources from mortgage certificates as well as classical mortgage loans and commercial bank loans. An assessment of existing economic systems would indicate an imbalance in systems for funding housing construction. The relative participation of individual funding systems for housing construction approved by the Concept of Housing Construction should change substantially (Figure 2).

Figure 2: Shares of Three Funding Systems for Housing Construction: Current and Future Prospects

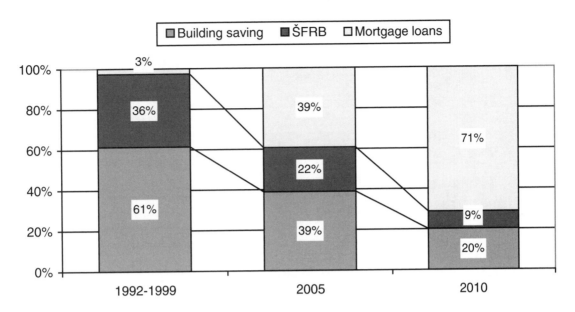

Conclusions

For the Slovak economy to continue to perform as regards the funding of housing construction, individual participants will have to continue to meet their objectives.

The development of housing construction will depend significantly on the availability of financial resources, particularly for: construction of rental apartments in the private sector and in the public rental sector; investments in technical infrastructure on building plots; and the development of mortgage banking.

As regards the capital and financial markets in the Slovak Republic, participation of foreign financial institutions is necessary to provide resources for funding, particularly to fund the construction of apartments in the public rental sector. According to the results of negotiations, foreign financial institutions require state guarantees before providing funds. With regards to meeting economic criteria, the state cannot come close to providing such guarantees for a sole area, particularly if the municipalities that benefit from those funds are able to provide reasonable and sufficient guarantees on their own.

In promoting housing construction, particularly in the public rental sector, a change in the attitude of foreign financial institutions should be valuable as to the provision of liability.

The Slovak Republic actively co-operates with international institutions to provide resources. For instance, co-funding for rental apartments for lower-income groups is currently being handled in co-operation with the Development Bank of the Council of Europe from the Bank's resources and those of municipalities.

HOUSING FINANCE IN SLOVENIA

by

Barbara Staric-Strajnar[*]

Macroeconomic characteristics

Slovenia is a small country in the middle of Europe on the Adriatic Sea. It has an area of 20 273 square kilometre, bordering with Italy, Austria, Hungary and Croatia. According to the 1991 census, Slovenia had a population of 1 988 million, of which 90% are Slovenes with Italian and Hungarian minorities.

Following the criteria of the International Monetary Fund, Slovenia is one of the best-performing Central and Eastern European economies in transition. The country is classified as one of the first countries in transition to overcome the slump that resulted from their transformation in the early 1990s. Economic growth was restored in 1993, reaching an annual rate of 4% in 1993-98. Unlike most other countries in transition, Slovenia has managed in recent years to maintain economic growth while also maintaining its foreign trade balance (no current account deficits in the balance of payments) and relatively sound public finances (no major public finance deficits). Internationally comparable indicators show that Slovenia is closing the gap between itself and the developed countries. In 1998, Slovenia achieved 69% of the average GDP per capita in the European Union (measured in purchasing power). With a GDP of ECU 13 700 per capita (based on purchasing power), Slovenia is catching up with Greece and Portugal, two EU member states.

Table 1: Macroeconomic Indicators

	1994	1995	1996	1997	1998	1999	2000
GDP (USD billion)		18.7	18.9	18.2	19.5	20.01	
GDP per capita (USD)		9 431	9 471	9 161	9 874	10 050	
Gross fixed capital formation (% of GDP)	20	21	22	23.5	24.5		
Inflation (annual, %)	19.8	12.6	9.7	9.1	8.6	6.6	8.9
Gross wage (monthly average, USD)	424	502	579	647	709	777	861
Net wage (monthly average, USD)	269	320	367	409	447	490	542

In 1999, Slovenia began to accelerate the implementation of structural reforms and the process of harmonisation of Slovenian legislation with the *acquis*, but is still lagging in the sphere of bank privatisation. Inflation trends were dictated mostly by tax reform, which nevertheless had no serious effects in terms of liquidity problems and high inflation. The introduction of a value added tax (VAT)

---

[*]   Chief, Housing Department, Ministry of Environment and Spatial Planning, Slovenia

in the second half of last year resulted in rising prices, which were boosted further by the increase in world oil prices. The official exchange rate against the Euro rose by 4.4%. The year 1999 was characterised by strong fluctuations in foreign exchange rates, triggered by the dynamic of exports, where the Bank of Slovenia adjusted the foreign exchange policy to market conditions by intervening in the foreign exchange market. In 1999, economic growth reached 4.9%. The most dynamic activities in 1999 included construction, trade and trade in real estate. Last year's unemployment rate was 13.6%. Economic indicators for 2000 point to economic growth of 3.5% to 4%.

Housing sector overview

Housing needs

Slovenia has a population of 1.913 million, 640 195 households and 652 422 dwellings, of which only 625 697 are occupied. Overall, 66.9% of the population reside in separate residential buildings, and the remainder in multi-apartment buildings. The ratio between owner-occupied dwellings and available rented housing is 88:12. The geographic distribution of available rental housing shows that unoccupied dwellings are most frequently found in locations where there is no demand for them, although overall, the housing supply, particularly of rental housing, does not keep up with demand. One problem is the insufficient occupancy of specific dwellings and multi-apartment buildings due to the poor mobility of the population. The gap between housing supply and demand is widening in Slovenia (14 674 housing units were built in 1981, but a mere 6 200 in 1998); this in turn rapidly increases the prices of newly constructed dwellings and of commercial rentals. The drastic fall in the construction of new housing can be blamed mostly on financial legislation adopted in 1991, which did away with practically all contributions, including those intended for housing construction. In order to boost the housing supply and to lay a solid foundation for the formulation and implementation of an adequate housing policy, the National Assembly adopted the National Housing Program in May 2000. This sets out the premises, conditions and measures of housing policy for 2000-09. According to the National Housing Program, Slovenia will have to build, or otherwise acquire, an annual total of 10 000 housing units, of which 2 000 are envisaged as social-rented dwellings intended for people with the lowest incomes, 2 500 as non-profit-rented dwellings for people who are not at risk socially but who lack the financial capacity to buy or build their own housing, 500 as commercial-rented dwellings, and 5 000 as owner-occupied dwellings and multi-apartment buildings.

Table 2: Statistical Data on Housing

	1994	1995	1996	1997	1998	1999
Total number of dwellings	672 282	677 918	684 146	690 146	696 749	702 949
Dwellings per 1 000 inhabitants	338	341	344	348	352	354
Average surface area per dwelling (m^2)	69.7	70.0	70.3	70.7	95	92
Average surface area per dwelling constructed (m^2)			105.6	105.7		
Dwellings constructed	5 522	5 636	6 228	6 085	6 518	6 200

Privatisation

The Housing Act, adopted in 1991, the year Slovenia gained independence, laid down a legal basis for the abolition of socially owned housing property by introducing privatisation -- enabling all tenants to purchase the dwellings in which they lived at that time at very favourable prices, with a repayment period of up to 20 years. The privatisation process lasted from 1991 to 1993. Prior to privatisation, the ratio between owner-occupied and rented housing was 67:33; after privatisation the ratio reached 88:12 in favour of owner-occupied housing.

The exceptionally high percentage of owner-occupied housing places Slovenia at the top among European countries in that category; this also has certain negative effects, however, since the large number of owners obstructs the effective management and maintenance of buildings. Among the new owners who acquired their property at an exceptionally favourable price are people whose income does not suffice to settle even the most basic liabilities associated with ownership. Municipalities still own 26 000 dwellings, which is 32% of the total number of rental dwellings available.

Of the funds acquired through privatisation, 20% was used to found and finance the operation of the Housing Fund, which has been the largest provider of favourable housing loans in Slovenia. Since 1995, housing funds have also been allocated from the national budget.

Privatisation of land was undertaken based on the Privatisation of Socially Owned Real Estate Act of 1997, which provided that the relevant real asset become the property of the natural or legal person who was using that asset when conditions of socially owned property were in place.

Housing policy

Slovenia's housing policy is set out in the National Housing Program, adopted in May 2000. The public interest in the planning of housing construction, reconstruction and spatial distribution of housing is defined in the Slovenian Constitution, which stipulates that the state shall create opportunities for citizens to obtain proper housing.

Relatively few citizens are capable of successfully addressing their housing problems, either by purchasing dwellings or residential buildings or by renting commercial-rented dwellings. Most citizens can gain access to suitable housing only if the local community or the state plays an active role in this. The provision of social-rented housing for people with the lowest incomes is the responsibility of local communities, which are obliged to finance the provision of social-rented dwellings from municipal budgets. The task of providing non-profit rental dwellings was vested in non-profit housing organisations, that is, legal persons established for the provision and management of non-profit dwellings. These non-profit organisations must contribute 30% to 40% of their own funds, obtaining the remaining amount from the Housing Fund in the form of favourable loans for a period of 25 years. There are currently 60 registered non-profit housing organisations in Slovenia, which are entered in the Register of Non-profit Housing Organisations kept at the Ministry of the Environment and Physical Planning. Non-profit housing organisations must make dwellings built with funds from the Housing Fund available for rent pursuant to the Regulations on Making Non-profit Rented Dwellings Available for Rent. The adoption of the National Housing Program opened up the possibility for municipalities to buy or build social-rented dwellings with funds obtained from the Housing Fund under the same conditions as non-profit housing organisations. Citizens who wish to address their unresolved housing problems by buying or building their own dwellings or residential buildings have the possibility of obtaining a favourable housing loan from the Housing Fund, or of joining the National Housing Saving Scheme. However, the possibility of obtaining a favourable loan from the Housing Fund is available only to those citizens who are resolving their housing problems for the first time, where priority is given to young families, families with a large number of children, disabled persons, and families with disabled family members. Irrespective of their status, all individuals who are prepared to save money in the form of monthly instalments deposited with one of the selected banks can join the National Housing Saving Scheme. In addition, as part of their provision of loans for housing schemes, commercial banks offer increasingly favourable loans, with interest rates that are increasingly competitive with those offered by the Housing Fund.

Every year the Slovenian government allocates a share of budgetary funds to add capital to the Housing Fund; the capital of the Fund currently totals more than SIT 40 billion (USD 174.18 million), which is used for long-term housing loans.

Table 3: Long-term Loans Offered by Commercial Banks for Housing Purposes

Year	1996	1997	1998	1999
Total amount (USD)	173,363,200	209,035,200	267,373,400	366,624,800
Share of the balance (%)	2.2	2.3	2.5	3.0

Types of tenancy

Eighty-eight percent of housing available in Slovenia is owner-occupied, intended to meet the housing needs of owners and their families, while the remaining 12% is rental housing.

Table 4: Types of Tenancy Offered by the Municipal Housing Fund
(data approximate)

Owner-occupied	520 000
Commercial-rented	6 000
Social-rented	5 300
Employer-provided	10 000
Non-profit-rented	80 000

Types of subsidies

The changes made to housing legislation at the end of 1999 instituted two types of subsidies: "object" subsidies and "subject" subsidies. Object subsidies are intended for owners of rental dwellings, and subject subsidies for tenants of rental dwellings, including social-rental and non-profit-rental dwellings.

Mortgage loans

Development of the mortgage loan system in Slovenia

Mortgage crediting in comparison to other European countries is still relatively undeveloped in Slovenia. Banks use mortgage as collateral when providing credit to the corporate sector. Recently, mortgages have also been increasingly used in housing finance, yet their importance in housing finance is still modest.

Data from a survey by the Ministry of Finance in February 2000 indicate that total mortgage loans outstanding at the end of 1999 amounted to USD 945 million, or 4.7% of GDP (Table 5). Lenders are predominantly banks, which account for 95% of all mortgage loans outstanding. Insurance companies account for 5% of such loans outstanding.

Table 5: Mortgage Loans in Slovenia (1998-99)

	1998		1999	
	USD million	% of GDP	USD million	% of GDP
Mortgage loans outstanding	916	4.1%	945	4.7%
Extended by banks	863	3.8%	891	4.4%
To individuals	27	0.1%	48	0.2%
To corporations	836	3.7%	843	4.2%
Extended by insurance companies	53	0.2%	54	0.3%
Housing mortgage loans given to the individuals by banks	27	0.1%	48	0.2%

Source: Survey of MOF, 2000; Insurance Supervisory Agency, 2000

Mortgage loans represent about 8% of total bank assets, and 15% of all bank credits, indicating a relatively small use of mortgage as collateral in securing banks credits. Banks use mortgage as collateral primarily in credits to the corporate sector. Almost 95% of all bank mortgage loans were extended to the corporate sector, and only 5% to individuals. It is worth note that only 3% of all outstanding bank loans to individuals are secured with collateral.

Table 6: Mortgage Loans by Banks by Maturity

	Total		To individuals	
	1998	1999	1998	1999
Up to 1 year	36%	36%	0%	0%
1 to 5 years	45%	41%	9%	9%
5 to 10 years	18%	20%	49%	51%
10 to 20 years	2%	2%	42%	40%
Over 20 years	0%	0%	0%	0%
Total	100%	100%	100%	100%

Source: Survey of MOF, 2000.

Mortgage loan maturity (Table 6 above) is relatively short: 77% of total mortgage loans outstanding are of original maturity of up to five years. As regards mortgage loans to individuals, which are basically housing loans, the maturity is longer. Loans with maturity of up to 10 years account for 60% of all loans. Considering that with housing loans, borrowers generally are interested in the longest possible maturity, we can say that the maturity is relatively short in this field, and that the mortgage housing loan sector in Slovenia has not reached its full potential as regards loan maturity. Long-term mortgage loans with maturity over 20 years do not exist in Slovenia.

The role of mortgage loans in housing loans in Slovenia

Housing loans in Slovenia amounted to USD 500 million in 1999. Banks accounted for almost 60% of the total, making them the most important lender, ahead of the state Housing Fund, with 40% of total outstanding housing loans (Table 7).

Unfortunately, mortgage loans still play a smaller role in housing finance than they do in more developed financial systems. The role of mortgage loans is gaining importance, however. The share of mortgage housing loans in all housing loans nearly doubled from 1998 to 1999, but it is still relatively low at 9.5% (Table 7).

Table 7: Housing Loans to Individuals

	1998		1999	
	USD thousands	Share	USD thousands	Share
Housing loans given to individuals				
By banks	267 523	57.27%	298 528	59.63%
By savings banks	12	0.00%	72	0.01%
By savings and loans undertakings	385	0.08%	426	0.09%
By the Housing Fund	199 229	42.65%	201 642	40.27%
Total	467 149	100%	500 667	100%
Of which: Housing mortgage loans given to individuals by banks (share)	26 992 (5.8%)		47 668 (9.5%)	

Source: Survey of MOF, 2000; Bank of Slovenia, 2000; Housing Fund of the Republic Slovenia.

The relatively uncompetitive mortgage housing loan market is also reflected in very different interest rates charged for such loans by banks. Table 8 shows average rates and range of minimum and range of maximum rates as reported by banks in the survey conducted by Ministry of Finance. It should be noted that these rates are real interest rates which come on top of basic interest rate which is a 12 months average of consumer price index. The latter is currently on the level 0.7% per month.

Table 8: Average Interest Rate of Housing Mortgage Loans to Individuals by Banks (1999)

Average interest rate	Base rate + 5.8%
Minimum interest rate	Base rate + 3.0% - 7.5%
Maximum interest rate	Base rate + 5.2% - 12.0%

Source: Survey of MOF, 2000

Major impediments to development of mortgage loan market in Slovenia

The central problem in real estate finance in Slovenia is the inability for the financial sector to engage in true and long term secured lending, that is, lending where a real asset serves as collateral for loan repayment.

For an asset to serve as collateral, it must be possible as a last resort for the lender to have swift and sure access to ownership of the asset upon non-payment by the borrower. Effective foreclosure and eviction procedures, a sound registration system, and mortgage banking regulations are required for the emergence of efficient mortgage finance for real estate.

All above-mentioned conditions are only partially met in Slovenia. There are already some relevant pieces of legislation in place, however some important are still missing. So, there is legislation regarding credits and crediting. Legislation also defines mortgage loan. On the other hand, there is also legislation regarding bonds its issuing and generally regarding trading in securities. But, both parts are not linked or connected in something what we call mortgage banking legislation. There is no legislation regarding mortgage banking, which would define and regulate issue of mortgage bond and mortgage bank as such. As a consequence banks are not in position to assure long term sources for financing their mortgage credits what on one hand reflects in shorter maturity of mortgage loans and on the other in relatively small proportion of mortgage loans in total loans. If the banks increase

154

mortgage lending with present average maturity of the loan in their credit portfolio they would increase maturity mismatch of their balance sheet positions.

As regards effective foreclosure procedures Slovenia adopted relatively modern legislation two years ago which substantially improved the position of lender in the case of default of the borrower. Nevertheless, the banks still report very long procedures in practice and many of them still feel that legislation is protecting borrowers more then lenders.

The third very important element is land and title register. There is also legislation regarding this in Slovenia and land register has been in place for more than two hundred years. The problem, however, is integrity of the register and the fact that the registry is not up to date. The biggest problem of integrity is that apartments were not entered in the register in the past decades. So, in the case of apartments it is more difficult to get mortgage loan. Also, foreclosure and eviction procedures in cases of not registered real estate are not so clearly and detailly stipulated by the law. So, creditors find themselves in even worse situation in the case that the borrower is unable to repay the loan than in cases that the real estate is registered. As also mentioned, procedures to enter real estate and of signing a mortgage are very lenghty and also relatively expensive.

In the following paragraphs legal and regulatory framework as well as supporting infrastructure is briefly explained to be completed with short description of the project which is currently in progress in Slovenia and has a goal to do away with present, above mentioned, deficiencies which present major impediment in development of mortgage loan market in Slovenia.

The legal and regulatory framework for mortgage lending

The matter of mortgage is regulated in The Basic Property Law Relations Act (1980). It defines, that mortgage is acquired with the entry into Land Registry on the basis of mutual agreement between banks and pledger or in the basis of Law. It also defines the common mortgage, the real estate and its fruits, transfer (cession) of claims with collateral in real estate, cease of mortgage, relations between debtors if there is more then just one, relations between creditors and pledger, etc. The Obligations Act defines general characteristic of the obligations as well as other contracts known, except modern contract such as leasing, factoring, know-how contract etc. Obligations Act also defines credit contract. The Securities Act defines bond, regulates who can issue bonds, what are major elements of a bond, and how the bond can be traded.

Supporting infrastructure – land and title registration

This is defined in Land Registry Act (1995). The Land Registry (LR) is a public book, (information in LR is public and everyone has the right to see it) run by the special division of Court of Justice, which contains the information about real estate, rights of possession and other rights concerning real estate (like mortgage), owners of real estates etc. As mentioned before all these rights are gained, acquired and also limited and ceased with the entry into Land Registry. All these affect mortgages, too. The mortgage is entered in LR only if there is a proof of the existing claim for which the mortgage was established and title to acquire the mortgage (in the Law or the agreement). Submitter of the entry can be either legal or natural person but this person must have the interest to carry out entry in LR. For example, the warrantor is entitled to propose such an entry in LR. Obliteration of mortgage can only be done by a pledger if following conditions are met: the entry of mortgage in LR was done more then 20 years ago; the pledgee is unknown or inaccessible to Court of Justice; no assert to claim was made in the past 20 years. With no opposition in 45 days the Court of Justice allows the obliteration of mortgage in LR. Notwithstanding, the obliteration is always allowed for mortgages older then 25 years (entered in LR more then 25 years ago). The obliteration of mortgage in LR does not affect the existence of claims.

Slovenia has recently also adopted Act Determining Special Conditions for Registering the Ownership of Individual Parts of Buildings with the Land Register (1999) which enable the registration of the ownership of apartments or other individual parts of building in the LR.

Foreclosure

In this area Slovenia has adopted in 1998 new Execution of Judgements in Civil Matters and Insurance of Claims Act, which completely defines execution of judgements in civil matters. Execution on real estate is performed in next steps: entry in the LR, determine the real estate price (evaluation of real estate), sail of this real estate in auction and final the repayment to creditors. On the some real estates the execution is not allowed. The law also regulates Insurance of Claims.

Project on housing finance and mortgage reform

Slovenia is aware of importance of developed mortgage system and mortgage loan market as a cornerstone of effective housing finance. On the other hand developed mortgage market can also substantially contribute to the depth of financial market in Slovenia especially that one of the capital market.

In order to do away with current shortages in the legal and regulatory framework as well as in supporting infrastructure as it is in land and title register Slovenia launched a big Real Estate Modernisation project. The project is also partially supported by the loan of the International Bank of Reconstruction and Development and funds acquired from the PHARE program. The project has a duration of four years and is expected to complete in 2004.

Table 9: Projects Related to Housing Finance and Mortgage Reform

Projects	Objective
Land and building cadastre	Setting up of databases of all buildings and land parcels
Land register	Gradual reduction of the backlog with the assistance of the computerised Land Register
Apartment registration development	Accelerate registration of ownership rights, including common areas, apartments and non-residential properties
Agriculture land use monitoring	Setting up a database of agricultural land use
Real estate tax and valuation system development	Development of a methodology for mass appraisal real estate and the development of a new real estate taxation and valuation system
Housing finance and mortgage reform	Define a suitable system of mortgage banking and prepare legislation regulating the implementation of mortgage banking thus enabling efficient and safe mortgage finance for real estate
Legal framework for property ownership	Harmonisation or levelling of the legislation regarding real estate ownership material rights with European Union material law codes
Project co-ordination and strategic studies	Assurance of operative assistance for the co-ordination of project set-up and implementation

The project covers various aspects of real estate starting with establishing modern fully computerised register which will be complete in scope and will provide for the registration of the most important multipurpose data on all real estate records and last but not least up to date registration with maximum delay in registration of up to 6 days in the year when the project will be completed. Among other aspects covered by the project are also housing finance including development of mortgage banking, valuation of real estate, taxation of real estate and so on.

The Ministry of Finance of the Republic of Slovenia is responsible for the subproject Housing Finance and Mortgage Reform. The aim of the subproject is creating an efficient legal groundwork for the development of mortgage banking in Slovenia in order to pave the way for effective housing financing.

Housing finance systems

Housing Fund

There are different sources of financing for different types of housing supply in Slovenia. The state annually allocates funds from the national budget for adding capital to the Housing Fund, which gives loans for:

- − Purchase or construction of dwellings owned by natural persons;

- − Construction of non-profit-rented dwellings owned by non-profit housing organisations;

- − Construction of social-rented dwellings owned by local communities.

Table 10: Balance Sheet of the Housing Fund   (thousand tolars)

	1999	1998
Cash	70 626	21 936
Securities	83 711	69 923
Placements to banks	1 356 150	2 142 600
Short-term loans	6 851 319	5 319 131
Deferred costs, accrued revenues and other assets	274 279	195 670
Long-term loans	32 456 958	26 797 241
Investments in clients' capital	74 290	69 993
Tangible fixed assets	3 400 961	3 029 551
TOTAL ASSETS	**44 568 294**	**37 646 045**
Long-term liabilities	2 382 691	2 497 203
Short-term deposits	1 537 108	1 611 892
Accrued costs, deferred revenues and other liabilities	295 253	466 427
TOTAL LIABILITIES	**4 215 052**	**4 575 522**
Capital	39 737 142	32 555 851
Reserves	386 872	359 546
Long-term reservations	229 228	155 126
TOTAL CAPITAL	**40 353 242**	**33 070 523**
TOTAL LIABILITIES AND CAPITAL	**44 568 294**	**37 646 045**
Adopting Liabilities	1 238 350	583 784

Table 11: Profit and Loss Statement (thousand tolars)

	1999	1998
Interest revenue	3 553 255	3 268 021
Interest expense	(433 316)	(322 504)
Extraordinary and other revenue	860 533	520 791
Revenue from acquired socially-owned housing units	29 201	35 617
Purchase money gained through Article 130 of the Law	1 581 897	1 522 769
TOTAL REVENUE	**5 591 570**	**5 024 694**
Bad and disputable debts value adjustment	151 453	(62 019)
Other expenses	(611 915)	(640 873)
Long-term reservations	(62 313)	(155 125)
PROFIT*	**5 068 795**	**4 166 677**
Allocation of revenues from investments to revaluation reserve	(2 513 450)	(2 049 924)
CAPITALISATION	**2 555 345**	**2 116 753**

Note: *) Tax exempt

The Housing Fund of the Republic of Slovenia was established on 19 October 1991 by the Housing Law as an independent public corporation in its own right and with its own account. According to the standard classification, the Housing Fund of the Republic of Slovenia belongs to banking agencies, which include banks and other financial institutions.

The Government of the Republic of Slovenia approved the statute, the investment policy, the financial plan, the annual and business reports, and the appointment and acquittal of the director of the Housing Fund of the Republic of Slovenia. The Government of the Republic of Slovenia approved also the Managing Board of the Housing Fund. The Housing Fund of the Republic of Slovenia finances the National Housing Programme, i.e. stimulates the housing construction, the reconstruction and maintenance of housing by granting loans at favourable interest rates to citizens and non-profit housing organisations.

Local communities are allocated additional funds by the state every year, intended for the construction of adequate social-rented dwellings. These funds have been allocated from the national budget to municipalities since 1996 in the amount of USD 6.9 – 8.7 million which is sufficient for an annual 20-300 social-rented dwellings and approximately 2 000 subsidies for rents.

Natural persons who wish to buy a dwelling or residential building may, if they fulfil the conditions determined by law, request for a loan from the Housing Fund, take out a loan with one of the commercial banks, or join the National Housing Saving Scheme.

Non-profit housing organisations must ensure 30 per cent of their own funds for the construction of non-profit-rented dwellings, where the remaining funds are provided by the Housing Fund in the form of favourable loans.

Active housing policy measures and the consistent implementation of the National Housing Programme are expected to increase the total amount of public and private funds intended for the construction, reconstruction and acquisition of dwellings from the current 2.1 per cent (in 2000) to 2.4 per cent of GDP in 2009.

The Housing Fund has hitherto approved nearly 159.000.000 USD of loans with a favourable interest rate taken out by natural persons, while non-profit housing organisations have constructed 2,272 dwellings by taking advantage of the favourable loans financed by the National Fund.

National Housing Saving Scheme

In March 1999 the Slovenian government adopted the National Housing Saving Scheme as the systemic basis for promoting long-term saving, including premium-granting for the purpose of increasing the extent of favourable long-term housing loans.

The National Housing Saving Scheme promotes long-term saving, making it more attractive by granting state-financed premiums and using bank interest for long-term savings deposits. Savers participating in this scheme can obtain a favourable housing loan, given that the banks are obliged to provide savers with a loan which must be at least double the sum they have managed to save and which is subject to a pre-set interest rate. The interest margin amounts to 0.8 per cent, which enables the banks to cover their operating costs incurred by the implementation of the scheme, where banks may not charge additional costs for approving the loan and for its management.

The National Housing Saving Scheme ensures the same interest rate for all savers' long-term savings deposits, and the same interest rate for housing loans on the same basis, depending on the length of the saving and loan period of course.

The system of granting state premiums to savers participating in the National Housing Saving Scheme in the form of adding a specific premium amount at the end of every year of saving increases overall return and thus makes long-term saving more attractive; it also promotes regular monthly saving. The state carries out the National Housing Saving Scheme via the Housing Fund and selected banks.

The right to a housing loan is transferable not only to spouses or partners but to children and grandchildren.

Table 12: National Housing Saving Scheme

Saving period	5 years	10 years
Saving interest	TOM+1.65%	TOM+3.00%
Premium	8.33% of annual savings (1 month saving amount)	10.42 of annual savings (1.25 month saving amount)
Loan period	10 years	20 years
Loan interest	TOM+2.45%	TOM+3.80%

Note: TOM is the basic interest rate

Contracts on saving within the National Housing Saving Scheme began on 1 July 1999. By 30 April 2000, 25 524 contracts had been concluded as part of the National Housing Saving Scheme, as many as 91.2% for a period of five years.

According to data as at 30 April 2000, savers most frequently opt for a monthly instalment of SIT 10 000 (USD 44.6), as 37.6% of all savings contracts have been concluded for this amount. This is followed by SIT 20 000 (USD 89.2), 28.9% and SIT 30 000 (USD 133.8), 18.9%.

Taking into account the balance of concluded contracts and saving amounts as at 30 April 2000, the monthly payment of savers within the National Housing Saving Scheme amounts to SIT 591 million (USD 2.5 million) in total, which means that SIT 601 million (USD 2.7 million) are required for premiums, to be drawn from the national budget by July 2000.

RECENT DEVELOPMENTS IN EUROPEAN MORTGAGE MARKETS

by
Judith Hardt[*]

Introduction

European property and mortgage markets are structurally very different for many reasons. Powerful factors are at work, bringing about significant changes. These factors include:

- Deregulation and consolidation

- The internal market

- The single currency

- The e-economy, and

- Revised bank capital requirements.

Deregulation of the financial services sector continues at an unequal pace across Europe. Consolidation or cross-border mergers and acquisitions are a more recent feature despite reluctance by certain governments to liberalise their markets and a desire to encourage national champions.

The achievement of an internal market in the provision of financial services, including mortgage credit, remains an ongoing process, as does growth in cross-border business such as commercial property lending. The Commission's latest attempt to achieve an internal market, the 1999 Financial Services Action Plan, has, some would argue, an overly ambitious completion date of 2005.

The introduction of a single currency has led to increasing integration of both the Euro-11 and the 15 hitherto autonomous economies. The single currency has major implications for European property markets and the financial systems that serve them. Property and mortgage markets remain intrinsically domestic, although as we move toward the creation of a deep and liquid single capital market this will change with property portfolios valued in Euro across Europe and loan books bought and sold in Euro.

The combined impact of e-commerce and technology on mortgage lenders and mortgage borrowers looks likely to reconfigure the mortgage credit sector and the way lenders do business.

---

*   Secretary General, European Mortgage Federation. The European Mortgage Federation, based in Brussels, is the leading organisation representing mortgage lenders at European level. Its members are mortgage banks, savings banks, building societies and insurance companies. Together they grant over 70% of mortgage loans (residential and commercial) in Europe. This article is based largely on "Hypostat 1989-1999", a 10-year statistical survey on mortgage and property markets in the European Union, published by the European Mortgage Federation.

Since the vast majority of mortgage loans remain on the balance sheets of European lenders the current review of bank capital requirements is of fundamental importance for mortgage lenders.

This paper will therefore seek to highlight the major differences between European mortgage markets and to explain the principal funding mechanisms that serve them; and examine the potential impact that factors of change will have on future developments.

European mortgage markets

Mortgage lending has grown substantially over the past decade

Mortgage lending is a growth industry in Europe. The volume of mortgage loans outstanding in the EU and Norway has increased at a remarkable rate, more than doubling in nominal terms over the period 1989-99, and amounting to around Euro 3.1 trillion at the end of 1999, approximately 33% of GDP. Mortgage markets retain strong national characteristics, however, and their economic importance varies from country to country. The largest markets, in terms of volume outstanding, are Germany, the United Kingdom, France and the Netherlands. The markets that have grown most in 1988-98 are Portugal, Spain, Ireland and the Netherlands. Figure 1 illustrates the phenomenal growth of residential mortgage lending over the last decade.

Figure 1: Residential Mortgage Loans in the EU and Norway[1/]

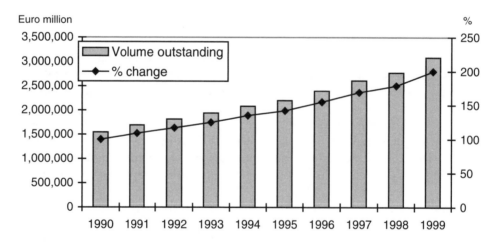

Note: 1) Denmark is not included in 1990 and 1991.
Source: European Mortgage Federation

The impressive expansion of European mortgage markets since the late 1980s is the result of a number of factors, of which deregulation in the financial sector and historically low interest rates (as a consequence of preparation for the introduction of the single currency) stand out. This environment has led to intense competition on mortgage markets across Europe and greater affordability of housing, creating favourable conditions for high demand for mortgage loans.

Increased competition, coupled with rapid technological advances, has pushed mortgage lenders to develop new financial products and new methods to market these products. Product innovation will have to continue to keep up with the needs of increasingly sophisticated and financially astute customers. As the completion of the single currency approaches, Euro-denominated mortgage products that can be sold across borders have emerged. The Internet in particular is seen as an important distribution channel. As more and more customers gain access to the Internet and become comfortable with it, the growth in its use will be rapid. Data from Find, the financial services directory, suggest that personal loans and mortgage loans are the most popular subjects on the Internet since they involve an important financial commitment.

European mortgage markets retain strong national characteristics

The dynamic growth of mortgage markets has outpaced GDP growth over the same period, thereby increasing its weight in the national economies. However, as Figure 2 shows, the importance of mortgage markets differs widely across the different EU member states. In Denmark, the Netherlands, the United Kingdom and Germany, the volume of residential mortgage loans outstanding is equivalent to 50% of GDP or more, in contrast to countries such as Italy, Greece and Austria, where it is equivalent to less than 10%.

Figure 2: Size of Mortgage Markets in the Economy
(Loans outstanding as a % of GDP, end-1998)

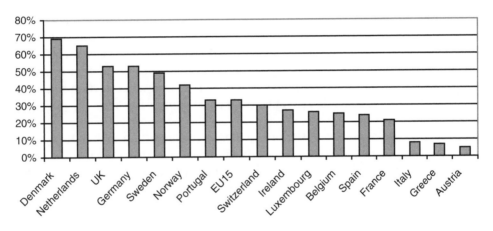

Source: European Mortgage Federation and national sources, Eurostat (GDP figures)

The large differences in the size of the mortgage markets in the national economy reflect the fact that mortgage markets retain strong national characteristics. There are considerable differences across countries due to differences in the types of lenders and consequently also differences in the types of products granted such as the duration of mortgage loans, the type of mortgage interest rate and loan-to-value (LTV) ratios. Some of these differences are illustrated in Table 1 and 2 below and are mostly the result of differences in the political and historical environments and in the legal and regulatory frameworks in which mortgage lenders operate.

Table 1: Typical Mortgage Products

	United Kingdom	Germany	Spain	France
Maturity of a loan	25 years	25-30 years	10-15 years	15 years
Type of interest rate	Reviewable	Renegotiable, Reviewable	+/- 90% reference	50% reference 50% fixed

Source: European Mortgage federation

Table 2: Loans Amount, Maturity and LTV Ratios in European Countries (1999)

Country	Mortgage loan	Original maturity	Loan-to-Value	
	(EUR)	(years)	Average	Absolute max.
Denmark	107 000	30	80%	80%
Germany	174 000	25-30	67%	100%
Greece	35 000	15	43%	
Spain	67 500	15	75%	80%
France	80 000	15	67%	
Ireland	92 000	20	61%	95%
Italy	62 000	10	50%	80%
Netherlands	122 000	30	72%	125%
Austria	105 000	25-30	54%	100%
Sweden	136 000	up to 30	80%	100%
United Kingdom	105 000	25	70%	100%
Norway	108 000		70%	80%

Note: Conversion rates for non-Euro area countries are: EUR/DKK=7.4627, EUR/GRD=330.300, EUR/SEK=8.5625, EUR/GBP=0.6217, EUR/NOK=8.0765.
Source: European Mortgage Federation and national sources

The typical maturity of a mortgage loan can vary from 10 years in some southern countries to as much as 30 years in Denmark or Germany. Different approaches to consumer regulation result in only a handful of products offered in some countries, compared to over 4 000 products currently on offer in the UK. In certain countries, fixed-rate mortgage products predominate. In others, variable rates are more common. In certain countries, the introduction of tight consumer protection rules has resulted in mortgage credit becoming increasingly separated from its sources of funding.

For example, complex rules on the variation of mortgage interest in Belgium, which require the change in interest rate to be linked to government bond indices rather than to the true cost of funds for mortgage lending, introduce an interest-rate risk. If interest rates on the loans and funding source diverge, doing business may become uneconomic. Rules, which limit prepayment penalties charged to consumers, also complicate the funding process, and may induce a dangerous situation of mismatching.

The differences across mortgage markets are also the result of differences in the property market (stock of dwellings, housing tenure structure, owner-occupation, private and social rental, financial instruments used to finance the housing sector, etc.) and in the construction industry (number of building permits issued, housing completions, number of transactions, etc.). The general economic situation will also have a direct impact on the mortgage market. When the economy is growing and employment is rising, households increase their demand for housing and for housing finance. Despite economic convergence in Europe, there remain significant differences in the fundamental macroeconomic variables (GDP, unemployment, inflation, etc.) which shape the development of the mortgage markets.

European mortgage lenders

Figure 3 shows that mortgage loans are granted by a large variety of different types of mortgage lenders. They range from specialised credit institutions (mortgage banks, building societies, Bausparkassen and other specialist mortgage lenders) to savings banks, mutual and co-operative banks, and universally active commercial banks. European mortgage banks are different from US mortgage companies (which are also called mortgage "banks"). These types of lenders are Monetary Financial Institutions (MFIs), and together they grant more than 90% of the mortgage loans in the EU.[1] The remaining mortgage loans are granted by non-MFIs, which include other financial intermediaries (e.g. umbrella companies established to hold securitised mortgage assets through mortgage-backed securities, generally known as special purpose vehicles), insurance corporations and other sectors.

Figure 3: Market Shares by Type of Institution and Type of Lender
(% based on volume outstanding, end-1998)

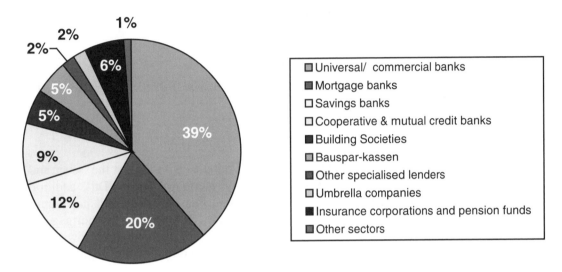

Note: The category "commercial banks" includes mortgage loans funded by the issuance of mortgage bonds that are granted by the largest "mixed" mortgage bank in Germany.
Source: European Mortgage Federation and national sources

Funding of mortgage loans

Retail deposits

Mortgage lenders in Europe use a large variety of methods to fund mortgage loans. The method used depends largely on the type of mortgage lender and varies considerably from one country to another. In the EU, the most common source for mortgage loans is funds obtained via retail deposits in one form or another (deposits with agreed maturity, deposits redeemable at notice or overnight deposits). The European Mortgage Federation estimates that retail deposits fund 62% of the volume of residential mortgage loans outstanding. Other "general" funding instruments will include loans from other MFIs (for instance, a parent company) and bank bonds. Mortgage loans will also rely on the own resources (equity capital) of the lending credit institution and insurance premiums (in the case of insurance corporations). Dedicated savings refers to deposits collected through the *Bausparkassen* system in Germany and Austria. The various funding methods are illustrated in Figure 4. Table 3 provides more detail on retail deposits in respective countries.

Figure 4: Funding Methods Used in the EU
(% based on volumes outstanding, end-1998)

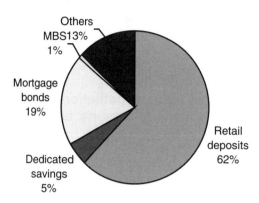

Source: Estimations based on contribution from EMF national members and own calculations

Mortgage bonds

A mortgage bond is a security giving the holder of the bond a claim against the issuer and enjoying a degree of special security because it is backed by mortgage loans. This additional security significantly reduces the risk to the bondholder, meaning that he or she will not require as high a return as with a similar bond not backed by mortgage loans. The issuance of mortgage bonds allows lenders to obtain funding at a reduced borrowing cost (relative to unsecured borrowing) in the capital market. It is therefore a cost-efficient method of funding a mortgage loan. Figure 5 illustrates how mortgage bonds function to finance housing.

Table 3: Overview of mortgage loan funding methods by country (1998)

	Residential mortgage loans outstanding	Own resources (equity)	Specialised funding		General funding	
	(End 1998 in EUR ban)		Mortgage bonds	MBS	Deposits	Other
Austria[1][2]	10	1%	7%	-	38%	54%
Belgium	56	Yes	-	Minor	>50%	Yes
Denmark[1]	122	-	100%	-	-	-
Finland	34	yes	yes	-	90%	10%
France	262	minor	21%[4]	3%	76%	-
Germany	1 013	-	yes	yes	yes	yes
Greece[1]	7	-	-	-	100%	-
Ireland	21	6%	-	0.7%	60%	33%
Italy	81	yes	-	yes	yes	yes
Netherlands	221	4-8%	7%	Minor	major	10%
Norway	54	3%	1%	-	48%	48%
Portugal	32	yes	yes	-	yes	-
Spain	123	5%	6%	3%	major	yes
Sweden[3]	99	yes	70%	-	-	30%
UK	647	-	-	yes	yes	yes

Note: 1) European Mortgage Federation members only, 2) Includes commercial mortgage loans outstanding, 3) Refers to housing credit institutions only, 4) of which 4% points bonds issued by CRH.

Figure 5: Mortgage Bonds

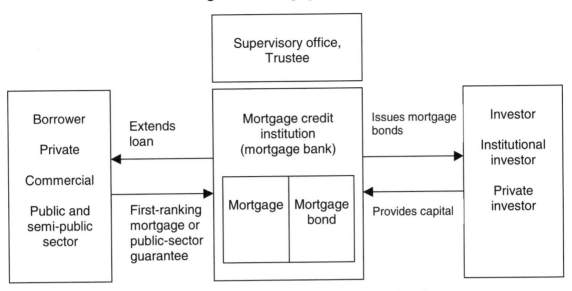

Source: Based on Prof. Dr. Klaus Spremann & Dipl.math.oec. Klaus Kränzlein (1996)

Mortgage-backed securities

Typically, the production of a new mortgage loan follows three phases: originating of loan, grouping or bundling of loans, and funding of loans. Securitisation, however, "unbundles" this process. The credit institution creates a legal entity known as a Special Purpose Vehicle (SPV) and sells mortgage loans that it has originated ("receivables") to this SPV. The purpose of the SPV is to isolate the receivables and the associated cash flows from the originator and to perform certain other closely related operations (such as restructuring of cash flows and credit enhancement). The SPV issues the securities which are sold to investors. (If the originating institution continues to participate, it is usually as "service," that is, a collector of principal and interest payments and processor of other related back-office functions.) This process is illustrated in Figure 6.

Figure 6: Mortgage-Backed Securities

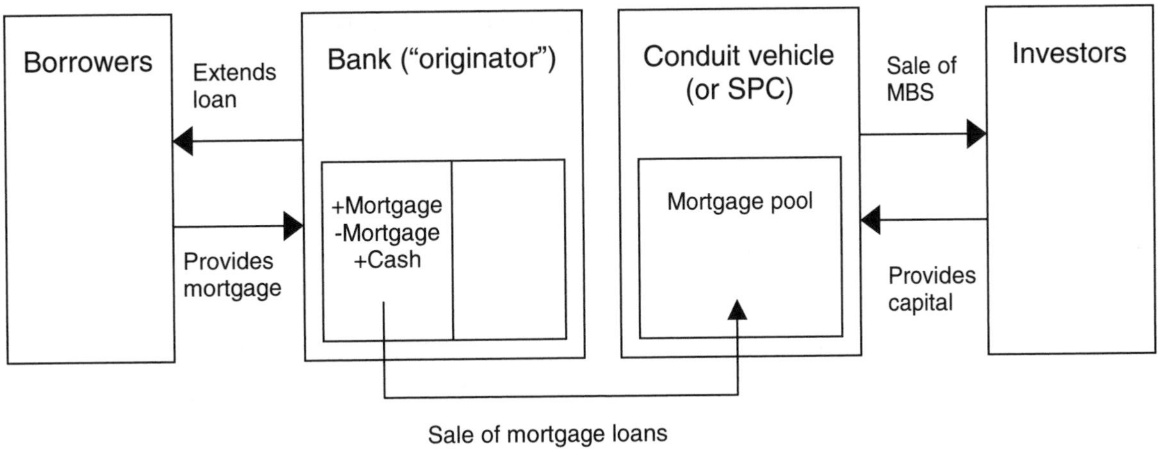

Borrowers	Extends loan	Bank ("originator")		Conduit vehicle (or SPC)	Sale of MBS	Investors
		+Mortgage -Mortgage +Cash		Mortgage pool		
	Provides mortgage				Provides capital	

Sale of mortgage loans

Source: Based on Prof. Dr. Klaus Spremann & Dipl.math.oec. Klaus Kränzlein (1996)

Figure 7: European MBS: Market Size and Importance as a Funding Instrument (1999)

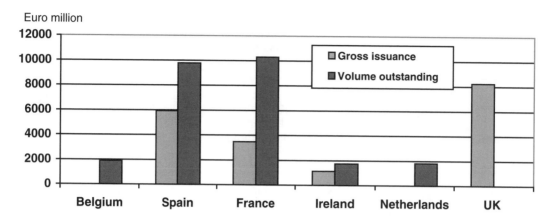

Note: Belgium refers to 1998.
Source: European Mortgage Federation

The Bausparkassen system

Contract savings for housing (CSH) systems provide housing finance with funding obtained from loan-linked savings deposits. CSH programs may be offered through banking institutions, as in France, or specialised savings and loans institutions, known as *Bausparkassen*, in Austria and Germany. Participants in these systems are eligible for subsidies and/or tax relief from the state upon completion of the savings contract. The participant agrees to save an agreed amount over a prescribed period in return for a commitment by the lender to provide a loan, at specified terms, for the purchase or renovation of owner-occupied housing. The contract typically entitles the saver to a mortgage loan in the future at below-market rates. Contract savings programs offered through general depository institutions are open systems, as the institutions can draw on other sources of funds to meet the contract loan commitments. *Bausparkassen* are closed systems reflecting the fact that contract loans are funded almost entirely by contract savings deposits.

Likely future developments

The current situation of fragmented mortgage and property markets is increasingly subject to external factors of change that should, in the long run, lead to a greater degree of integration.

Deregulation and consolidation

Until the 1980s, housing finance systems tended to be tightly regulated by national authorities, in particular because of the danger of mismatching in long-term finance but also because many governments wanted to favour access to home-ownership at the lowest possible cost.

There were restrictions on the activities of institutions (Italy), balance sheet restrictions (UK), restrictions of specific mortgage instruments to specific institutions (France, Germany) or regulations of the terms of mortgage contracts (Belgium).

Increasingly, deregulation has removed such restrictions and in the process changed the nature of financial institutions offering mortgage credit. In the United Kingdom, many building societies have converted into banks, while in Italy, a new law abolished the principle of specialisation and transformed all mortgage lenders into universal banks allowed to engage in all types of banking activity. As a consequence, the type of institution offering mortgage credit is no longer as important as the types of mortgage product which are offered.

As a counterbalance to increased deregulation and liberalisation, regulators and super-regulators such as the UK's Financial Services Authority are increasingly aware of the need for improved supervisory co-ordination and review in the light of the growth of cross-border financial services conglomerates and the operation of e-banks outside the market for which they have been licensed.

As a measure of consolidation in the EU banking market, the European Central Bank estimated in April 2000 that the share of bank assets accounted for by the top 20 European banks had risen from 35% in 1997 to 41% in early 1999.

The internal market

The internal market program, which was completed in 1992, had a significant impact on mortgage markets across the EU. Markets once regulated on a national level were suddenly subject to EU directives. In particular, the solvency ratio and own-funds directives had a significant impact on mortgage credit institutions in Europe.

In principle, the single market program should have led to the opening up of national mortgage markets to Europe-wide competition. The principle of home country control should have meant that mortgage lenders would be free to provide services across EU borders, but be regulated by their own national supervisory authorities. In practice, the single market for mortgage credit has not really developed, since governments have not been keen to allow lenders from member states where consumer protection legislation is less strict to compete on an unequal basis with domestic lenders. Further, the absence of tax harmonisation has resulted in fiscal obstacles to cross-border mortgage credit.

Indeed, in its latest progress report on its 1999 Financial Services Action Plan, the European Commission seems to have shifted its focus from retail to wholesale aspects of financial services. This may be a recognition by the Commission of the difficulties inherent in trying to complete an internal market for mortgage credit and that such an objective remains an ongoing process -- a process that may be assisted by other factors of change such as e-commerce and the introduction of the single currency on 1 January 2002.

The single currency

The introduction of a single currency, more than any other event, is changing the face of mortgage lending in the European Union. The Euro will:

- Eliminate exchange rate risks;
- Reduce transaction costs;
- Improve price transparency; and
- Reduce interest rate risk through economic policy co-ordination.

In the "core" countries the single currency has seen maintenance of the environment of low inflation, low interest, long-term views and stability. In the "peripheral" countries such as Ireland, inflation has re-emerged. Low interest rates have created concerns in several countries with respect to asset price inflation, including increasing house prices. In the run-up to the launch of the single currency, governments were concerned over their loss of control over interest rates as a tool of economic policy, the view being that one size does not fit all

The introduction of the single currency has affected capital markets. There is now an established Euro-denominated bond market, which is less volatile than the earlier national markets. This should favour more long-term instruments such as mortgage bonds and MBS. The policy of governments as well as the approach of private issuers is geared toward the creation of as deep, liquid and transparent a capital market as possible. The current nationally based securities markets are being transformed into a single market with common conventions as stock exchanges merge. The reduction of government debt has also left more room for private debt instruments, which had been crowded out of the market. Finally, the progressive integration of national capital markets into a single supranational marketplace offers the potential for economies of scale hitherto impossible in the smaller economies. In particular, this should favour the development of techniques such as securitisation.

It is also likely that access to cheap, low-interest long-term funding on the capital markets will favour recourse to fixed-rate funding instruments such as mortgage bonds and MBS, to the detriment of variable rate instruments in the form of savings deposits. Higher yield instruments increasingly attract savers, and this has led to the drying up of the traditional funding instruments of savings and co-operative banks. In addition, mortgage bonds have been included by the European Central Bank in its Tier 1 list of eligible assets for use in open-market policy. As outlined elsewhere in this paper, a number of Member states are working to adapt their mortgage bond legislation to ensure that it conforms to the Tier 1 criteria.

Changes on the capital markets are feeding through to the mortgage markets. Indeed, mortgage markets underwent a fundamental change resulting from the convergence of economies in advance of the locking together of the currencies. Interest rates on mortgage loans in the 11 participating countries have converged considerably, and until recently had fallen to record low levels.

The single currency should lead to greater cross-border opportunities for mortgage lenders, and more competition will benefit consumers. The lack of exchange rate risk and greater price transparency open up opportunities for borrowers to take out loans in other Member states, and the remaining obstacles to cross-border mortgage lending are becoming more apparent. Considerable efforts are being made by the European Commission to liberalise and harmonise financial services, which could lead to greater integration of markets.

Finally, such developments may result in change on the property markets. Stable economic conditions should result in greater price stability of housing, while lower interest rates should improve access to owner-occupied housing. The loss of national government control over monetary policy may, however, lead to governments making greater use of fiscal instruments to control the economy, and the property sector risks being particularly affected.

The "e-economy"

The Internet is playing a decisive role in opening up European mortgage markets, as it allows EU-wide market penetration at relatively little cost (no expensive branch network needs to be established). On-line mortgage lending is currently a growth area, with both existing and new players looking to build their share of on-line originations from the initial borrower inquiry through to the granting of a mortgage loan.

In the US, more than 15% of new mortgage loans are initiated through the Internet. According to a study by Forrester Research, the American Internet consultants, the US online mortgage market is expected to grow from USD 18.7 billion to more than USD 91 billion in 2003. Forrester further predicts that mortgages will account for more than 10% of the whole on-line market. Almost two-thirds of American lenders expect to be able to process credit applications on-line by the end of this year. More generally, Datamonitor predicted in April 2000 that the number of Europeans using Internet banking would grow by 30% to more than 20 million users by 2004.

The Internet is, of course, a vehicle for price transparency and more informed consumer choice. At present it is more often a source of information for comparison-shopping than a means to take out a mortgage loan.

Although e-commerce and the Internet are primarily a distribution means to target borrowers and sell mortgages, they also allow lenders to raise funds from depositors. The jury, however, is still out on the success or suitability of using an Internet bank for the latter purpose. The Internet may become instrumental in the globalisation of the capital markets. Already there is evidence that housing markets are becoming global and that the single currency is accelerating the integration of property markets in Europe.

Increasingly, EU countries are adopting US mortgage securitisation models. This encourages standardisation and may create opportunities for American lenders and mortgage technology vendors to expand into these markets. Likewise, it could benefit the funding side by accelerating the standardisation and marketing of various funding instruments to investors.

The European Commission's directive on certain legal aspects of electronic commerce that was adopted in May 2000 is the first attempt to regulate, at a European level, one of the fastest developing fields of the economy. Member states have 18 months to modify their national legislation accordingly.

Indications are that the mortgage industry will initially take advantage of the new information and communications technologies to speed up home buying, accelerate the mortgage process and improve transparency, but it will take some time before cross-border mortgage lending develops fully and benefits from an appropriate legal framework.

Revision of bank capital requirements

The Basel Committee on Banking Supervision and the European Commission are currently reviewing bank capital requirements. The current discussions in Basel and Brussels will lead to a new set of prudential rules that will apply to all credit and financial institutions. The new regulatory own funds requirements are likely to revise the current risk-weighting scheme by taking into consideration a broader range of risks (credit and market risks but also operational, legal and reputation risks). Internal rating, market discipline and supervisory related issues are also a focus of both regulators.

The review of regulatory capital requirements is of fundamental importance for mortgage lenders in Europe since the vast majority of their mortgage loans remain on-balance sheet and are capital intensive (i.e. 50% or 100% weightings).

This contrasts with the system in the United States, where more than 50% of mortgage loans are removed from the balance sheet through securitisation, thus freeing up the lender's own funds. US government-sponsored enterprises (Ginnie Mae, Fannie Mae and Freddie Mac) buy most of the loans from mortgage lenders and sell them into the secondary mortgage market.[2] In so doing they convert 50% risk weight assets into 0% (Ginnie Mae) or 20% (Fannie Mae, Freddie Mac) risk-weighted MBS. This creates an incentive for lenders to "swap" their mortgage portfolios for lower-risk-weight MBS portfolios. The GSEs are also _not_ subject to the same own fund requirements as mortgage lenders. Thus the total capital held against securitised assets is substantially less in the US than in Europe.[3] These powerful agencies also benefit from government support that reduces their funding costs by as much as 50 basis points. The existence of these agencies is a major reason for the high percentage of loans securitised in the US.

Europe's secondary mortgage markets mirror the diversity and the history of primary mortgage markets. Mortgage bonds issued by specialised mortgage banks and credit institutions have been a major funding instrument in several countries for more than 100 years. Mortgage banks, as portfolio lenders, fund their mortgage assets through the issuance of mortgage bonds, and have to rely solely on their financial strength and strict regulations to ensure the soundness of their mortgage bonds. Mortgage-backed securities issuers rely on the quality of the collateral and various structuring techniques to create high-quality securities. In Europe, there is competition between on-balance and off-balance sheet instruments on the basis of the intrinsic quality of the issuing institution and the securities issued. The emergence and standardisation of mortgage financing instruments should be encouraged as European lenders use a wide variety of methods from mortgage bonds to securitisation to fund their mortgage loans.

The current proposals, influenced by the American off-balance sheet approach, could put European mortgage lenders at a disadvantage. In particular, current proposals that would accord a lower risk weight (20%) for highly rated mortgage securities could create opportunities for capital arbitrage and could put portfolio lenders at a competitive disadvantage as it would be less capital intensive to buy mortgage and asset-backed securities than to have a mortgage book. The vast majority of mortgage loans in Europe (over 98%) remain on the banks' balance sheets and are capital-intensive (i.e. 50% or 100% weighting).

Apparently there is agreement on the part of the regulators to maintain the current regulatory treatment (i.e. 10% weighting) of mortgage bonds according to Article 11 (2) of Directive 89/647/EEC on the Solvency Ratio. The European Mortgage Federation believes that the weighting of mortgage-backed securities should relate to the credit risk and there should be no supervisory discrimination between instruments except on the basis of a comparison of credit quality.

Conclusion

European primary mortgage markets have been growing more quickly than GDP and have proved surprisingly resistant to change, though both mortgage and property markets are tightly governed by national law. Differences in tax and subsidy rules, consumer protection rules and the fact that mortgage lending has always been considered as a local business, with various ways of providing mortgage credit, will mean that the achievement of a single European market in the mortgage credit field can only take place in the longer term.

However these structural differences are increasingly subject to the factors of change, which strive to impose a certain level of integration.

Following the introduction of the single currency, indications are that we are moving toward a European capital market in which the funding of house purchases will be an integral part of that market, via funding instruments ranging from mortgage bonds to mortgage-backed securities. Savings or retail deposits remain the most common way to access funds for lending purposes; but in the low-interest-rate environment existing up until recently they have become increasingly subject to competition.

Mortgage bonds, the second most popular source of funds, and mortgage-backed securities, both specialist mortgage instruments, are proving particularly attractive in this new environment. The development of a single capital market has led to new opportunities for the wholesale funding of mortgages, resulting in new products on the primary markets.

Legislative progress in the creation of a single market for the provision of mortgage credit has been painstakingly slow. On the other hand, one has to be optimistic about the likely impact of the business drivers of changes, such as the Internet and the single currency on a macro level, and cross-border commercial property lending on a micro level.

The review of bank capital requirements being undertaken by the Basel Committee and the European Commission will influence the business environment faced by mortgage lenders for the next 15 years at least. How funding instruments are treated is of crucial importance for lenders in both the European Union and the accession countries.

NOTES

1. In 1997, the European Mortgage Federation classified the different types of mortgage lenders according to the ESA95 framework. ESA95 is the European System of national and regional accounts 1995, which was introduced by a Council Regulation of 25 June 1996. It provides a methodology for common standards, definitions, nomenclatures and accounting rules, intended to be used for compiling accounts and tables to be drawn up on comparable bases for the purposes of the Community. The Regulation is binding in its entirety and directly applicable in all Member states. Mortgage lenders are classified as follows: (i) **Monetary Financial Institutions (MFI)** includes universal/commercial banks ("commercial banks"), mortgage banks/mortgage credit institutions ("mortgage banks"), savings banks, mutual and co-operative banks, building societies, *Bausparkassen*, other specialised mortgage lenders; (ii) **other financial intermediaries** (with the exclusion of insurance companies and pension funds) refers to umbrella companies established to hold securitised mortgage assets through mortgage-backed securities, generally known as special purpose vehicle ; (iii) **insurance companies and pension funds** refers to insurance companies; and (iv) **Other sectors.**

2. Ginnie Mae is an agency of the US Government, and its securities benefit from a full faith and credit guarantee. Fannie Mae and Freddie Mac are government-sponsored enterprises (GSEs) that are owned by the public and benefit from certain charter advantages. They issue corporate guarantees which are widely viewed as being implicitly backed by the Government.

3. For example 2% against a Fannie Mae MBS (1.6% by the lender and 0.4% by Fannie Mae) as compared to 4.8% for loans funded by mortgage bonds in Europe (4% by the mortgage bank and 0.8% by the mortgage bond investor.)

INTERNATIONAL MODELS OF HOUSING FINANCE: HOUSING SYSTEMS IN THE WESTERN AND TRANSITION ECONOMIES

by

Mark Stephens[*]

Introduction

One of the striking features of housing finance systems in the West is the degree of diversity. Despite developments such as the liberalisation of capital flow and the development of a single market and currency within most of the European Union, housing finance systems have remained robustly reluctant to converge. This is important because housing finance systems play an important role in shaping each country's wider housing system. Since the form that the wider housing system takes has important social and economic consequences, it follows that the development of housing finance systems is far more than a technical exercise. Hence, the way in which housing finance systems are developed in transition economies will be of crucial importance in shaping the housing systems of the future.

This chapter illustrates some of the options available to transition economies by identifying the key features of housing finance systems found in the Western capitalist economies. These features help to explain the kind of housing systems that have emerged. Three types of housing system (or model) are identified -- the Southern European model, the Homeowner model, and the Balanced Tenure model. Of course, not every country fits neatly into these models. But the countries selected share sufficient characteristics to be discussed in this way. The distinct social and economic impacts of each are discussed. The chapter then discusses these systems in relation to the transition economies.

The Southern European model

The countries of Southern Europe exhibit very high levels of owner-occupation, ranging from about 68% in Italy to nearly 80% in Spain. However, these very high levels are not the product of particularly well-functioning housing finance systems. Rather, they are the legacy of constrained tenure choice. Typically, private rental sectors were weakened severely by decades of rent controls, the impacts of which were exacerbated by periods of high inflation. A notable feature of the Southern European countries is that significant social rental sectors were never developed, and are of little importance. In part this reflects the distinctive welfare regime in these countries, which some have labelled "rudimentary" but which is more accurately characterised as "family-based." In other words, the state has traditionally played a relatively minor role in welfare, which instead has been provided by extended families.

---

[*] Lecturer, Department of Urban Studies, University of Glasgow, UK

Nevertheless, the state has been active in housing finance systems. Spain, for example, has a history of privileged funding for housing development. Banks were obliged to set aside funds for state-favoured projects, including housing, until the 1980s. These subsidies were aimed at promoting construction, although they became more related to individual circumstances in the 1970s. Due to rent control, construction normally took the form of owner occupation. In the 1980s, the system was transformed into one whereby mortgages are provided with interest rates subsidised by the state and related to household income. However, it is sometimes necessary to consider whether interest subsidies are needed because the (inflationary) economy demands high interest rates, or whether housing is fundamentally unaffordable without subsidy. The widespread prepayment of subsidised mortgages in favour of market-based loans after Spain's currency devaluation in the early 1990s suggests that inflation, or inflationary expectations, have contributed to the front-end loading problem that often prompts subsidy.

Table 1: Characteristics of the Southern European Model

	Level of Owner Occupation (%)	Loan-to-value Ratio (%)	Loan Duration (years)	Mortgage Debt (% of GDP)
Spain	78	75	20	22
Italy	68	40	15	7
Greece	76	70-75	15	6

Source: Maclennan *et al.* (1998)

As democracy was restored in Spain and as the country prepared to join the European Community, the Spanish Government made a concerted effort to deregulate the finance system. Compulsory investment ratios were abolished. The state mortgage bank was privatised. There was a huge expansion of mortgage credit, as the system moved toward market pricing.

However, weak foreclosure laws in Southern Europe have hindered the development of housing finance systems. In Italy, the foreclosure process can take as long as seven years. Inadequate foreclosure systems are a factor in explaining the relatively low loan-to-value ratios found in these countries (40%-75%), the relatively short duration of mortgages (15-20 years) and the low level of mortgage debt in the economy (as low as 7% of GDP in Italy).

The Southern European model has important social and economic consequences. The most important is that there is limited access to mortgage credit. Given the lack of tenure choice, the limited access to mortgage credit also implies limited access to housing. Unsurprisingly, informal lending, especially on an intergenerational basis, is a crucial feature of the Southern European countries. This is inefficient and inequitable. It is inefficient because those able to lend may not be related to those wishing to borrow. It is inequitable because a key determinant of access to housing is luck of birth, with advantage and disadvantage passing down the generations.

Some commentators have noted the rising age at which children leave the parental home as a result of being unable to access housing, as well as the postponement of marriage and having children. The housing finance system appears to contribute to demographic ageing, which in turn causes problems for funding pensions.

The low levels of mortgage debt in the Southern European countries means that housing is relatively detached from the macroeconomy, in contrast to the countries that belong to the Homeowner model. However, inefficiency in the housing finance system seems likely to contribute to labour market immobility, although this may be offset by the development of private rental housing in urban areas for the most mobile sections of the work force.

The Homeowner model

The Homeowner model is found in the mainly English-speaking countries, where owner-occupation levels are generally 65% to 70%. A culture of owner-occupation exists in these countries: owner-occupation is regarded as being somehow a morally superior tenure, which carries connotations of having a stake in society. In the United States, home-ownership is seen as an important component of the "American Dream." In the United Kingdom, politicians talk about the "property-owning democracy."

Table 2: Characteristics of the Homeowner Model

	Level of Owner Occupation (%)	Loan-to-value Ratio (%)	Loan Duration (years)	Mortgage Debt (% of GDP)
Canada	64	95	30	41.2
UK	68	100	25	57
US	67	95	30	54

Source: Maclennan *et al.* (1998)

Although these countries now have liberalised housing finance systems, with clearly established property rights and generous valuation systems, it would be wrong to attribute the growth of owner occupation to these characteristics alone. In the United Kingdom, privatisation of state-owned housing has added some two million homes to the homeowner total in the past 20 years. Tenants of local authorities have been able to purchase their houses at discounts of up to 70%, the generosity of the scheme being made possible by the erosion of housing debt by inflation, the legacy of a significant stock of inter-war social rental housing, and the use of rent pooling. Australia and Canada have operated interest subsidy schemes for homeowners in the past. Fundamental housing affordability has also been a factor in the growth of owner-occupation, especially in the 1950s and 1960s. For example, the availability of cheap suburban land and the growth of car ownership assisted the growth of home-ownership in the United States and Australia.

It is clear that the state plays an active role in promoting home-ownership in these countries. In the United Kingdom, tenure choice has been restricted by rent controls, which have reduced the private rental sector to the smallest in the European Union. Many once privately rented properties were sold by landlords into owner-occupation, sometimes to the tenants themselves. While mortgage interest tax relief is no longer available in Canada, Australia and the United Kingdom, homeowners' imputed rental income and capital gains are commonly untaxed. These factors tend to lower the real user cost of capital for owner-occupiers and place it in a privileged position in relation to renting and other investments.

The high loan-to-value ratios seen in these countries, which certainly help to widen access to mortgage credit, are derived in part from the favourable (for the lender) legal framework for property rights and foreclosure. However, they are also achieved by credit enhancement (loan insurance), which takes both public and private forms. In the United States and Canada, state institutions (such as the US Federal Housing Agency) insure some mortgages, and quasi-state organisations (such as Fannie Mae) purchase these loans and securities them. In the United Kingdom, high loan-to-value ratio loans (over 75%) are generally covered by a system known as mortgage indemnity guarantees (MIGs). The borrower pays a premium to protect the lender from losses arising from default and foreclosure.

The Homeowner model has clear limitations. Owner-occupation levels seem to peak at around 70%. Attempts are being made in the United States to raise owner-occupation rates very marginally through education and counselling programs, particularly targeted at low-income and minority ethnic groups. The development of sub-prime lending and the possibility of greater use of risk pricing can have a limited and marginal impact. Indeed, evidence from Australia suggests that the fundamental unaffordability of owner-occupied housing is leading to falling homeowner rates among younger households. Consequently, the 70% homeowner rate, maintained for 30 years, may soon begin to fall. It is therefore important to recognise that an efficient finance system accompanied by favourable supporting institutional structures (legal and valuation systems) cannot overcome the two inherent barriers to owner occupation: the front-end loading of costs faced by everyone using mortgage finance, and what might be described as fundamental or long-term unaffordability for other households, arising from low lifetime incomes.

The Homeowner model does indeed extend access to home-ownership by increasing the availability of mortgage credit, but not to everyone. Consequently, it has distinctive social and economic consequences. High loan-to-value ratios and the expansion of home-ownership to lower-income households increase the risk of default and foreclosure. This affects only a small proportion of borrowers in any one year, yet it adds up to a significant social problem. In the recession of the early 1990s, 10% of the households accepted as being homeless by local authorities in England were former owner-occupiers. The role of the state in facilitating mortgage protection insurance, or in providing social assistance for mortgage payments, has been a subject of debate in Australia and the United Kingdom. The growth of low-income home-ownership in the United Kingdom arising from the sale of social rental dwellings to sitting tenants has raised questions of the "sustainability" of home-ownership, in particular the danger that the stock may deteriorate over time if owners cannot afford to pay for repairs and maintenance.

Tenure polarisation is a particular problem that arises in countries that have adopted the Homeowner model. By stretching home-ownership down the income scale, renting, especially social renting, becomes a strong indicator of poverty. Evidence from the European Union reveals the extent to which social rental housing is residualised in the United Kingdom in comparison to France, the Netherlands and Germany (Stephens and Burns, forthcoming). The dilemma for public policy is that the more home-ownership is extended down the income scale, the greater the exclusion of those who still cannot gain access to it.

The links between the housing system and the macroeconomy have become more pronounced over the past two decades. Liberalised finance systems may also facilitate housing market instability. There has been a history of house price volatility in countries that deregulated their mortgage systems in the 1980s. While some of this arose from the sudden expansion of mortgage credit, the nature of housing as a part-asset makes it ripe for speculative bubbles. These speculative bubbles are likely to be exacerbated when the supply-side of the housing system is impaired by any combination of the following: scarce land supply, restrictive planning laws, and a construction industry suffering from inefficiencies or labour shortages. Further pressures occur in "hot spots" as a result of uneven economic development.

While a developed housing finance system does not provide the kind of barriers to mobility found in the Southern European model, especially when transaction costs are low, the differential performance of regional housing markets can contribute to immobility. Workers in areas of low house price inflation may be unable to afford housing in areas of high house price inflation; workers in low demand housing areas may be unable to sell their houses in order to move; and workers in areas of high house price inflation may be reluctant to move to areas of low house price inflation for fear that they will be unable to afford to return to the high inflation areas. This "mobility trap" was observed by John Muellbauer in the 1980s.

The role of personal housing wealth is also important, both for individuals who may convert housing wealth into income, sometimes to supplement pensions, and the economy, which may experience increased levels of consumption. The vastly different roles of home-ownership, mortgage-related debt, its interest rate structure, and housing equity within the European Union pose a particular challenge for macroeconomic management under the European single currency. This issue is discussed further in Maclennan, *et al.* (1998; 2000).

The Balanced Tenure model

Several European countries display characteristics of the Balanced Tenure model, but the best example is Germany. The key feature of the Balanced Tenure model is that owner-occupation is at much lower levels than in most other Western countries. It is below 40% in Germany (and is only around 42% in the former West Germany). Owner-occupation is balanced by a large and vibrant private rental sector, which, in the case of Germany, is about the same size as the owner-occupied sector.

Table 3: Characteristics of the Balanced Tenure Model

	Level of Owner Occupation (%)	Loan-to-value Ratio (%)	Loan Duration (years)	Mortgage Debt (% of GDP)
Germany	38	80	30	51
Austria	54	80	30	32

Source: Maclennan *et al.* (1998)

This situation arises in part from a housing policy that has treated the privately rented sector more favourably than in other countries -- in terms of rent controls and taxation. Additionally, the private rental sector was enlisted to provide *social* rental housing. Private landlords received subsidised loans, but had to rent properties at controlled rents with a limited rate of return. However, when the loan was repaid, the landlord becomes free to let the property on free-market terms. Thus, the private rental sector is continually replenished by properties that used to count as being *social* rentals. The slow-down in the rate of construction of social rental dwellings since the 1970s means that there is now a rapid decline of the social rental sector.

The German finance system is also regulated in such a way as to restrict access to mortgage credit. Finance is provided by specialist institutions -- mortgage banks, savings banks and *Bausparkassen*. These are now generally located within integrated ownership structures that produce packaged loans. The mortgage banks are efficient, but conservative. Legally, loan-to-value ratios are limited to 60% on loans backed by mortgage bonds, and the valuation system is conservative. Germany employs the "mortgage lending value" system, which attempts to establish the long-term value of a property. This is generally lower than the market value approach used in many English-speaking countries. Further finance can be gained from contract-savings schemes run by *Bausparkassen*, whereby a savings contract is rewarded with a cheap loan (and sometimes a bonus for lower income groups). The availability of a time-limited (to eight years) depreciation allowance has also sent out a powerful financial incentive to households to postpone house purchase. This was replaced by a time-limited tax credit (with high income limits) in 1996, which avoids some of the discrimination experienced by low-income groups under the previous system. It should perhaps be added that Germany's record of low inflation probably has created less of a financial incentive for home-ownership than exists in countries with higher rates of owner-occupation, although the front-end loading effects would be lower.

The Balanced Tenure model suppresses demand for owner-occupation (by encouraging households to delay entry into owner occupation) and limits access to it (by restricting access to mortgage credit). It does, however, provide choice by creating a sustainable private rental sector, which is sometimes absent in the Homeowner and Southern European models. The presence of a viable private rental sector also means that the restrictions on mortgage credit do not have the same adverse social effects on household formation that is a feature of the Southern European model. It also has the advantage that there is less tenure polarisation than is found in the English-speaking countries. The housing market tends to be more stable than in the English-speaking countries, and the links between housing wealth and consumption are weaker.

The transition economies

While there were differences between the housing systems established by the Communist governments in Central and Eastern Europe, they shared a similar logic, which has led some academics to refer to an "East European model of housing" (Tosics and Hegedüs, 1998). At the heart of these systems were state-dominated social rental systems, characterised by very low rents, administrative allocation systems, and often a reliance on non-traditional building technologies. Compared to the West, housing was relatively homogenous, and with minimal rents it once was described as being "a ration provided with wages" (Donnison and Ungerson 1982, p.107). This reflected the system of "individual" wages in the socialist system that necessitated the supply of heavily subsidised essential goods and services (in contrast to the "family" wage commonly established in Western Europe). In virtually all of the Central and Eastern European countries, a degree of "marketisation" within the housing systems was encouraged in the 1970s and 1980s, once it became clear that the state would be unlikely to meet the housing aspirations of the whole population. Marketisation took various forms, but included the encouragement of housing co-operatives, especially in more urban economies such as Czechoslovakia, East Germany and Poland, and the promotion of self-built owner-occupied housing in Hungary, and subsidies for owner-occupation in more rural economies, such as Yugoslavia, Bulgaria and Romania (Donnison and Ungerson, 1982).

The most common theme in housing reform in the transition economies has been the privatisation of state housing, normally sold to existing tenants at below-market prices. The extent of privatisation varied considerably between countries. In Albania, more than 90% of the stock was sold to sitting tenants in the first half of the 1990s; in Romania, around 85%. Conversely, the Czech Republic, Slovakia and Poland privatised no more than 6% of their social rental housing in this way (Hegedüs *et al.*, 1996).

In relation to the models presented earlier in this chapter, it appears that two distinct housing systems are emerging among these transition economies: one with distinct parallels with the Southern European model and one that shares some of the characteristics of the Balanced Tenure model.

Combined with the legacy of (usually) rural (and sometimes suburban) owner-occupation, privatisation has raised owner-occupation to internationally high levels in many of the transition economies (Table 4). The Southeast European countries, along with Hungary, Slovenia and Lithuania, fall into this category. Indeed, home-ownership in each of these countries (Lithuania excepted) is higher than in any member state of the European Union.

These countries appear to exhibit some of the key features of the Southern European model, notably the combination of a high level of home-ownership with housing finance systems that have yet to be fully developed. Hence, the ability to access intergenerational transfers has become a key determinant of a household's ability to enter owner-occupation. With vibrant private rental sectors failing to emerge (they are often restricted to serving niche markets such as wealthy foreigners) and increasingly residualised social rental sectors, the ability to access owner-occupied housing coincides with the ability for a household to form. Within these countries, mobility is also likely to be problematic.

Table 4: Tenure in Some Transition Economies (1994)

	Public Rentals	Private Rentals	Other Rentals (Co-ops)	Owner-Occupied	Other (Co-ops)
Czech Republic	27.6	4.7	6.1	42.2	19.4
Hungary	13.0	1.0	-	86.0	0.0
Poland	25.4	5.2	13.5	41.7	14.2
Slovakia	26.0	0.5	0.5	51.6	21.4
Slovenia	8.9	3.4	0.0	87.7	0.0
Central-East Europe	23.1	3.9	8.2	52.0	12.8
Albania	2.0	-	0.0	98.0	0.0
Bulgaria	6.6	3.2	0.3	89.7	0.0
Croatia	10.6	3.7	-	84.5	1.2
Romania	7.8	3.0	0.2	88.9	0.2
SE Europe	7.6	3.1	0.2	89.1	0.3
Estonia	56.0	5.0	3.0	30.0	6.0
Latvia	54.0	5.0	2.0	39.0	0.0
Lithuania	12.9	8.5	0.0	78.6	0.0
Baltic countries	36.4	6.5	1.3	54.4	1.3
Total Central and Eastern Europe	18.6	3.8	5.9	64.2	7.5

Source: Hegedüs *et al.* 1996, cited by Pichler-Milanovich (2001)

Many of the other countries share some of the characteristics of the Balanced Tenure model. Like Germany the home-ownership sector in such countries as the Czech Republic, Poland, Slovakia, Estonia and Latvia is relatively small. According to the Association of Germany Mortgage Banks (VdH), the Czech Republic, Slovakia, Poland and Latvia have adopted legislation to support mortgage bonds. As in Germany the loan-to-value ratio on these instruments is restricted to 60% (except in the Czech Republic, where it is 70%) and valuations are based on the more conservative mortgage lending value (again with the exception of the Czech Republic, where the market valuation system is used). The main difference with Germany is that the balance of the rental sector is reversed: large social rental sectors remain in place while private rental sectors have failed to develop. Nevertheless, the social rental sector in the Czech Republic, Poland and Slovenia (at around 25%) would not look out of place in Western Europe. Estonia and Latvia, with social rental sectors that exceed 50%, still look more like traditional centrally planned economies.

Within these broad categories, the lack of tenure choice in the countries that share many of the attributes of the Southern European model implies that the need to develop liberalised mortgage finance systems is pressing on both equity and efficiency grounds. Where privatisation has created low-income home-ownership, questions of the long-term maintenance of the stock clearly arise, with additional logistical challenges where the stock is made up predominantly of flats rather than houses. Even with an efficient housing finance system, it seems likely that fundamental affordability problems will remain for significant sections of the population. Whether public resources should be directed toward enabling such households to enter home-ownership, or toward creating rental alternatives is another issue. Meanwhile, the countries with lower levels of home-ownership probably have more choice in determining the kind of housing system that they wish to create. A German-style banking and valuation system seems to imply that access to mortgage credit may be limited, in which case the prospect of a more socially mixed rental sector is a more realistic objective than in the neighbouring countries.

Conclusions

Each of the models discussed in this chapter displays the essential features of intermediation: funds are mobilised from savers and packaged into loans for borrowers, with default, interest and other risks dealt with in various ways. But they also respond to the legal system that establishes property rights and provides security and to the principles of valuation, which vary between countries. Consequently, the housing finance systems help to shape quite distinct housing systems -- each of which has its advantages and disadvantages. The main point is that it is the choice of housing system that should drive the choice of housing finance system, and not the other way around. After a decade of reform in the transition economies, some countries have gravitated toward the Southern European model, and are likely to benefit from the development of their housing finance systems. Others appear to have adopted a more cautious approach toward home-ownership, and as such probably have more choice concerning the future direction of policy.

REFERENCES

Donnison, D. and Ungerson, C. (1982). *Housing Policy.* Harmondsworth: Penguin.

Hegedüs, J., Mayo, S., and Tosics, I. (1996). "Transition of the Housing Sector in the East Central European Countries." *Review of Urban and Regional Development Studies*, Vol. 8, No. 2, pp. 101-136.

McCrone, G., and Stephens, M. (1995). *Housing Policy in Britain and Europe.* London: UCL Press.

Maclennan, D., Muellbauer, J., and Stephens, M. (1998). "Asymmetries in Housing and Financial Market Institutions and EMU." *Oxford Review of Economic Policy*, Vol. 14, No. 3, pp. 54-80.

---- (2000) "Asymmetries in Housing and Financial Market Institutions and EMU" (updated version) in Jenkinson, T. (ed.) *Readings in Macroeconomics.* Oxford. Oxford University Press.

Pichler-Milanovich, N. (2001) "Urban Housing Markets in Central and Eastern Europe: Convergence, Divergence or Policy Collapse." *European Journal of Housing Policy*, Vol. 1, No. 2, forthcoming.

Stephens, M. (2000). "Convergence in European Mortgage Systems Before and After EMU." *Journal of Housing & the Built Environment*, Vol. 15, pp. 29-52.

Stephens, M., and Burns, N. (forthcoming). Report to the Joseph Rowntree Foundation.

Tosics, I., and Hegedüs, J. (1998). "Centrally Planned Housing Systems," in van Vleit, W. (ed.) *The Encyclopaedia of Housing*, London: S.

THE STRUCTURE AND EVOLUTION OF AMERICAN SECONDARY MORTGAGE MARKETS, WITH SOME IMPLICATIONS FOR DEVELOPING MARKETS

by
Robert Van Order[*]

Introduction and summary

From the end of World War II to the 1970s, American mortgage markets were easy to understand. They were dominated by depository institutions (mainly savings and loan associations or, more broadly, thrift institutions or simply "thrifts"), which were induced, by both regulation and tax incentive, to hold most (about 80%) of their assets in mortgages. The mortgages were financed with low-cost, short-term, government-insured deposits. The thrifts provided all the major aspects of mortgage lending, and they held the overwhelming majority of mortgages. They originated loans, serviced them (collecting payments and managing defaults) and were the ultimate investors, both accepting the risk of borrower default and raising money to finance the mortgages.

The use of short-term deposits to fund mortgages posed two problems for thrifts. First, deposits posed liquidity risk. That is, while thrifts generally enjoyed a stable source of core deposits, there were times when deposits flowed out of thrifts (or did not grow fast enough to keep up with the market), and they did not have an elastic source of funds with which to replace them. Second, deposits' short maturities, combined with holdings of long-term fixed-rate mortgages, led to a duration mismatch that became quite risky. In the early 1980s, when interest rates increased rapidly, many institutions had large losses and became insolvent on a mark to market basis. These losses, as well as some regulatory changes, led the thrifts to focus primarily on adjustable-rate mortgages (ARMs) from the mid-1980s to the present. It is clear, in retrospect, that interest-rate risk was the beginning of the collapse of the thrift industry in the 1980s.

About half of all mortgages now end up in secondary markets, where they or their derivatives compete with a wide range of securities in the capital markets. This occurs primarily through the three major secondary market institutions, Fannie Mae, Freddie Mac and Ginnie Mae. These three are primarily in the business of purchasing mortgages and packaging them into easily tradable securities (or funding them with debt), for which they manage the risk of default. A major change in mortgage markets, brought on largely by the secondary markets, has been the unbundling of the four major aspects of mortgage lending: origination, servicing, funding and accepting credit risks. This is most evident on the investment side. Investors in mortgages need not be involved in originating or servicing mortgage loans, or dealing with credit risk. Pools of mortgages (mortgage-backed securities) now trade in national and international markets, almost as efficiently as Treasury securities.

---

[*]   Chief Economist, Housing Economics and Financial Research, Freddie Mac, USA. This article does not necessarily represent the opinions of Freddie Mac.

183

An effect of this has been to allow thrifts to avoid interest-rate risk. They can originate fixed-rate loans and sell them, but make money from servicing them; they can hold ARMs financed with short-term deposits; they can use derivative securities (e.g., options and forward contracts on Treasury bonds) to hedge the risks of long-term mortgages; they can hold "derivative" securities (discussed below) which have varying degrees of interest-rate risk, or they can hold debt backed by mortgages with varying degrees of call protection.

Liquidity problems have also been addressed. Initially this was done through the Federal Home Loan Bank system. This system, created in the 1930s, lends money to qualified thrifts and banks in the form of loans that are over-collateralised by pools of mortgages, which are kept on the balance sheet of the thrift or bank borrower. More recently there have been solutions in the form of repurchase agreements and brokered deposits, which allow banks and thrifts to bid for deposits almost as if they were issuing debt; and, of course, there are sales of loans into the secondary market, which have become the main source of liquidity.

Mortgage rates are now determined by capital markets in general and are largely independent of the ups and downs of the thrift industry, though they are subject to the ups and downs of capital markets in general. Because the system is based largely on bond-like instruments with access to the entire capital market, it is, taken as a whole, now quite liquid.

While these changes have generally increased the efficiency of the mortgage market, they have also generated some special management problems. The main management concern for Fannie Mae and Freddie Mac, the main actors in the secondary market, is risk management. The primary risks are interest rate and credit risk, but there are also management and operations risks. The unbundling that has come with secondary markets increases the dependence of the various participants in the market upon one another, and enhances these risks. This makes it necessary for Fannie and Freddie to monitor the behaviour of people on whom they depend and to worry about whether they have the right incentives.

Recent developments in information technology have increased competition in the mortgage industry, both among the institutions in it and between the primary and secondary market institutions, and they have changed the way that the above-mentioned risks are managed. In some ways the market is coming full circle. The availability of the same technology in all parts of the markets is increasingly making the distinction between primary and secondary markets irrelevant, and the extent of unbundling is decreasing.

An accurate description of the structure of the mortgage market now can be summarised as one of duelling charters. That is, there are two major charters in the industry. One is depositories (traditionally thrifts but also including banks[1]). These use the deposit market as a way to attract funds. The other charter is for the government-sponsored enterprises (GSEs), Fannie Mae and Freddie Mac, which use the capital or bond markets. The charters have similarities, particularly in the form of implicit and explicit guarantees, and differences, for instance in regulation. Both are clearly viable, each with about a 50% market share. The distinction between primary and secondary markets is no longer very important. There are simply two ways (e.g., via a savings and loan or via Freddie Mac) of getting money from the capital markets to the mortgage market.

The rise of the secondary market in the last 20 years has involved implicit and explicit government support, but government support has dominated mortgage markets since the 1930s. Fannie Mae and Freddie Mac do not represent an increase in government support so much as a change in the nature of support from the depository charter (mainly thrifts in the past) to the GSE charter. Competitive balance between the two charters depends largely on which charter is more exploitable, and that depends partly on the balance between the information advantages of the depositories and the fund-raising economies of the secondary market.

There are lessons from all this that can be exported, but not directly. Many developing markets do not have the infrastructure -- the current bond market, for example -- to support a secondary market like the US market; management problems, particularly the adverse selection problems, are likely be much more problematic in developing markets; government-sponsored enterprises like Fannie Mae and Freddie Mac may be difficult to regulate and can expose a government to bailout costs or collapsed markets; and the creation of specialised secondary market institutions such as Fannie and Freddie may or may not add much to the ability of the mortgage market to attract funds.

Many countries have an existing depository system, banks, that can support a mortgage market. Bank-oriented systems are capable of providing the essential service of secondary markets, which is to connect capital markets in general (rather than just deposit markets) with mortgage markets, either as direct issuers of bonds (on balance sheet) or via off-balance-sheet securitisation managed by banks. There is also the option of tapping deposit markets, which can also draw funds from capital markets.

What can be exported from US experience is the idea that with the right legal and regulatory structure it is possible to have well-functioning mortgage markets that are integrated with capital markets and which have minimal subsidy. You can make money at this!

This paper focuses on the structure and evolution of the American secondary mortgage market in terms of the interactions between the primary and secondary market as well as some management principles that are important to the secondary market. The next section presents a brief history. After that I turn to the economics of the secondary market, with a focus on special management issues. Following are discussions about the management of different risks and some public policy issues. The last section provides comments on applications of the US model to developing markets.

Some history

The primary (i.e., origination) mortgage market in the United States has been dominated historically by depository institutions and mortgage bankers who, unlike European mortgage banks, act as dealers and servicers in mortgages rather than investors. After origination, mortgages are either held in portfolio (e.g., by a traditional savings and loan) or sold into the secondary market. While there has always been a secondary market in the United States, until recently it was informal and *ad hoc*.

The rise in the secondary markets in the 1970s and especially in the 1980s came about largely because of standardisation of pools of mortgages brought on by three government agencies: the Federal Home Loan Mortgage Corporation (Freddie Mac), the Federal National Mortgage Association (Fannie Mae), and for government-insured loans, the Government National Mortgage Association (Ginnie Mae). Annual sales of mortgages to these three institutions have risen from USD 69 billion in 1980 to more than USD 700 billion in 1998; they now own or are responsible for about half of the outstanding stock of single family mortgages.

Fannie Mae, the oldest of the agencies, was established in the 1930s as a secondary market for newly created Federal Housing Administration (FHA) loans. These were government-insured but during the Great Depression had trouble gaining acceptance by private investors. For most of its history Fannie Mae operated like a national savings and loan, gathering funds by issuing its own debt (short-term debt rather than deposits) and buying mortgages that were held in portfolio, but because it held government-insured mortgages it accepted almost no credit risk. This was a particularly useful function during credit crunches when deposit-rate ceilings limited the ability of savings and loans to raise money. Fannie Mae was probably a useful countercyclical tool before deposit rates were deregulated in the early 1980s, because it was, in effect, the only "deregulated" savings and loan.

In 1968 because of budget pressures from the Vietnam War, Fannie Mae was moved off budget and set up as a private, government-sponsored enterprise (GSE). In the 1970s, it switched its focus toward conventional (not government-insured) loans, which do have credit risk. It receives no government funding, and its operations are separate from "on-budget" parts of the government. Ginnie Mae was created as a successor to the old Fannie Mae; its purpose was to handle Fannie Mae's policy-related tasks and to provide a secondary market for government-insured loans. It is on the federal budget as a part of the US Department of Housing and Urban Development.

Ginnie Mae was responsible for promoting the major innovation in secondary markets, the mortgage-backed security (MBS). An MBS is a "pass-through" security. The issuer, typically a mortgage banker, passes through all of the payments from a pool of mortgages (both principal and interest, net of fee) to the ultimate investors, who typically receive pro-rata shares of principal and interest payments. The issuer also guarantees the payment of interest and principal even if the borrower defaults (the issuer is covered by government insurance for almost all foreclosure costs), and Ginnie Mae guarantees timely payment even if the issuer does not make the payments. Hence, its guarantee is on top of the federal insurance and the issuer's guarantee. This has proven valuable in marketing government-insured loans. Because it enhances other existing guarantees its costs are small. It has actually made money from the relatively small (0.06% per dollar of loan balance) annual fee it charges. As with most pass-through securities, Ginnie Maes are subject to interest-rate risk.

Freddie Mac was created in 1970 to be a secondary market for the thrifts. At the time it dealt only with thrifts, and Fannie Mae dealt with mortgage bankers. Now both institutions deal with the same originators. Like Fannie Mae, it is a private, government-sponsored enterprise (GSE), and it too is off-budget. It initiated the first MBS program for conventional loans in 1970. Fannie Mae began its conventional MBS program in 1981. Both institutions' MBSs are similar to Ginnie Mae's; both protect investors against credit risk but not interest-rate risk. Neither Fannie nor Freddie does more than a negligible amount of federally insured mortgages, which almost always go into Ginnie Mae pools.

Because Ginnie Mae is on-budget, its securities have a "full faith and credit" federal guarantee. Because Freddie Mac and Fannie Mae are private corporations, neither has an explicit guarantee, but both have a nebulous, "implicit" or "conjectured" guarantee, because investors believe that if these institutions went under the government would protect debt-holders (though it has no legal obligation to do so). This allows the GSEs to borrow (or sell mortgage-backed securities) at interest rates lower than they would otherwise. Both are regulated by the Department of Housing and Urban Development for their public purpose missions and by the Office of Federal Housing Enterprise Oversight (OFHEO) for safety and soundness. Fannie Mae and Freddie Mac are now quite similar and compete in the conventional mortgage market, as buyers of mortgages, and in the securities markets as sellers of mortgage-backed securities and issuers of debt. The primary benefit of the implicit guarantee is that while Fannie and Freddie would still be strong companies (probably in the low AA range, according to recent "stand-alone" ratings by Standard & Poors) without their charter, they borrow at better than AAA rates with it. This saves them from 0.20% to 0.50% (currently around the middle of this range) in borrowing costs. As a result, borrowing rates for loans eligible for purchase by Fannie and Freddie are lower than other rates. Both Fannie and Freddie consistently make returns on equity in excess of 20%.

Since the early 1980s, secondary markets have developed beyond the "plain vanilla" mortgage-backed security and have attracted funds through partitioning MBSs into "derivative securities." This is because a pro rata share in a pool of 30-year fixed-rate mortgages is not what all investors want.

While MBSs have virtually no credit risk, they have two types of interest-rate risk: the usual risk of any long-term security that its value will fall when rates rise, and a second risk similar to that of callable bonds, because borrowers have the option to refinance (or call the bond), and they tend to do this when rates fall. Hence, upside gains are limited. This call risk is difficult for many investors to evaluate because borrowers' prepayment behaviour is difficult to predict; and because some investors work harder than others to assess prepayment risk (by gathering data and using sophisticated statistical models) there is the risk that less-informed investors are selected against, ending up with the loans with the worst prepayment characteristics.

Beginning in 1983 with the first collateralised mortgage obligation (CMO), issuers and Wall Street dealers have created derivative securities, which take pools of mortgages and pass through the payments in non-pro rata ways. The first CMO established groups of "tranches" that received principal payments in sequence; the first tranches receiving interest plus the first X number of dollars in principal payments, the second tranches receiving the next Y number of dollars in principal payments, etc. In this way a complicated 30-year callable security was broken into a sequence of short-, medium-, and long-term bonds, which could be sold to different types of investors. This carving up of the mortgages does not eliminate interest-rate risk, but it does allow the risk to be allocated more efficiently.

Complications in tax law limited the use of the first round of CMOs. Tax reform in 1986 created the Real Estate Mortgage Investment Conduit (REMIC), which solved most of the remaining tax problems. REMICs are much the same as CMOs (the names are often used interchangeably), but they and CMOs have become much more exotic, carving up the cash flows from a pool of mortgages in complicated ways. They can now be tailored to specific investor needs, but because of their complicated nature (some REMICs now have 50 tranches or more) REMIC tranches are often difficult to evaluate without computer simulation. No two tranches are exactly alike; they are often less liquid than straightforward pass-throughs. Some particular tranches are quite risky, in that sizeable losses occur if interest rates move either up or down. The central problem is that the REMIC must be self-contained, so that it can pay off all claims under any circumstance (such as extremely rapid prepayments). This means that if one tranche assures investors a more stable level of prepayments (e.g., a tranche that looks like a five-year bond under most conditions) another tranche has to absorb the extra prepayment risk. Residual tranches are sometimes referred to as "hazardous waste."

Both Fannie and Freddie also fund mortgages with debt. Most of the debt is long-term callable debt that is issued in a way that hedges against interest-rate risk, or short-term debt that is combined with derivatives to produce synthetic long-term callable debt. Investors prefer callable debt to pass-through securities. If debt is callable, the circumstances under which the debt will be called are more transparent than the circumstances under which borrowers will prepay. Also, the risk of being selected against is minimal, and if it is not callable, Fannie and Freddie take the call risk. Hence, Fannie and Freddie can raise money at lower cost by issuing debt even after adjusting for option costs. The risk to Fannie and Freddie is that the models they use to estimate when borrowers will prepay will be inaccurate and/or their hedges will not work. For instance, it has been the case in the 1990s that borrowers prepaid faster than expected when interest rates fell, leaving Fannie and Freddie with the risk of having to reinvest at lower rates before they can call their debt.[2]

The share of debt financing has increased sharply for both GSE's, especially Freddie Mac, and is now around 40%. An accurate way of thinking about Fannie and Freddies' operations is that they buy mortgages that are financed with a portfolio of securities made up of pass throughs, comprising 60%, and various types of debt (and derivatives) comprising 40%. Variations in this mixture affect their exposure to interest rate risk, and both companies almost always take on credit risk regardless of the means of funding.

The economics of secondary markets

Most mortgages are now sold into the secondary mortgage market. This is especially true for fixed-rate mortgages (FRMs), which are typically 60% to 85% of the market. Virtually all government-insured loans become mortgage-backed securities. About 50% of conventional mortgages are now sold to either Fannie Mae or Freddie. There is also a growing "private label" secondary market, which operates primarily in the market for conventional loans that exceed the Fannie/Freddie loan size limit (currently USD 252,000 for single family houses) that is around 10% of the market.

The reasons the secondary market was started in the United States are not entirely the same as the reasons for its continuation. The evolution of the secondary market has been a product of a variety of factors, many of which are of largely historical interest. For instance, deposit-rate ceilings, which limited the ability of savings and loans to raise money for mortgage loans, were a major factor in the rising importance of Fannie Mae in the 1960s and 1970s, and the creation of Freddie Mac in the 1970s, but deposit-rate ceilings are no longer an issue. Similarly, the inability of banks and savings and loans to operate nationally was important, but national deposit markets and liberalised branching rules have limited the importance of this.

The main reason for the important role of secondary markets today, and for their rapid increase in the 1980s, is that secondary markets have generally been an efficient, low-cost and stable way to raise money and manage cash flows. This is primarily because of economies in raising money "wholesale" in the capital markets, in processing the purchase and servicing of large numbers of mortgage loans, and in managing risks, through diversification. Fannie and Freddie have an implicit guarantee, moreover, which gives them a benefit comparable to deposit insurance for depositories.

Depositories also have a low-cost source of funds in the form of insured deposits, but this has not been as elastic a source of funds as the one coming from capital markets in general, which the secondary market can tap quickly. As a result, depositories sometimes have trouble raising money quickly, especially relative to Fannie and Freddie. This is particularly true for FRMs because secondary markets have excellent access to long-term funds, through long-term debt, MBSs and hedging, whereas depositories have traditionally (though this has been changing) been confined to the deposit market, which is primarily short-term; that makes it more difficult for them to hold FRMs without exposure to interest-rate risk. However, as discussed below, the depositories remain a major source of funds, particularly for ARMs, but also for FRMs. They are increasingly capable of using their charter to find ways of getting to capital markets.

Unbundling

The traditional savings and loan performed all aspects of the mortgage bundle: it originated the mortgage, serviced it, took the risk of default (perhaps along with a private or government insurer) and raised money in the deposit market to fund it. The secondary market evolved largely by unbundling this package. The major contribution of the "Agencies" (Ginnie Mae, Fannie Mae, and Freddie Mac) has been to facilitate the money-raising part of the bundle by taking on credit risk and packaging mortgages, so that they could be sold as relatively homogenous securities or financed with homogenous debt in the capital markets. This allowed separation of the funding part of the bundle from the other three parts and has helped to lower mortgage rates.

All four aspects of the mortgage bundle can now be unbundled. The US secondary market is now composed primarily of: mortgage originators, large in number and small in scale, which sell or act as agents for a relatively small number of mortgage servicers; mortgage servicers, which sell mortgages into the secondary market and either keep the servicing or sell servicing rights to other mortgage servicers; and secondary market institutions and mortgage insurers, which take on credit risk; and investors who buy mortgage-backed securities. The last function has become further unbundled with the advent of derivative securities (REMICS, CMOs, etc.).

For instance, interest rates on 30-year fixed-rate mortgages in the US in the 1990s were generally about 8%. If a borrower takes out such a mortgage and it ends up securitised by Fannie or Freddie, the money and paperwork will flow approximately as follows:

1. The borrower will pay about 1% of the mortgage balance to the originator, e.g., a mortgage broker, mortgage banker or a depository, to cover expenses involved in originating the loan. The borrower will then make principal and interest (at an 8% annual rate) payments necessary to pay off the loan in 30 years.

2. The loan will be serviced by a mortgage banker or a depository, who will manage the payment flows. The servicer will typically receive 0.25% per year of mortgage balance for the service. The servicing rights to a pool of mortgages can be sold to another servicer. Large mortgage bankers acquire their servicing portfolios primarily by buying them from other mortgage originators.

3. The loan will be put into a pool with other similar loans and sold as a mortgage-backed security on which Fannie or Freddie will accept the credit risk. For this service they will receive about 0.25% (currently less), of which about 0.05% will cover expected default loss. If the loan has a down payment of 20% or less, there will be a private mortgage insurance policy, which typically will cover the first 25 cents on the dollar if there are foreclosure losses and for which a fee, roughly equivalent to a 1% increase in borrower's interest rate, will be charged.

4. The mortgage-backed security made up of these will be sold through dealers at whatever price the market will fetch, competing with Treasuries, corporate bonds etc. Investors can be institutions such as life insurance companies or pension funds, or they can be depositories or individuals. The pool will have a coupon rate of 7.5% (the 8% paid by the borrower minus servicing and secondary market charges). The pool might be carved up (by an investment banker) into a CMO for which there will be different pay-offs by class.

If the mortgages are debt-funded there will be a similar process. Most of the time Fannie and Freddie do their debt funding by repurchasing their own pass-throughs and issuing debt to fund the repurchase.[3]

This unbundling takes advantage of scale economies (where they are important) and division of labour and promotes competition among the suppliers of the various bundles, but it does not occur without cost. The cost is that the players that focus on one part of the bundle depend on players in the other parts of the unbundling to perform services for them as expected (e.g., originate good loans) when it is not always in their interest to do so. That is, there is a "principal-agent" problem: the principals (ultimate investors) depend on agents (the institutions originating and servicing the loans) to perform as promised, even though it may not be profitable for them to do so.

The key element of the principal-agent problem is information asymmetry: if originators did not have superior information about the loans they deliver to investors and insurers, there would be no limit to what the secondary market could buy because of its lower costs.

For Fannie Mae and Freddie Mac the major principal-agent issue has come largely from the reliance on originators and servicers to originate good loans and service them properly. The major risks are that sellers, with superior information about loans, will adversely select against them, keeping good loans and selling the ones that are riskier than they appear to be, relaxing monitoring, underwriting poorly, etc.; or if they intend to sell, making loans that are of low quality either deliberately (occasionally there is actual fraud) or through sloppy underwriting. This is often referred to as moral hazard.

The interests of sellers and servicers are not always the same as those of Fannie and Freddie. For instance, mortgage originators make money based largely on their volume of business. They may have no inherent interest, other than their reputation, in the quality of the loans they originate once they are sold. This is particularly true for institutions that are in danger of bankruptcy. Mortgage servicers do have a stake in mortgage performance because delinquent mortgages are more costly to service. However, servicers benefit from scale economies, and therefore have incentives to service lots of loans, and their stake in actual foreclosure is small. Hence, to control credit risk, Fannie Mae and Freddie Mac need to do things that align the incentives of a large number of servicers (there are currently over 2,000, although a relative few do most of the servicing) with their own.

Historically, operating a market on the scale of the current secondary market has required that investors not have to spend resources monitoring the credit risk of individual loans. Hence, the burden of controlling credit costs has fallen on the performance of mortgage insurers, who insure loans with down payments of 20% or less; on underwriting guidelines, which attempt to define the parameters of an acceptable mortgage; on the ability to provide incentives to induce originators to make good loans and monitor agents' performance; and ultimately on the ability to foreclose on borrowers who do not make payments.

This is all in contrast with the traditional, bundled savings and loan (portfolio lender) which had all the elements of the bundle under its control and should be less worried that the part of the firm that originates mortgages will take advantage of the part of the firm that evaluates credit risk.[4]

The balance between the role of the secondary markets and the role of traditional portfolio lenders has depended largely on the balance between economies of scale and fund-raising that the secondary market brings, with the advantages of control over important risks that the traditional portfolio lender brings. That this balance has been favourable to the secondary market for single-family mortgages has been due primarily to advantageous circumstances in the market for single-family houses and may not be replicable for other type of loans or in other countries. The most important favourable circumstances are the relatively good information available about house values (because houses trade fairly frequently and are relatively, if imperfectly, easy to appraise) and the ability to use a house as a security (this comes from foreclosure laws and registration). These factors mean that lenders have a good idea of homeowner equity at loan origination and can foreclose and thereby minimise losses, so that homeowner equity is a good deterrent to default. As a result, a major concern of institutions that accept credit risk is the probability of equity becoming negative. This risk is subject to some control from diversification (we may not know much about how many houses in a given neighbourhood will fall in price so much as to leave owners with no equity, but we have a better idea of how many will on a nationwide basis); it can also be analysed statistically, along with characteristics such as borrower credit history.

Another important part of the framework is the right of mortgage originators to sell mortgages without notifying the borrower and with no tax and minimal transfer costs. Indeed, most borrowers do not know (or care) if their mortgage has been sold. Similarly, servicing rights can be sold or transferred without the borrower's permission, notification happening only because the borrower needs to know where to send payments.

The ability to treat houses and mortgages almost like commodities and default risk almost like a financial option (a "put" option, which gives the borrower the right to exchange the home for the mortgage) is a major factor in the success of the secondary market. To the extent that this is all that matters (or is all that can be measured), information asymmetries become much less important. Default costs then depend primarily on the initial loan-to-value ratio, which is known to everyone; on the probability of house value falling by enough to trigger default, which is not known equally well by everyone but which can generally be estimated reasonably well by the secondary market; and on other factors that can be diversified away.

These advantages are not common to most other markets. For instance, lending for rental housing is quite different. It is much more difficult to evaluate apartment building property values (these properties are much more heterogeneous, they trade less frequently, and incentives for inaccurate appraisals are greater), and incentives to take care of the property are weaker when owners are not also occupants.

While single-family housing has great informational advantages, it is clear from both experience and research that there is more to credit risk than simply down payment and equity build-up. Risks have been shown to vary by neighbourhood, borrower characteristics (especially credit history), and other factors. Hence, even given initial down payment, there is still much potential for those with better information surreptitiously to pass risks through to the secondary market. For the secondary market to survive it must control other, hard-to-measure, sources of risk, so that default risk can be treated in a simple and quantitative manner. This probably means trying to avoid risks that are hard to quantify and/or involve serious information asymmetries, and are therefore difficult to price, while working hard to gather objective information about default risk. This is especially the case in the current low-inflation environment. We can no longer count on rapid house price appreciation to build up borrower equity and solve credit problems.

Managing risks

The major risks taken by Freddie and Fannie can be summarised as follows:

- Credit risk, which is the risk from loss due to default;

- Interest-rate risk, which is the risk of change in value of the firms assets and/or liabilities when interest rates change;

- Business risk, which is the risk that a firm takes when making or providing a new product or service; and

- Management and operations risk, which is the risk that management and/or systems will break down.

Historically, the first two risks have been most important for institutions involved in mortgage lending. The beginning of the savings and loan debacle in the US was due to interest-rate risk caused by the use of short-term deposits to finance long-term mortgages and the run-up of interest rates in the late 1970s and early 1980s. Credit risk has been less an issue for single-family mortgages in the US, primarily because house prices have generally been increasing and homeowners have generally had too much equity in their houses to default. However, some parts of the country have had serious real estate recessions (e.g., the Southwest, especially Texas, in the middle and late 1980s, and New England and California more recently), and inflation slowed and default risk increased in the early 1990s.

All of the risks categories are related. For instance, one way of avoiding interest rate risk is to engage in sophisticated portfolio management techniques, but these techniques can lead to operations risk because portfolio models and computer systems can break down. Similarly, business risk and credit risk are related because business risk is likely to show up as credit risk from new and unfamiliar business lines.

Despite the complicated interactions among these risks, I shall discuss them and the way that Fannie and Freddie approach them, one at a time.

Credit risk

Because the secondary market relies on third parties to originate and service mortgages, the nature of the risks depends on managing what these third parties deliver. It is here that principle-agent problems are potentially most serious. As described above, the centre of the conflict is that mortgage originators and servicers make money primarily from origination and servicing fees and generally do not have a direct interest in credit risk.

The underlying choice issues for both buyers and sellers in the secondary market can be summarised as follows. The secondary market has to worry about the principal-agent issues discussed above. Fannie and Freddie traditionally have published guidelines that specify what is clearly acceptable while allowing lenders to go outside the guidelines if there is a compensating factor, such that credit risk is unchanged (i.e., that the loans still be "investment quality"). For instance, a high down payment may be enough to compensate for a bad credit history or high mortgage payment relative to borrower income. However, guidelines do not clearly specify what the tradeoffs are: lenders are meant to exercise their own judgement subject to our review; if they are conservative, the guidelines can be a series of hoops through which borrowers must pass, rather than a set of tradeoffs. There is a potential punishment to lenders who go outside the bounds and deliver excessively risky loans: the GSEs do quality-control sampling of loans and can make sellers repurchase the loans, at some cost; and if they deliver too many low-quality loans they may not be allowed to sell more mortgages to the GSEs.

Hence, the choice problem for the lender who wants to sell mortgages has been that it can sell standard mortgages, which it almost certainly will not have to repurchase and/or it can sell non-standard mortgages for which there is some risk of repurchase. Not selling (or not originating) non-standard loans is safer but may mean missing some profitable business. Good originators can choose to sell non-standard mortgages at relatively low risk of repurchase. There is a further choice, of course, which is either to violate the rules deliberately or be overly aggressive about what is creditworthy and make money from origination and servicing fees until caught. The fact that entry into and exit from the mortgage servicing businesses are relatively easy makes this a tempting strategy in some circumstances (e.g., firms in financial trouble, "gambling for resurrection").

There is something inevitable about all this. The secondary market needs to be flexible, but it needs to protect itself, and as a result it needs to have a way to punish lenders who exploit the guidelines. Lenders, especially non-portfolio lenders, need to worry about repurchase risk. For the secondary market to survive and to take advantage of the economies it has, it has to confront the principal-agent problem, which means that it has had to be more conservative in the loans it accepts than local portfolio lenders such as savings and loans and more concerned with quantifying risks. Competition between Fannie and Freddie for the purchase of new mortgages tends to keep both institutions at some sort of margin between the benefits from volume and the costs of adverse selection.

An important aspect of controlling risks has been attempts to align the various interests by requiring servicers to keep some sort of interest in their loans. One good example is the creation of valuable servicing contracts, which can be transferred if performance is bad. For instance, in the Ginnie Mae, market servicers are required to charge 44 basis points for servicing, but it costs less than this to service the loans. This extra income does not show up as higher interest payments for borrowers; rather it is a forced investment, which servicers must make to be able to service the loans. Most loan originators would prefer to charge a lower servicing fee so that when the loans are sold into the secondary they have a higher coupon rate and can be sold at a higher price. This would give the servicers the money up front rather than as an investment in the pool of mortgages, which could be lost or taken away (the value of the right to service a pool of mortgages is on the order of 1% of the value of the pool). If the servicer does not fulfil its obligations to Ginnie Mae, Ginnie Mae has the right to take all of the servicer's Ginnie Mae servicing and sell it, and it has this before any other claims (e.g., loans from banks) on the servicer.

There are similar incentives in Fannie Mae and Freddie Mac servicing, and an active market in trading servicing contracts has developed. This has facilitated the development of scale economies in servicing mortgages. Because these contracts are, in effect, annuities whose income stops when the mortgages prepay, servicing contracts are subject to interest-rate risk, and mortgage servicers are becoming increasingly aware that they are forced to be portfolio managers and hedge against interest rate risk.

This all helps, but it does not always provide sufficient assurance that good loans will be originated or sold in the first place. This has been exacerbated by the advent of mortgage brokers, who make money from origination and have no stake after that. Indeed, Freddie Mac data indicate that loans originated by third parties do have higher default rates.

Recent advances in information technology are bringing about important changes in how risks are managed and on competition in the industry. A major innovation has been the use of technology to evaluate credit risk. Fannie and Freddie have both developed automated underwriting systems that allow rapid decisions about what they want to purchase and what they do not want; the decision to accept can be made in five minutes and loans can be closed in five days, all at lower costs than before.

Fannie and Freddie have both developed statistical credit-scoring models, which use down payment, credit history and a variety of other variables to evaluate credit risk. These scoring models use much (but not all) of the same sort of information available to the depositories (which are now using similar models) and they promise to use the information better (partly because they are using very large data sets), so that there is great potential for reducing the principal-agent problems discussed above, and much less need to delegate authority to mortgage originators. The statistical models automatically calculate the tradeoffs among different risk factors. This provides originators with greater clarity about what is acceptable; and indeed, once a loan is accepted, there is no repurchase risk as long as the information provided is accurate. On the other hand, automated underwriting lowers the value-added of the originator, whose underwriting role is increasingly confined to loans that are at the margin, or for which data are incomplete or otherwise not useful.

Automation is producing a trend toward what might be called rebundling, as the secondary market takes control over more of the underwriting process. In the future it promises to allow entry into other riskier parts of the market and to price individual loans based on their individual risk, so that there will be fewer rejections.

Interest rate risk

Both Fannie Mae and Freddie Mac finance most (about 60%) of their purchases with pass-throughs. Securitisation effectively avoids almost all interest-rate risk.[5] This is a marked change from the way mortgages were financed in the past. As discussed above, savings and loans traditionally were short-funded, which exposed them to considerable interest-rate risk. It is also the case that Fannie Mae, before it introduced its pass-through securities in the early 1980s, was short-funded, and suffered from interest-rate increases as well, to the point where it was probably insolvent on a mark-to-market basis. Securitisation passes interest-rate risk on to investors, who must then manage it. And many mortgage-backed securities go into derivative securities; this allows interest-rate risk to be allocated among different investors in accordance with the types of risk they wish to take on. This effectively pushes unbundling yet one stage further.

Both Fannie Mae and Freddie Mac also have sizeable holdings of mortgages that are funded by debt, rather than mortgage-backed securities. However, having learned from the experiences of the early 1980s, neither company is short-funded; both rely largely on long-term, callable debt or its equivalent (short-term debt and derivatives like interest-rate swaps and caps and floors) to finance long-term mortgages.

Nonetheless, both companies' portfolios involve some interest-rate risk, because callable debt is not a very precise hedge against mortgages, because while mortgages are like callable bonds, it is difficult to predict with much precision how rapidly people will prepay when interest rates fall and because hedges do not always work as expected. As discussed above, it is difficult to set up a portfolio of callable debt that will be (optimally) called in a way that matches the way that borrowers prepay mortgages.

There is a further problem with prepayment risk: there is much potential for adverse selection based on differences in prepayment behaviour across borrowers. Clearly, there is much more to modelling prepayment behaviour than simply the ruthless exercise of an option. If depositories can tell which borrowers are likely to be less ruthless in exercising options they can select against the secondary market.

This is a very broad issue, because selection problems arise at all levels of trading mortgages (e.g., some traders in mortgage-backed securities invest in information about prepayment characteristics of different mortgage pools, raising lemons at all levels), and it is beyond the scope of this paper to pursue this in detail. The main point is that there is potential for selection against the secondary market based on local information about mobility and ability to refinance, particularly as current secondary-market credit scoring models do not generally take prepayment risk into account.

This provides important incentives for the secondary market (SM) to continue the trend away from pass-through funding and toward debt funding. This is because it has superior information about prepayment risk relative to MBS investors. It can exploit this information and fund mortgages with the equivalent of callable debt, which investors prefer to pass-through securities because of the greater predictability of the call option (partly because of the lesser chance of being selected against (for example by traders with better information) if they buy MBS pools). This, of course, exposes the SM to risk from mistakes in its prepayment models, but that may be the best place to locate that risk.

Hence, there is a need for balance. There is more money to be made, on average, by financing mortgages with debt (over half of Fannie Mae's and Freddie Mac's profits come from income from the 40% of their portfolios that are debt-financed), but there is also risk. This risk is not just from the imprecision of using debt to finance mortgages, but because of management risks from controlling a large portfolio of debt and other hedging devices. Debt also provides flexibility. For instance, in 1994 when the CMO market fell apart and in 1998 when some hedge funds were dumping MBSs, it was useful to have debt financing as an alternative.

Business risk

Business risk comes primarily from the risk of the unknown that is associated with new business lines. This is largely limited by Fannie Mae's and Freddie Mac's charters, which limit them to residential mortgages. However, within this category there is potential of unknown new risks. For instance, the extension of the statistical models used in automated underwriting to new and riskier areas may be potentially profitable, but it runs the risk of losses from bad parameters.

Management and operations risk

To a large extent these risks are the same for secondary-market institutions as for most other businesses. An area worth emphasising, given the size of Fannie Mae's and Freddie Mac's mortgage portfolios, is that of computer systems. Most Freddie Mac employees are involved in processing information, either about mortgage purchases or mortgage prepayments, monthly mortgage payments, the sale of mortgage-backed securities or payoffs to security holders. Freddie Mac currently has around eight million individual loans in its portfolio, each of which is supposed to make monthly payments, which generally must be passed on to investors. It bought more than two million loans in 1998, and it lost about two million due to prepayments. All of this must be monitored, placing a great deal of responsibility on systems.

Capital, risk and public policy

The safety and soundness of GSEs (as well as depositories) has been a major public policy concern for some time. This is because an implicit guarantee and the implicit benefits that go with it can lead to misallocation of resources and/or bailout costs. The major concern has been whether or not GSEs (like depositories in the past) will undertake excessive risk-taking.

At some level almost all risks can be managed, particularly in the sense of keeping the risks from bankrupting the company. One way to achieve the latter is for the company to finance a large share of its investments with equity rather than debt. This is particularly important from a public policy standpoint if the financial institution has an explicit or implicit government guarantee and if it is risky. The amount of capital needed to keep a company solvent with high probability depends on how risky its business is.

But debt-equity decisions also involve principal-agent conflicts. Both depositories and the secondary market institutions have an incentive to put up as little of their own money as possible, so that they can leverage their guarantee. Having to make regular interest payments forces discipline on management, which also benefits shareholders, and in the US, interest expenses are deductible but dividends are not, providing a tax incentive to issue debt rather than equity.

Hence, there is a potential conflict between a guarantor's needs for safety and the shareholders' profit motive. The conflict is not inevitable. Because Fannie Mae and Freddie Mac have a valuable charter, which no one else has, they have incentives not to take on too much risk and not to be undercapitalised, lest they lose their franchise. Recent studies have generally found that Fannie and Freddie take on relatively little risk, both because of limits on risk-taking in their charters and, probably more important, because of their valuable franchises. A major factor in the risk-taking by thrifts in the 1980s was the fact that free entry and competition from the rest of the capital markets greatly diminished the value of the thrift franchise.

Nonetheless, the potential for risk-taking is real. This means that the government has to worry about safety and soundness, particularly about whether the institution has enough capital relative to its risk. Much progress was made along these lines with respect to Fannie Mae and Freddie Mac in 1992, when legislation set up capital standards, but safety and soundness remain controversial issues. The centrepiece of the new standards is the use of stress tests, which simulate the companies' performance through stressful environments involving scenarios when risks have taken a particularly bad turn. The legislation requires that both companies have enough capital to survive 10 years of stress, in three different scenarios that involve both serious interest-rate and credit risk; actions are prescribed in the event capital is insufficient.

These capital requirements also present important management issues. Traditional capital standards specify required ratios of accounting capital to assets. It is relatively easy to see how these ratios are moving, and they generally move slowly, giving management time to adjust to change. Stress test standards are more realistic (accounting capital was misleading during the 1980s, allowing many institutions which were economically insolvent to appear to be solvent in an accounting sense), but their results can be quite volatile. Hence, management in its planning must estimate the probability of stress test results becoming bad, and will probably want to build a cushion against unforeseen changes.

Finally, while it is clear that Fannie and Freddie cause mortgage rates to be lower than they otherwise would be, there is debate over whether that is a good thing. It can be argued that lower rates represent a subsidy that distorts capital flows. It can also be argued that homeownership is socially beneficial, and Fannie and Freddie make contributions to promoting homeownership and stabilising markets, improving resource allocation. As yet, we do not have much empirical work to evaluate these differing propositions.

Applications to developing markets

Can the benefits and/or lessons of the US secondary market be exported? Some can. But it may be that the principal-agent problems discussed above will be more difficult to manage in other countries. The most important first steps may be to develop laws for foreclosure and develop good systems for recording title and transactions. The lessons of the secondary market do not come from the details of how it operates in the US (e.g., the use of sophisticated capital markets instrument like CMOs). These details probably cannot and need not be exported. Depository-based systems can, with the right laws and regulations, do much the same thing as secondary markets. Indeed, about 80% of the increase in homeownership rates that took place in the US from the 1940s until the present took place by the 1960s, with a system that was largely depository-based, with virtually no secondary market (and without access to much information about borrower credit history).

The success of Fannie and Freddie has come in part from the fundamental simplicity imposed on them by their charters. The simplicity is that Fannie and Freddie function primarily as conduits with the capital markets, so that they work with market forces rather than against them. They have focused primarily on a particular part of the bundle, guaranteeing credit risk, primarily of single-family mortgages. They have done this primarily by relying on others, mainly mortgage originators and servicers, private insurers and investors to accept most of the risk. As discussed above, however, we are beginning to see rebundling, largely because of innovations not widely applicable elsewhere. Simplicity has required a large infrastructure, which should not be taken for granted.

What US experience has shown, both before and after the advent of secondary markets, is that with the right legal and regulatory framework (in particular the ability to foreclose and evict, which makes it possible for houses to act as real collateral) and a reasonably stable macroeconomy, you can make money in single-family mortgages. Linking mortgage markets with capital markets, moreover, can be done with minimal or no subsidy. While government has provided a backup role, it can be argued that this role has involved rather small borrowing costs (for Fannie and Freddie it is hard to argue that subsidies in the form of low borrowing costs, for example, are more than 0.5% at the most) and largely controllable subsidies; its essence has been moving with the market.

Applications?

Many countries do not currently have effective ways of linking lending markets with capital markets. Secondary markets might be a particularly good way of tapping international capital markets. This does not, however, mean that creating a GSE like Fannie or Freddie is a good idea:

1. The selection issues discussed above are likely to be more formidable in developing markets, where asymmetric information may be a bigger problem, because mortgage originators will have access to all sorts of local information and where access to things like credit history, historical data and automation will be difficult. Underwriting will be left to originators, which inevitably will be able to select the best loans for themselves. This is worsened if foreclosure costs are high, so that the house is not good security.

2. Banks are often in a position to access bond markets as well as deposit markets. A Fannie or Freddie-like institution might have no funding advantage over banks. Anything they could do banks could do, funding with deposits or bonds, and without the selection problems a secondary market institution would have.

3. Much of the infrastructure for unbundling would have to start from scratch.

4. A new regulatory scheme would have to be set up, with possibilities for abuse and risk-taking. For instance, a major effort to control interest-rate risk would be necessary. As was the case in the US, taking interest-rate risk (long-term assets funded with short-term debt, possibly complicated with prepayment risk) can lead to trouble very quickly. Compounded by adverse selection problems, there is potential for insolvency, bailout costs and/or market collapse.

These, of course, are things regulators will have to worry about with banks as well. A central question is whether new GSEs (banks are, after all, essentially GSEs too) add to risk and whether existing institutions like banks can do what GSEs can do. Different countries will have different answers.

There is no reason in principle to not simply equip the private sector with a legal framework that will let it evolve and securities as it chooses, competing with banks, perhaps in the form of specialised mortgage lenders. Specialised portfolio lenders do not appear to be the direction in which mortgage markets around the world are moving. The distinction between thrifts and banks in the US is fading rapidly, and building societies in the UK have basically become full-service banks. Private securitisers have not been very successful in most countries, but there is no reason in principle for opposing them. A problem is that financial institutions in general might have automatic implicit GSE status. Hence, new institutions will have the potential to require future bailouts and/or to require new regulatory regimes even if that is not the original intention. In that case, explicitly chartered GSEs with accompanying regulation might be preferable.

This is not to say that there need not be a role for government, but it need not be in the form of creating a secondary market. Some form of government guarantee might be useful, particularly in attracting foreign investment. A major obstacle to getting a mortgage market off the ground can be the credibility of foreclosure laws, especially in countries where new laws have recently been adopted. It might be possible to provide guarantees designed to promote credibility, for instance by putting the banks in a position to take the first loss on mortgages, according to estimates of a reasonable level for normal losses (assuming the laws work) with the government taking the risk beyond that, which the government is better prepared to accept, by covering losses due to unenforceability of the foreclosure laws and other catastrophic losses.

This need not require creating a Fannie or a Freddie, but a GSE structure with private ownership and value-maximising incentives is likely to be a more efficient way of providing guarantees and starting up a mortgage market than is a state-owned corporation. A substitute for Fannie and Freddie, which is also a GSE, is a liquidity facility like the Federal Home Loan Bank system in the US, which takes very little risk, because it lends against over-collateralised pools of mortgages, but nonetheless also connects mortgage and capital markets. Clearly of concern with any GSE-type set-up, or any government intervention, are the details of the charter, responsibilities, incentives, etc., which will be filtered through a political process that may not get everything right.

It is a central fact of life that capital is scarce in developing markets. The most markets can do is allocate it efficiently.

NOTES

1.   Banks have become important participants in the mortgage markets as regulatory changes have diminished the distinction between banks and thrifts; it is now more accurate to think of them as simply "depositories".

2.   Callable debt is usually issued with the provision that it cannot be called before some future date. Fannie and Freddie try to issue portfolios of callable debt with different call dates to match the way mortgage borrowers prepay.

3.   This may seem like an odd way to hold mortgages, but there is a point to it. The point is that if Fannie or Freddie chose which loans to hold and which to sell, the market will assume it is being selected against and will be reluctant to hold the securities. When the securities are repurchased they are purchased by Fannie and Freddie traders with the same information (about pools) as everyone else, mitigating the selection problem.

4.   That is not to say that there is no risk. Compensation schemes could induce conflicts of interest inside the firm. The point is that conflicts inside the firm are easier to resolve.

5.   I say almost all because there are some remaining risks that come from the ability to predict borrower prepayments. For instance, prepayments are not passed through immediately, which expose Fannie Mae or Freddie Mac to costs from "float."

List of Lead Speakers

Opening Remarks

Mr. William Witherell,
Director, Directorate for Financial, Fiscal and Enterprise Affairs, OECD

Mr. Eigil Mølgaard,
Deputy Secretary, Ministry of Economic Affairs, Denmark (Chairman of the Workshop)

Session I: Housing Finance in Transition Economies: What Is It and What Should It Be?

Part A: Main Features of Well-Functioning Housing Finance Systems

Mr. Robert Van Order,
Chief Economist, Housing Economics and Financial Research, Freddie Mac, USA

Mr. Mark Stephens,
Lecturer, Department of Urban Studies, University of Glasgow, UK

Ms. Daniela Grabmullerová,
Director, Housing Policy Department, Ministry for Regional Development, Czech Republic

Part B: Current Situations and Strategies

Mr. Takahiro Yasui,
Principal Administrator, Directorate for Financial, Fiscal and Enterprise Affairs, OECD

Mr. Marek Zawislak,
Director, Housing Finance Systems Department, State Office for Housing and Urban Development, Poland

Ms. Barbara Staric-Strajnar,
Chief, Housing Department, Ministry of Environment and Spatial Planning, Slovenia

Session II: Development of Mortgage Loan Business

Part A: Practical Aspects of Mortgage System Designing

Mr. Jose Landa,
Mortgage Director, Auritec-GMAC/RFC

Mr. Tim Lassen,
Association of German Mortgage Banks, Germany

Mr. Erik Österlöf,
Vice President, Stadshypotek AB, Sweden

Part B: Effective Management of Mortgage Loan Business

Mr. Claude Poirier-Dufoy,
President, Canada Mortgage and Housing Corporation

Mr. Inesis Feiferis,
President, Mortgage and Land Bank of Latvia

Ms. Debra Erb,
President, Societas, USA

Session III: Institutional Arrangements and Funding Strategies: Pros and Cons

Part A: Alternative Funding Strategies and Risks

Ms. Judith Hardt,
Secretary General, European Mortgage Foundation

Mr. József Csomos,
Deputy Chief Executive, FHB Land Credit and Mortgage Bank, Hungary

Mr. Aloyzas Vitkauskas,
Managing Director, Housing and Urban Development Foundation, Lithuania

Part B: Institutional Arrangements

Mr. Thierry Dufour,
Crédit Foncier, France

Mr. Andreas Zehnder,
Managing Director, European Federation of Building Societies

Mr. Herbert Pfeiffer,
Director, First Construction Saving Bank, Slovak Republic

Session IV: Practical Steps for Establishing Housing Finance Systems: Strategies, Implementation and Role of Government

Mr. Robert Buckley,
Principal Economist, World Bank

Mr. Shunichi Kuwata,
Manager, Public Relation Division, Government Housing Loan Corporation of Japan

Mr. Igor Jakobson,
Chairman, Estonian Housing Foundation, Estonia

Concluding Session: Future Work

Mr. Takahiro Yasui,
Principal Administrator, Directorate for Financial, Fiscal and Enterprise Affairs, OECD

Mr. Eigil Mølgaard,
Deputy Secretary, Ministry of Economic Affairs, Denmark (Chairman of the Workshop)

OECD PUBLICATIONS, 2, rue André-Pascal, 75775 PARIS CEDEX 16
PRINTED IN FRANCE
(14 2002 01 1 P) ISBN 92-64-19674-9 – No. 52223 2002